"This volume offers a significant collection of international perspectives on how and where educational language policy happens, and how language teachers and stakeholders can impact policy. The collection presents both the work of rising stars and established scholars. It will be of value to both scholars and students of LPP and how it affects practice."
—*Terrence G. Wiley, Professor Emeritus, Arizona State University, and Immediate Past President of the Center for Applied Linguistics*

"This volume offers many examples of current research, carefully reported, to expand the knowledge and skills of investigators, educators, and decision makers concerned with English language learning and teaching. It is a timely and valuable contribution."
—*Mary McGroarty, Northern Arizona University*

"This groundbreaking book examines language education policy through a wide lens. Taking into consideration how language teaching professionals, institutions, and other key stakeholders shape a broad range of educational issues, the editors and contributing authors of this volume lucidly illustrate the complexities surrounding language policy development and implementation. This book will be an important resource for language policy and planning scholars and everyone else who is interested in educational linguistics."
—*Peter De Costa, Assistant Professor, Michigan State University*

GLOBAL PERSPECTIVES ON LANGUAGE EDUCATION POLICIES

Presenting research on language policy and planning, with a special focus on educational contexts in which English plays a role, this book brings readers up-to-date on the latest developments in research, theory, and practice in a rapidly changing field. The diversity of authors, research settings, and related topics offers a sample of empirical studies across multiple language teaching and university contexts. The fifth volume in the Global Research on Teaching and Learning English series, it features access to both new and previously unpublished research in chapters written by TIRF Doctoral Dissertation Grant awardees and invited chapters by respected scholars in the field.

JoAnn (Jodi) Crandall is Professor Emerita of Education at the University of Maryland, Baltimore County, USA. She is a past president of TESOL, WATESOL, and AAAL, and a founding and current member of the TIRF Board of Trustees.

Kathleen M. Bailey is Professor of Applied Linguistics in the TESOL/TFL Programs at the Middlebury Institute of International Studies at Monterey and at Anaheim University, USA. She is a past president of both TESOL and AAAL, as well as the current president of TIRF.

GLOBAL RESEARCH ON TEACHING AND LEARNING ENGLISH

Co-published with The International Research Foundation for English Language Education (TIRF)

Kathleen M. Bailey & Ryan M. Damerow, Series Editors

Crandall & Bailey, Eds.
Global Perspectives on Language Education Policies

Carrier, Damerow, & Bailey, Eds.
Digital Language Learning and Teaching: Research, Theory, and Practice

Crandall & Christison, Eds.
Teacher Education and Professional Development in TESOL: Global Perspectives

Christison, Christian, Duff, & Spada, Eds.
Teaching and Learning English Grammar: Research Findings and Future Directions

Bailey & Damerow, Eds.
Teaching and Learning English in the Arabic-Speaking World

For additional information on titles in the Global Research on Teaching and Learning English series visit **www.routledge.com/books/series/TIRF**

GLOBAL PERSPECTIVES ON LANGUAGE EDUCATION POLICIES

Edited by
JoAnn (Jodi) Crandall and Kathleen M. Bailey

A co-publication with The International Research Foundation for English Language Education (TIRF)

First published 2018
by Routledge
711 Third Avenue, New York, NY 10017

and by Routledge
2 Park Square, Milton Park, Abingdon, Oxon, OX14 4RN

Routledge is an imprint of the Taylor & Francis Group, an informa business

© 2018 Taylor & Francis

The right of JoAnn (Jodi) Crandall and Kathleen M. Bailey to be identified as the authors of the editorial material, and of the authors for their individual chapters, has been asserted in accordance with sections 77 and 78 of the Copyright, Designs and Patents Act 1988.

All rights reserved. No part of this book may be reprinted or reproduced or utilized in any form or by any electronic, mechanical, or other means, now known or hereafter invented, including photocopying and recording, or in any information storage or retrieval system, without permission in writing from the publishers.

Trademark notice: Product or corporate names may be trademarks or registered trademarks, and are used only for identification and explanation without intent to infringe.

Library of Congress Cataloging-in-Publication Data
Names: Crandall, Jo Ann, editor. | Bailey, Kathleen M, editor.
Title: Global perspectives on language education policies /
  edited by JoAnn (Jodi) Crandall and Kathleen M. Bailey.
Description: New York ; London : Routledge, 2018. | Series: Global
  Research on Teaching and Learning English Series | Includes
  bibliographical references and index.
Identifiers: LCCN 2017040092 | ISBN 9781138090811 (hardback) |
  ISBN 9781138090828 (pbk.) | ISBN 9781315108421 (ebook)
Subjects: LCSH: Language policy—Research—Methodology. | Language
  planning—Research—Methodology. | Language and languages—
  Research—Methodology. | Language and languages—Study and
  teaching—Research.
Classification: LCC P40.5.L35 G46 2018 | DDC 306.44/9072—dc23
LC record available at https://lccn.loc.gov/2017040092

ISBN: 978-1-138-09081-1 (hbk)
ISBN: 978-1-138-09082-8 (pbk)
ISBN: 978-1-315-10842-1 (ebk)

Typeset in Bembo
by Apex CoVantage, LLC

 Printed in the United Kingdom
by Henry Ling Limited

This book is dedicated to the memory of Dr. James E. Alatis, one of TIRF's founding Trustees. Issues related to language education planning and policy were of great importance to him throughout his professional life in his positions in the U.S. Department of Education, at Georgetown University, and as the executive director of TESOL. Jim mentored many doctoral students at Georgetown, and we believe that he would be pleased with the work of these authors.

CONTENTS

Foreword   *xiii*
Joseph Lo Bianco

Preface   *xviii*
Kathleen M. Bailey

Acknowledgments   *xxiv*
JoAnn (Jodi) Crandall and Kathleen M. Bailey

1 Introduction   1
JoAnn (Jodi) Crandall and Kathleen M. Bailey

PART 1
The Teacher as Language Planner and Policy Maker   21

2 Whither Mother Tongue (in) Education? An
Ethnographic Study of Language Policy
in Rural Primary Schools in Pakistan   23
Aziz U. Khan

3 Agentic Responses to Communicative Language
Teaching in Language Policy: An Example
of Vietnamese English Primary Teachers   34
Duc Manh Le

x Contents

4 Examining Brazilian Foreign Language Policy and Its
Application in an EFL University Program: Teacher
Perspectives on Plurilingualism 46
Angelica Galante

5 Refugee Women in the United States Writing
Themselves Into New Community Spaces 56
Nicole Pettitt

PART 2
Adoption or Adaptation of Educational
Language Policies by/in Institutions 71

6 Policy Borrowing in University Language Planning:
A Case of Writing Centers in Japan 73
Tomoyo Okuda

7 Economic Markets, Elite Multilingualism, and Language
Policy in Nepali Schools 84
Bal Krishna Sharma

8 Linguistic Diversity and the Politics of International
Inclusion: Challenges in Integrating International
Teaching Assistants at a University in the
United States 95
Nicholas Close Subtirelu

9 Official and Realized Hiring Policy of Assistant
Language Teachers in Japan 106
Takahiro Yokoyama

PART 3
Perspectives of Diverse Stakeholders
on Educational Language Policy and Planning 117

10 Policy and Practicality in Timorese Higher Education:
Lessons From Lecturers in Development-related
Disciplines 119
Trent Newman

Contents **xi**

11 The Absence of Language-focused Teacher Education
    Policy in U.S. K12 Contexts: Insights From Language
    Socialization Research in a Ninth-grade
    Physics Classroom   130
    Sarah Braden and MaryAnn Christison

12 Bilingualism for All? Interrogating Language
    and Equity in Dual Language Immersion
    in Wisconsin   141
    Laura Hamman

13 Media Discourses of Language Policy and
    the "New" Latino Diaspora in Iowa   153
    Crissa Stephens

PART 4
Identity and Individual and "Invisible"
Language Policy and Planning   **167**

14 Rethinking Culturally and Linguistically Diverse
    Students' Perceptions of Family Language Policies
    and Identities in an American Afterschool Program   169
    Yu-Chi Wang

15 Digital Literacy, Language Learning, and
    Educational Policy in British Columbia   181
    Ron Darvin

16 Small Stories of/in Changing Times in Paraguay:
    A Resource for Identity Work in Language Policy
    Appropriation   192
    Katherine S. Mortimer

17 Challenges of Language Education Policy Development
    and Implementation in Creole-speaking Contexts:
    The Case of Jamaica   205
    Shondel Nero

xii Contents

18 Summary and Concluding Observations   219
G. Richard Tucker

About the Contributors   *226*
Index   *230*

FOREWORD

New Scholars, New Scholarship, New Optimism:
The Language Policy Revival Continues

Since its current revival commenced in the early years of the new millennium, the field of language policy and planning (LPP) has become richer in the stock of concepts used to interpret language problems in society, the methods deployed to investigate and explore language issues, the settings in which such research takes place, and the range of issues studied. This revival contrasts with the weak state the field had been reduced to in the late 1980s. At that time, even in academic programs devoted to the study of language in society, distinguished scholars such as Robert Kaplan could observe that language planning studies were a marginal concern, of interest to few people, and even in academic programs "only a handful of universities in the world offers anything more than a random course in language policy/planning" (Kaplan, 1994, p. 3).

That this situation was ever the case is an indictment of academic scholarship and of imagination, but also an indicator of the disciplinary silos that dominate much of academic life. A further reason why formal LPP studies had declined as much as Kaplan noted in 1994 is surely because few topics in the language sciences in general and applied linguistics in particular (or perhaps I should be bold and say no topic in any of the language sciences at all) connect so strongly to application. In short, LPP is where the rubber hits the road in the academic exploration of things linguistic. LPP is a topic that ties together what we study academically with what is decided and enacted in the real world, with direct consequences for students, indigenous or immigrant people, and many others. This distinction between studies of LPP and 'real world' LPP is critical. Whereas academic scholarship had shrunk in the early 1990s, not only in the realm of public

xiv Foreword

administration and the management of public resources, but also in many private and personal domains, actual LPP never declined. Whether it is the formal process of allocating funding to teach children languages, either their home languages or languages 'foreign' to them; to make decisions about refugee applications; to determine citizenship; to deliver hospital, medical, and legal services; to run drivers' license tests; or to negotiate with banks abroad and customers at home: All these practical and everyday things in the multilingual and multi-literate world we live in are sites and problems of language interaction, and in all of them decisions are made about language, whether or not academics study these problems.

In academic institutions, there is an additional obstacle to the presence of formal academic LPP research and teaching. This challenge has to do with multi-disciplinarity. LPP research is necessarily multi-disciplinary, and so, like all similar fields of research, it faces the crisis of lacking a 'natural' academic home, given that most higher education institutions remain rooted in formal disciplines.

This volume can be thought of as dealing with settings, issues, and purposes for LPP. There are many institutional settings where LPP occurs, such as education, hospitals, libraries, corporations, government departments, nations, international organizations, and religious bodies. There is an equally broad range of issues that LPP investigates, such as literacy, single languages, multiple languages, language assessment, language ideologies, non-verbal languages, script, signs and linguistic landscapes, and language discrimination, to name a very small number. There is also a vast set of purposes that LPP research might aim to achieve in addition to knowledge creation, such as efficiency as dictated by authoritative bodies, rights as demanded by speakers of minority or minoritized languages, and the revival of languages that are shedding users and becoming restricted in uses. But language policy research is also often directed at the causes of nationalism, prejudice, politics, power, or simply technology. This wide range of settings, issues, and reasons for doing LPP means that the field almost defies categorization.

This important new volume is welcome because it makes a singularly outstanding contribution to each of these areas, expanding still further the settings studied, deepening the exploration of issues examined, and refining the purposes for doing so. The volume is very ably edited by JoAnn (Jodi) Crandall and Kathleen M. Bailey, themselves highly significant contributors to aspects of language policy and planning related to English language education, assessment, policy, and innovation in technology. One key aspect is the voice of teachers as language policy makers and as language planners, which, in a rare move in the academic literature on LPP, is given pride of place in this book. This recognition marks a critical shift in language policy studies over recent decades, away from the nation- or authority-centered approach to a more dynamic and conversation-centered understanding of deliberate language change in the hands of educational practitioners. Past conceptions of language policy and planning were limited to the actions of government bodies and to authoritative texts, like a national constitution. The main reason for these restrictions was a highly limited idea of what counts as language change, how it comes about, and which voices are prominent in setting off the processes of social transformation that are reflected in language and often produced by and through language innovations.

The contributions in the first part of the book, by Aziz U. Khan, Duc Manh Le, Angelica Galante, and Nicole Pettitt, are important installments in this transformed understanding of where language policy and planning occur, who its agents and practitioners are, and the processes through which it operates. In the interactions between mother tongue minority pupils in a rural Pakistan primary school—and with teachers, administrators, and parents—and in Vietnamese English classes at the primary level in communicative-oriented classrooms, we see mechanisms of teacher agency and pupil interaction as instances of language policy and planning practice, of how attitudes and communication practices shape the language abilities and views of young people. Galante shifts the focus to university-level plurilingual programming, and Pettitt to refugee adult women in U.S. writing programs. In both of these latter cases, a similar dynamic of interactive, interpersonal, and pedagogical language planning is animated.

The next part of the book explores institutional language policies in Japan, Nepal, and the United States. Tomoyo Okuda, Bal Krishna Sharma, Nicholas Close Subtirelu, and Takahiro Yokoyama enrich the understanding of language policy and planning processes by showing, collectively and individually, the dynamic processes of even quite formal kinds of policy. These are shown to be a result of both cross-national borrowing, and also of increasingly connected economic markets and relations between elite and non-elite populations, policies of minority inclusion, and relatively mundane administrative procedures of the hiring of staff. These processes of administration and management contain their share of ideology and values, and in these chapters they are shown to be sensitive to global systems that rely on the flow and movement of ideas and operations of management. In effect, whereas the settings can differ and what occurs in them can be radically different from one place to another, there is also an overarching, shaping context derived from the now rapidly advanced process of education globalization and transnationalism. The consequence of this globalization of procedures means that certain concepts and methods of language policy analysis are taking root almost everywhere.

In the next part the focus moves to the perspectives of diverse stakeholders in educational LPP. Here Trent Newman, Sarah Braden and MaryAnn Christison, Laura Hamman, and Crissa Stephens add Timor-Leste, U.S. K12 physics classes, and the U.S. states of Wisconsin and Iowa into the mix. With these new settings come new problems and new purposes. Newman documents the remarkable situation of lecturers in Timor-Leste higher education who need to interpret formal policy, which is inevitably general and sometimes vague, along with occupational demands in fields as different as tourism and coffee production, and multiple

xvi Foreword

languages with their different hierarchies and statuses. Braden and Christison turn our attention to teacher education from the compelling angle of language socialization in a content area (ninth-grade physics), underscoring the ubiquity of settings in which language norms are negotiated in interaction. Hamman and Stephens direct their analysis to U.S. states, sites of great variation rather than uniformity, as they look at the treatment of multiple languages, such as dilemmas with ideals of universalistic dual language provision in Wisconsin (Hamman) and contrasts between mainstream media representations of desirable language policy and the various vintages of Latino presence in Iowa (Stephens).

It is clear that the new sites of language policy are at all levels of spatial distribution (macro, meso, and micro), but also with new registers of action, from the authoritative top down to the transgressive bottom up, and other forms of directionality and temporality. This distribution occurs because we use language as communication to make or establish, implicitly or explicitly, norms for our communication. These norms are applied in our choices of talk and writing, in the patterns of relationships among multiple languages, varieties of languages, and other semiotic systems that constitute everyday 'verbal' interaction.

Completing what is already an impressively layered and significant expansion of the possibilities for LPP, the final cluster of papers pushes still further, exploring LPP through individual acts and performances of identity and even through invisibility. Yu-Chi Wang opens with a discussion of family language policy and identity from the perspective of student participants in an afterschool program, showing the rich levels of consciousness and perception that are present. Ron Darvin documents learning and education policy settings in relation to the presence of digital learning resources and literacies in British Columbia. Katherine S. Mortimer moves the discussion to Paraguay and shows how "small stories" can constitute a resource in people's work to reshape identities in response to received or outsider positioning of them. Nero's focus on Jamaica is no less complex and situated than Mortimer's. Nero pays close attention to the many layers of de facto language in education policy. She does so in settings of intra-language diversity, such as the diverse but hierarchically arranged varieties of English and Creole.

G. Richard Tucker, long one of the most original and inventive writers about language policy and planning and well ahead of the game of its new and diverse manifestations, provides an epilogue of reflections about this once endangered field of scholarship, which now enjoys robust new life. He is a trustee of TIRF, The International Research Foundation for English Language Education, which fosters multilingual research all over the world to improve education, scholarship, and communication across borders. TIRF, in its partnership with Routledge, is a perfect body to issue this fine book.

The individual parts of this book are fascinating, detailed, and scholarly displays of language policy and planning as it happens and where it happens, increasingly more diverse in both. The collective whole is a resource that stakes out a new public importance for the intersection of the language sciences and the many real worlds we occupy.

Joseph Lo Bianco
University of Melbourne, and TIRF Trustee

Reference

Kaplan, R. B. (1994). Language policy and planning: Fundamental issues. *Annual Review of Applied Linguistics, 14*, 3–19.

PREFACE

Please think of the following situations.

An EFL teacher must decide, moment to moment, whether to use English or the national language or a local language in class. The teacher knows that the national policy requires target language use, but the students' low level of language proficiency seems to demand explanations in their first language.

Parents in an English-dominant region must decide—if they have a choice—whether to enroll their children in monolingual schools or to locate programs which would allow the children to learn in a bilingual or multilingual curriculum.

A teacher in a family language and literacy program believes that using locally generated texts based on the learners' experiences would be more beneficial than using the required commercially produced textbook, which is largely unrelated to the reality of those learners' lives.

People in a small city learn about the success of a local dual language immersion program in the newspaper and on television. But a researcher wonders what stance the media authors have adopted and how their reports are related to findings of studies on language learning.

A country institutes a program that requires native speakers of an important world language to serve as assistant teachers in foreign language classrooms. Many of these foreign assistant teachers have very limited professional preparation (if any), and the local language teachers have mixed feelings about their presence.

Local teachers and educational administrators believe that developing school children's bilingual competence is both an asset and a right. They choose to develop a curriculum that will promote that competence, even though the new curriculum is not entirely in alignment with statewide policies.

University administrators in one country adopt (or adapt) policies and programs developed for a related need in another country. A researcher wonders how those 'borrowed' policies play out in reality.

School goals and policies about digital literacy influence learners' use of the range of technological tools available to them to some extent. But whether or not all the pupils have access to technology and guidance about how to use it at home is another matter, which influences the realization of the school goals.

Language teachers understand that the official language policy articulates particular goals and approaches, but limited local funding for resources does not support the implementation of those approaches and goals. In addition, the teachers have not been professionally prepared to carry out those goals in their lessons.

University professors teaching in a range of disciplines are faced with the question of using the national language, the colonial language, or the language(s) their students understand best. The situation is complicated because of the language(s) in which the textbooks are published. In addition, many of the professors themselves received their subject matter training in languages in which the students are not proficient.

In other university contexts, international graduate students are hired as teaching assistants (TAs) to support undergraduate students in a wide range of disciplines. Although these TAs have substantial knowledge and skill in their own fields of expertise, they are not native speakers of the language of instruction. Policies may or may not exist at the institutional (or even departmental) level to determine what proficiency in the language of instruction is necessary or desirable. The TAs' language skills (or lack thereof) are often blamed (by students, parents, legislators, etc.) for students' learning difficulties. But what about those learners? Are they making an effort to communicate effectively with their TAs? Is TA testing and training the answer to this problem, or is some more broadly envisioned cross-cultural communication training needed for the learners as well?

All these situations are related—either directly or indirectly—to language planning and policy issues in educational contexts.

Historical Context for this Volume

Since 2002, The International Research Foundation for English Language Education (TIRF) has been funding doctoral research on topical priorities determined by the Foundation's Trustees. When the Board of Trustees first decided that TIRF should support doctoral research, a meeting was held to establish the key issues to be funded. (See Duff & Bailey, 2001, for a discussion of the topics that were identified at that meeting.) Over the years, the TIRF Trustees have added new priorities and updated the existing ones to respond to developments in the field of language education.

According to TIRF's website, the term *language planning* "encompasses all the processes, formal and informal, overt and covert, which shape the direction and nature of change in language" (TIRF, 2013, para. 1). In contrast, *language policy* "involves explicit decisions usually taken by authorities to influence the function, structure, or acquisition of a language or language variety in a particular

xx Preface

speech community, an institution or in a geo-political space, such as a nation" (TIRF, 2013, para 1). The website adds that recently there has been an increase of "practical language planning and policy making as a result of economic globalization, increased population movements, and the expansion of communication technologies linking all parts of the world in real time. Global English is a key part of these phenomena" (TIRF, 2013, para. 2).

TIRF's Mission Statement

Indeed, the Foundation's mission statement specifically addresses language policy as its final point:

> TIRF's vision is that in the 21st century, personal and social value accrues to individuals who are proficient in English and in some additional language. Therefore, TIRF's mission embodies four major goals:
>
> - to implement a research and development program that will generate new knowledge and inform and improve the quality of English language teaching and learning;
> - to promote the application of research to practical language problems;
> - to collect, organize, and disseminate information and research on the teaching and learning of language; and
> - to influence the formation and implementation of appropriate language education policies, recognizing the importance of indigenous languages and cultures worldwide, and of English as an international language (TIRF, 2010, para. 2).

In selecting language planning and policy as a research priority for funding and now as the focus of the fifth TIRF-Routledge volume, the Trustees decided to address this fourth goal in depth.

Doctoral Dissertation Grants

TIRF's research priority on language planning and policy was first adopted in 2013, at the urging of TIRF trustee Joseph Lo Bianco, an internationally recognized expert on language policy and planning issues. (See, for example, Lo Bianco, 2005, 2009, 2010; Lo Bianco & Freebody, 2001.) Since that time, the Foundation has funded 13 doctoral studies on this important topic. And in this, the fifth volume in the TIRF-Routledge series, Global Research on Teaching and Learning English, the majority of the chapters are based on the research of TIRF's grantees who have addressed this important constellation of issues.

The TIRF James E. Alatis Prize

In addition to funding Doctoral Dissertation Grants, the TIRF Trustees have chosen to emphasize the importance of language planning and policy by instituting the TIRF James E. Alatis Prize for Research on Language Policy and Planning in Educational Contexts. Jim Alatis was a member of the original task force established by Joy Reid, the then-president of Teachers of English to Speakers of Other Languages (TESOL). The members of that task force explored the possibility of establishing a foundation to support research in our field. Jim then served as a member of the Board of Trustees for many years and was voted "Trustee Emeritus" by his Board colleagues. Jim supported TIRF, both intellectually and financially, throughout his life, and members of his family have continued that tradition since his death in 2015.

The annual Alatis Prize competition recognizes an outstanding chapter or article reporting on empirical research on language planning and/or policy. Selection criteria include "the quality of the work and its potential impact on the field of language policy and planning in educational contexts" (TIRF, 2015, para. 4). The first recipient of the Alatis Prize was Dr. Shondel Nero. Her article was entitled "De Facto Language Education Policy Through Teachers' Attitudes and Practices: A Critical Ethnographic Study in Three Jamaican Schools" (Nero, 2014). It appeared in the journal *Language Policy*. The second recipient was Dr. Katherine Mortimer, for her article, "Producing Change and Stability: A Scalar Analysis of Paraguayan Bilingual Education Policy Implementation" (Mortimer, 2016), which appeared in *Linguistics and Education*. We are very pleased that both of these authors have provided new chapters for the present volume.

Methodological Approaches

The empirical studies in this volume all utilized qualitative approaches to data collection and analysis, although within that broad paradigm there is a great deal of variety.

Several of the studies published herein report on parts of broader ethnographic research. The chapters by Braden and Christison, Khan, Pettitt, and Newman take this approach. Of course, in an edited volume, only a small portion of a larger ethnography can be presented. I encourage interested readers to seek out the larger works: Braden (2016), Khan (2014), Newman (forthcoming), and Pettitt (2017).

Many of these authors used interviews to solicit information. Newman and Sharma both used *focus groups*: "The focus group method involves a small group of people discussing a topic or issues defined by a researcher" (Cameron, 2005, p. 116). Newman also conducted interviews with individuals, as did Darvin, Subtirelu, Khan, Nero, Mortimer, and Braden and Christison. Three authors—Le, Galante, and Pettitt—used *semi-structured interviews*, in which the researcher employs a set of prepared questions, but uses "these questions as a point of departure for the interview and will not be constrained by them" (Nunan & Bailey, 2009, p. 313).

xxii Preface

Observation was also widely used as a data collection procedure in several of these chapters. Newman, Braden and Christison, and Nero all conducted classroom observations in the contexts they studied. Darvin observed two young Filipino immigrants in Canada as they used their computers. Mortimer, Pettitt, and Wang conducted participant observations—i.e., they were "engaged in the activities of the group they were studying" (Nunan & Bailey, 2009, p. 194), rather than maintaining their distance.

The data analysis procedures in eight chapters include policy document analysis—those by Mortimer, Nero, Yokoyama, Braden and Christison, Subtirelu, Khan, Okuda, and Stephens. Nero also analyzed textbooks in the Jamaican context.

Further data collection procedures included recordings of small group discussions (Wang), an online survey (Yokoyama), and a questionnaire for teachers (Nero). Both Braden and Christison's chapter and the one by Darvin involved the analysis of artifacts. Other analytic procedures included self-rating of proficiency (Yokoyama) and content analysis (Braden and Christison). Four studies used discourse analyses (Mortimer, Pettitt, Khan, and Wang). Two of those (Khan and Mortimer) refer specifically to narrative analyses. Two other chapters—those by Newman and Stephens—describe their use of intertextual and interdiscursive analyses. Only two of the chapters incorporated quantitative data collection and analyses. Both Okuda and Yokoyama use frequency counts as part of their broader interpretive analyses.

Concluding Comments

I am very pleased, as a co-editor of this volume, to share these outcomes of TIRF's focus on language planning and policy with our reading audience. On behalf of the Board of Trustees, I want to congratulate and thank the contributors. It is my hope that this book will be of great value to its readers and that its publication will help "to influence the formation and implementation of appropriate language education policies, recognizing the importance of indigenous languages and cultures worldwide, and of English as an international language" (TIRF, 2010, para. 2).

Kathleen M. Bailey
Middlebury Institute of International Studies at Monterey
Monterey, California

References

Braden, S. K. (2016). *Scientific inquiry as social and linguistic practice: Language socialization pathways in a ninth-grade physics class* (unpublished doctoral dissertation). University of Utah, Salt Lake City, Utah.

Cameron, J. (2005). Focusing on the focus group. In I. Hay (Ed.), *Qualitative research methods in human geography* (2nd ed., pp. 116–132). Oxford, UK: Oxford University Press.

Duff, P. A., & Bailey, K. M. (2001). Identifying research priorities: Themes and directions for the TESOL International Research Foundation. *TESOL Quarterly, 35*(4), 595–616.

Khan, A. (2014). *A study of the language attitudes and practices in the context of two elite English-medium schools in Pakistan* (unpublished doctoral dissertation). University of Auckland, Auckland, New Zealand.

Lo Bianco, J. (2005). Including discourse in language planning. In P. Bruthiau (Ed.), *Directions in applied linguistics* (pp. 255–263). Clevedon, UK: Multilingual Matters.

Lo Bianco, J. (Ed.). (2009). *China and English: Globalisation and the dilemmas of identity.* Clevedon, UK: Multilingual Matters.

Lo Bianco, J. (2010). Language policy and planning. In N. H. Hornberger & S. L. McKay (Eds.), *Sociolinguistics and language education* (pp. 143–176). Bristol, UK: Multilingual Matters.

Lo Bianco, J., & Freebody, P. (2001). *Australian literacies: Informing national policy on literacy education.* Melbourne, Australia: Language Australia Ltd.

Mortimer, K. S. (2016). Producing change and stability: A scalar analysis of Paraguayan bilingual education policy implementation. *Linguistics and Education, 34,* 58–69.

Nero, S. (2014). De facto language education policy through teachers' attitudes and practices: A critical ethnographic study in three Jamaican schools. *Language Policy, 13*(3), 221–242.

Newman, T. P. (forthcoming). *Localised heteroglossic higher education: Tracing the multilingual pedagogies of Timorese lecturers in development-related disciplines* (unpublished doctoral dissertation). Melbourne, Australia: University of Melbourne.

Nunan, D. C., & Bailey, K. M. (2009). *Exploring second language classroom research: A comprehensive guide.* Boston, MA: Cengage.

Pettitt, N. (2017). *Social positioning in refugee women's education: A linguistic ethnography of one classroom* (unpublished doctoral dissertation). Georgia State University, Atlanta, Georgia.

TIRF. (2010). *TIRF's mission statement.* Retrieved July 28, 2017 from www.tirfonline.org/about-us/

TIRF. (2013). *Language planning and policy.* Retrieved July 28, 2017 from www.tirfonline.org/research-grants/tirfs-research-priorities/language-planning-and-policy/

TIRF. (2015). *Alatis Prize.* Retrieved July 28, 2017 from www.tirfonline.org/grants-prizes/alatis-prize/

ACKNOWLEDGMENTS

We are very grateful to the following people, all of whom have helped bring this project to fruition:

- First, we want to thank our editorial assistants, Arvanoush Boudaghians, who managed the initial communications with the authors, and Kelly Donovan, who did a masterful job of word processing, managing files, editing, and indexing as the project continued. Their involvement was funded by a Wyckoff Professional Development Grant from the Middlebury Institute of International Studies at Monterey.
- Our publishing colleagues, Naomi Silverman, Karen Adler, and Emmalee Ortega, have been consistently supportive over the years of the TIRF-Routledge partnership.
- Ryan Damerow, TIRF's Chief Operating Officer and also a series editor, read the entire manuscript in a very short period of time and gave us valuable feedback.
- TIRF Trustees Joe Lo Bianco and Dick Tucker graciously supported this project by writing the foreword and the epilogue, respectively. Terry Wiley gave us his time and his insights on language planning and policy in educational contexts.
- Finally, we must express our deep gratitude to all the chapter authors, who are either TIRF Doctoral Dissertation Grantees or recipients of the TIRF James E. Alatis Prize for Research on Language Planning and Policy in Educational Contexts. Authors and editors in this TIRF-Routledge series forego any honoraria or royalties for their work so that any royalties realized from the sale of the books may be channeled directly into the Foundation's ongoing programs.

JoAnn (Jodi) Crandall and Kathleen M. Bailey, Editors

1

INTRODUCTION

JoAnn (Jodi) Crandall and Kathleen M. Bailey

This collection reports on language education policy research by 14 TIRF Doctoral Dissertation Grantees and the first two winners of the TIRF James E. Alatis Prize for Research on Language Policy and Planning in Educational Contexts. Language education policy, also variously referred to as educational language policy (Cooper, Shohamy, & Walters, 2001) or language-in-education policy (Plüddemann, 2015), involves policy decisions that can be realized through educational practices regarding the following:

- promotion of languages/varieties as mediums of instruction, including in bilingual/multilingual contexts;
- acquisition of additional (often official or international) languages;
- choice of languages for initial literacy and for teaching specific subjects such as science or technology;
- support for minority or indigenous/community languages;
- recognition of the linguistic resources of plurilingual individuals (Council of Europe, 2007); and
- decisions for which languages and skills are assessed.

Language education policy involves both top-down and bottom-up (Hornberger, 1997) planning and processes, also referred to by Coulmas (2005) as macro- and micro-choices. Macro-choices involve the "allocation of languages and varieties, the promotion of languages for education, and managing patterns of multilingualism," whereas micro-choices involve "daily decisions about classroom language use, such as dealing with gendered speech, dialects, and code-switching" (Coulmas, 2005, p. 6; Cf: Clyne, 2001 on micro-policy as a barometer of change and Baldauf, 2006 on the importance of micro-language planning in

2 JoAnn (Jodi) Crandall and Kathleen M. Bailey

ecological contexts). Language policy is also developed and implemented at the meso-level—that is, by institutions, programs, etc.

Ricento and Hornberger (1996) use the metaphor of an onion to describe the many layers of language education policy and the ways in which agents, levels, and processes "interact with each other" (p. 402). The outer layer is where official policy documents, laws, or regulations are created and promoted by national and supranational agencies. Such official policy statements can even be administered by consulates or embassies abroad. (See, for example, Yokoyama, this volume, on the administration of the Japanese English Teacher program.)

These laws or official policy documents are then "interpreted and modified" (Ricento & Hornberger, 1996, p. 409) in an array of smaller institutions (such as schools, universities, businesses, and community organizations, as well as the media) by diverse individuals, who have their own experiences, perspectives, and goals. In each of these contexts, institutions and individuals may adapt, transform, ignore, or reject the policy. In the case of language education planning and policy, schools and universities play a primary institutional role, determining the curriculum or texts, deciding on professional development initiatives, etc., although the media also have an important role (as Stephens, this volume, makes clear).

At the innermost layer are the teachers, who are central to "educational and social change and institutional transformation" (Ricento & Hornberger, 1996, p. 417) within their local contexts. They are "the heart of language policy" (Ricento & Hornberger, 1996, p. 417). Teachers enact the curriculum and through their practice ignore, resist, or adapt policy. For example, they may disregard the textbooks provided by a program or mandated by state policy and implement the practices they believe will be more effective with their learners, such as the use of the Language Experience Approach by a teacher of refugee women in the US (Pettitt, this volume), or adapt texts and provide additional resources, as illustrated by Vietnamese teachers attempting to implement communicative teaching with young learners (Le, this volume). In some cases, teachers may not even be aware that the policy exists, as in the case of a policy governing the use of Jamaican Creole in education (Nero, this volume).

Menken and García (2010) describe a dynamic language education policy in which the onion is "stirred" by numerous stakeholders (with a focus on teachers and teacher agency), rather than a bottom-up set of linear processes and practices. Teachers are more than interpreters of policy; they are active policy agents creating policy through their decisions and their practices (García & Menken, 2010). And educational policies are assessed in their importance by learners, as evidenced by the discussion of the relative importance of Chinese as a global economic language in Nepal (Sharma, this volume).

Responses to national policy are not always compliant, for a number of possible reasons. For example, whereas mother-tongue literacy may be permissible or even mandated, parents may not want the school to take time away from the study or use of mediums of instruction which are perceived to be more powerful. In

Introduction **3**

other cases, curricula, materials, or teachers who can teach through that language may not be available (Newman, this volume; Shohamy, 2006). The local language may be perceived as not adequately developed to use as a medium of instruction, as in the case of Tetun in Timor-Leste (Newman, this volume). In some situations, the language of the textbook may differ substantially from the language spoken by both teachers and learners, as in the case of Pashto in rural Pakistan (Khan, this volume). An additional challenge to policy is the lack of mandated competence or availability of professional development opportunities to address issues related to language by mainstream or subject matter teachers, as in the case of science teachers with English learners in the US (Braden & Christison, this volume); to communication by international teaching assistants in U.S. universities and their students (Subtirelu, this volume); or to implementing plurilingual policies in language classes (see Galante, on English as a foreign language classes, this volume). Conflicting policies also present a problem, such as the qualifications expected of Assistant Language Teachers in Japan (Yokoyama, this volume).

Globalization and internationalization policies at universities have led to questions of medium of instruction. In many contexts, the choice is English (Park & Pawan, 2016; Kling, 2016), although as Okuda (this volume) discusses, the choice can be Japanese in Japan. Additional to the choice of language is the choice of cultures which are represented or presented through the language (for example, cultures other than American and British, etc., in English as a foreign language class; see Galante, this volume). Internationalization efforts may also be part of an effort to promote changes in language teaching approaches, e.g., to focus on communicative competence through a communicative approach or to enhance understanding of a country and culture by international students, both of which are discussed by Okuda (this volume).

Language policy may also be explicit or implicit. For example, the United States has no official language, although a majority of individual states in the US have explicit language policies which designate English as the official language. However, New Mexico and Hawai'i have two official languages, as does the Commonwealth of Puerto Rico (Wiley, 2000).

As it moves from layer to layer, policy is "interpreted and modified" (Ricento & Hornberger, 1996, p. 409; Cf. García & Menken, 2010). Wiley and García (2016) have called for greater attention to the role of local agents (Cf. language planning arbiters, Johnson & Johnson, 2015) in policy implementation. (See Hamman, this volume, on the role of teachers, administrators, board members, and the community in implementing a district's first dual language immersion program in Wisconsin.) As Hornberger and Johnson (2007) indicate, policy documents "are nothing without the human agents who act as interpretive conduits between the language policy levels" (p. 258). Indeed, as Menken and García (2010) note, "At each level of an educational system, from the national ministry or department of education to the classroom, language education policies are interpreted, negotiated, and ultimately (re)constructed in the process of implementation" (p. 1).

But some language education policy is invisible. Families (and communities) may have a direct or indirect impact on language-in-education policy in their decisions of which language(s) to use at home, which language(s) to support in the education of their children, and which language(s) can best serve their children's and their family's social status. (See Curdt-Christiansen, 2009; King & Fogle, 2013; see as well the discussion of immigrant students' perspectives on language use in Wang, this volume.) Parental practices and socioeconomic realities also play a part in language policy. For instance, as Darvin (this volume) indicates, considering youth as digital natives or digital immigrants ignores the diverse ways in which youth use technology and the implications thereof for educational policy.

Identity also plays a powerful (although sometimes invisible) role in educational language policy, especially at the level of teachers and learners. When that policy changes, those who were governed by previous policies may find that they no longer meet the expectations or requirements of the current policy, although they may agree with its intent. See, for example, the relationships between identity and Guarani in Paraguay (Mortimer, this volume). As Johnson and Johnson (2015) make clear, language policy has a great deal to do with issues of power, prejudice, and identity.

Perspectives on language policy range from what Ruiz (1984) has referred to as language as a problem, as a resource, or as a right. Examples of these orientations or attitudes toward language policy or practices can all be found in the chapters in this collection.

Part 1: The Teacher as Language Planner and Policy Maker

Part 1 of this collection focuses on ways in which teachers, although they are "non-authorized policy actors," become "de facto language planner[s] and policy maker[s]" (McCarty, 2011, p. 15). In the four studies in this part, teachers develop educational language policy at the micro or local or bottom-up level, exercising agency in their choice of language, activities, or materials. Sometimes teachers make these choices in response to written policies, sometimes in the absence of these policies (e.g., Pettitt, this volume).

Most of the studies on teacher agency have focused on tertiary (especially university) contexts. (See, e.g., Hamid, Zhu, & Baldauf, 2014; Zacharias, 2013.) That observation makes the first two chapters in this part particularly important because they report on the ways in which primary teachers in two contexts (Pakistan and Vietnam) responded to changes in language education policy.

Aziz Khan's chapter, "Whither Mother Tongue (in) Education?: An Ethnographic Study of Language Policy in Rural Primary Schools in Pakistan," explores how two teachers "viewed and put into practice the recently introduced language-in-education policy of using the learners' mother tongue [Pashto] as the medium of instruction" (Khan, this volume, p. 23). Although the choice of medium of instruction was left to the provinces, the policy recommended the "teaching [of] English (the only official language), Urdu (the only national language), and one regional language as subjects" in primary schools, although Khan notes that the regional languages were "largely ignored" (this volume, p. 24). However, in the province of Khyber Pakhtunkhwa, where the majority of the population speaks Pashto, the regional language was reintroduced as a compulsory subject and even used as a medium of instruction in some schools. In his ethnographic and narrative study, Khan sought the perspectives of two rural primary teachers in a Pashto-medium government school in a small village, where English, Urdu, and Pashto were all taught, but with the textbooks for English and Urdu written in Pashto. Khan found that whereas the teachers expressed "great love and pride for their mother tongue," "they doubt[ed] its instrumental value" (Khan, this volume, p. 27). Moreover, the teachers believed that Pashto didn't need to be taught because their students all knew Pashto. They believed that time would be better spent teaching in Urdu or English. As Khan concludes, "Macro-level policy decisions regarding the medium of instruction had little relevance to how the teachers actually employed languages for teaching and learning at the micro-level in their rural primary schools" (Khan, this volume, p. 30), partially because of lack of planning for implementing the policy. It was, in the words of Pearson (2014), "a policy without a plan" (p. 51).

Duc Manh Le's chapter, "Agentic Responses to Communicative Language Teaching in Language Policy: An Example of Vietnamese English Primary Teachers," also focuses on teacher agency by primary school teachers in response to a new policy. In this case, it was a policy that "mandates a communicative language teaching approach" (Le, this volume, p. 36) and makes communicative competence the goal of English language learning. It also lowers the starting age for English from Grade 6 to Grade 3. Le interviewed six Vietnamese primary school teachers over a four-month period during their attempts to implement the policy and found they faced a number of difficulties: "insufficient professional support," i.e., "lack of sufficient professional training on how to teach communicatively" (this volume, p. 37); "overloaded and inappropriate teaching contents" (this volume, p. 38); "limited teaching resources" (this volume, p. 39); and "constrained language classroom settings" (this volume, p. 40). However, there were a number of ways in which teachers creatively compensated for these difficulties: by pursuing their own professional development, by relying on their professional knowledge of effective teaching practice in adapting the mandated textbook, by finding ways of engaging children in pairs or groups within their small spaces, and even by buying needed supplementary resources themselves. As Le concludes, these teachers, rather than being "passive policy recipients or teaching technicians" (Le, this volume, p. 41), "had the capacity to act as agents" (Le, this volume, p. 41).

Angelica Galante's chapter, "Examining Brazilian Foreign Language Policy and Its Application in an EFL University Program: Teacher Perspectives on

6 JoAnn (Jodi) Crandall and Kathleen M. Bailey

Plurilingualism," explores "the extent to which linguistic and cultural diversity represented in Brazilian foreign language policies aligns with the concept of plurilingualism" (Galante, this volume, p. 47) as expressed in the Common European Framework of Reference (Council of Europe, 2001, 2007). *Plurilingualism* usually refers to "the repertoire of varieties of language which many individuals use . . . [including] 'first language' and any number of other languages and varieties" (King, 2017, p. 6, drawing on work by the Council of Europe, 2007). When applied to language teaching, as Galante explains, it is "an approach to teaching languages that harnesses the use of students' knowledge of other languages, dialects, and cultures" (Galante, this volume, p. 47). The eight university EFL teachers in her study in Brasilia believed the inclusion of linguistic and cultural diversity topics was important, but three of them placed particular emphasis on American and British cultures, although one noted the importance of varieties other than "English from the United States or French from France" (Galante, this volume, p. 51). The teachers identified three benefits of including knowledge of other cultures and languages in the EFL classroom: "(1) connections among languages and cultures, facilitating the learning of new ones; (2) open-mindedness and respect toward other languages and cultures, and (3) development of critical global citizens" (Galante, this volume, p. 51). They also identified a number of challenges, including limited time for teaching English, limited knowledge about other languages and cultures by teachers and students, and limited focus on other cultures in the text, requiring teachers to do extra preparation to address diversity.

Nicole Pettitt's chapter, "Refugee Women in the United States Writing Themselves Into New Community Spaces," reports on part of a larger ethnographic study (Pettitt, 2017) of a family literacy program in the southeastern United States. It explicates one teacher's decision to use the Language Experience Approach (LEA), rather than adhering to the funder-provided textbook in a beginning adult ESOL (English for speakers of other languages) class. This program enrolled refugee women and their children (ages 0–5), with the goals of "preparing children for kindergarten and making ESOL available to women who needed childcare in order to attend" (Pettitt, this volume, p. 57). LEA is a participatory literacy approach (Freire, 1970; Shor & Freire, 1987; Spener, 1992) in which students' discussions about community or home events (Landis, Umolu, & Mancha, 2010)— often related to whole class experiences—serve as the basis for the development of reading (and writing) activities and materials. In this approach, the teacher serves as both prompter and scribe, eliciting information from the learners and in the process creating a text that they then copy and use for multiple learning activities. Pettitt describes several patterns of valued practice in this teacher's class, including the use of community as a "learning (con)text" (Pettitt, this volume, p. 63) and the importance of "learner voice" in producing the classroom text (Pettitt, this volume, p. 63). The author further notes that although the focus of the class was on learning English, the teacher also encouraged the students to use their own language and literacy repertoires (an example of plurilingualism). For these refugee women, the family literacy class provided a place where their experiences, thoughts, and languages were valued.

What these four chapters have in common is a focus on teacher agency: on the multiple ways in which teachers in their classroom practices and curricula reject or adapt language policies developed and promulgated by authorities who may have limited understanding of the community and classroom contexts in which the policies are expected to be implemented. The teachers relied on their knowledge of the local context and their learners' needs and goals to implement what they believed to be better educational language policies.

Part 2: Adoption or Adaptation of Educational Language Policies by/in Institutions

The four chapters in this part address the theme of adoption or adaptation of educational language policy by institutions. The authors examine policy issues in four very diverse contexts: writing centers in Japanese universities, Mandarin as a foreign language in Nepali private schools, international teaching assistants in U.S. universities, and Assistant Language Teachers in Japanese schools.

The first chapter, by Tomoyo Okuda, on "Policy Borrowing in University Language Planning: A Case of Writing Centers in Japan," analyzes the ways in which universities and educators selectively borrow and adapt educational policies and practices to meet national and local needs (Phillips & Ochs, 2004; Steiner-Khamsi, 2014). Her study of cross-national policy borrowing analyzes "the political rationales, power dynamics, and consequences of transferring educational systems, models, and concepts across contexts . . . [which] is not only a matter of adopting better educational practices, but also involves deeper political and economic interests and motives" (Okuda, this volume, p. 75), in this case, on the development of writing centers in Japanese universities. By analyzing government documents, university writing center webpages, and research articles, Okuda identifies a number of reasons why the writing center philosophy was borrowed in Japan and why writing centers "proliferate[d]" there (Okuda, this volume, p. 74). Okuda found that writing centers in Japan serve different functions for different clients: native speakers of Japanese can get help with their Japanese writing, or with their English writing, and international students can receive support in their Japanese writing. She notes that these centers have spread not only because of government policies promoting English and bilingualism in the workplace, but also because of "educators' interests in Western-based pedagogy . . . [and selective] borrowing . . . to match the Japanese higher education agenda" (Okuda, this volume, p. 80). More recently, the Ministry of Education has also emphasized the importance of communication skills in Japanese, with writing centers not only focused on Japanese writing, but also on their potential to foster active learning (a concept borrowed from Western educational philosophy) and academic socialization. In addition, writing centers have become one way to internationalize Japanese universities.

8 JoAnn (Jodi) Crandall and Kathleen M. Bailey

The next chapter, "Economic Markets, Elite Multilingualism, and Language Policy in Nepali Schools," by Bal Krishna Sharma, also investigates the effects of globalization on language policy and practices, but this time with an emphasis on the growth and influence of Mandarin Chinese in Nepal. Sharma analyzes "the role of economic markets, such as business and tourism, in shaping language policies that promote an 'elite' form of multilingualism in two Nepali private schools" in which English has long held dominant status, serving as the medium of instruction from kindergarten and as the language of communication among teachers and students (Sharma, this volume, p. 84). In this chapter, he analyzes policy issues involved in the decision by these two multilingual, elite private schools to offer Mandarin as a foreign language courses beginning in the fourth grade, asking what motivated the schools to implement the policy of offering Chinese courses and how the students make sense of and interpret that policy in terms of the relative value of learning Chinese and/or learning English. Sharma finds a "strong tie between language policy and political economy in these two schools" (this volume, p. 88). School administrators identified the largely economic value of offering Chinese for their students' employability and education, noting that students' parents are principally involved in business where Chinese is another useful international and regional language. The learners reported personal reasons for studying Chinese: to help a father in business or to study medicine in China. They perceive China as a world power, as well as a neighbor, and Chinese as an economically valuable language, but they still view English as the major international language, with Chinese more restricted to Asian contexts, but they also note its usefulness in Nepal.

In the next chapter, "Linguistic Diversity and the Politics of International Inclusion: Challenges in Integrating International Teaching Assistants at a University in the United States," Nicholas Close Subtirelu investigates the situation of nonnative speaking teaching assistants (TAs) at U.S. universities—a context that has received a great deal of attention since the early 1980s. For many years, the "foreign TA problem," as it was formerly called (see, e.g., Bailey, 1984, p. 3), was seen entirely as a result of some TAs' insufficient English proficiency. In spite of being highly qualified graduate students in their own disciplines, the nonnative TAs' spoken English and listening comprehension challenges were often perceived by their undergraduate students as the sources of teaching and learning difficulties. The related publications at the time dealt largely with the development of English language programs and/or testing procedures (see, e.g., Abraham & Plakans, 1988; Byrd & Constantinides, 1988; Hinofotis, Bailey, & Stern, 1981), or with students' perceptions of TAs' English (see, e.g., Briggs & Hofer, 1991; Hinofotis & Bailey, 1981). In recent years, however, this situation has been relabeled to focus on *international* teaching assistants (ITAs) instead of *foreign* TAs, and to acknowledge that the undergraduate students they teach should also have a role in promoting successful communication. Subtirelu's research in a large public university in the US asks what policies or support prepare students to successfully communicate with ITAs and what support ITAs have to prepare them for their teaching duties. He found little policy guidance or support for either and makes a compelling case for viewing the ITAs' work as a cross-cultural context. He argues that universities should provide training for the students to better understand nonnative speech and to better communicate with the ITAs, as well as providing better assessment of and support for the ITAs.

In the final chapter of this part, we continue a discussion about policy related to international teachers, but this time in Japan, with a focus on Assistant Language Teachers (ALTs), who are recruited to support English language instruction in the schools, especially in communicative language classes, and to promote internationalization. Takahiro Yokoyama, in "Official and Realized Hiring Policy of Assistant Language Teachers in Japan," examines the competing policies of the Ministry of Education, Culture, Sports, Science and Technology and the Ministry of Foreign Affairs regarding the qualifications and the major contributions of the ALTs and how those policies play out in hiring practices. ALTs can be qualified language teachers (although what that designation entails is not entirely clear) or can be strongly motivated to teach a foreign language. Additional evaluation is given for language teaching or general teaching experience, as well as for proficiency in Japanese. Drawing on an online survey, Yokoyama finds a higher percentage of ALTs with Japanese proficiency (self-reported at the intermediate level or above) than with qualifications in general education or teaching English to speakers of other languages (TESOL). He posits that the preference for selecting ALTs with Japanese proficiency may be the result of the government's policies of internationalization, but rather than promoting globalization through English in Japan, the objective is to promote "Japaneseness" (Hashimoto, 2009, p. 38). He recommends greater clarity in the policy for selecting ALTs and their placements because their major assignment is teaching English or assisting Japanese teachers of English.

As these four chapters reveal, a number of factors affect the implementation of institutional language-in-education policy and its adoption or adaptation to meet what may be competing or hidden agendas. Writing centers may be created to help students improve their English or Japanese writing skills, but they also may be used to encourage different teaching and learning approaches. Chinese may be adopted as another global language in private schools in Nepal because parents, students, and administrators all see its largely economic value. Depending on their roles, U.S. universities may need to adapt their policies to provide more linguistic and cultural support for both international teaching assistants and their students. Last, it might be useful to clarify competing policies affecting the hiring of Assistant Language Teachers for Japanese schools, especially if these ALTs are expected to (team) teach English.

Part 3: Perspectives of Diverse Stakeholders on Educational Language Policy and Planning

Part 3 of this collection offers perspectives from diverse stakeholders on educational language policy and planning. Included here are the voices of lecturers

10 JoAnn (Jodi) Crandall and Kathleen M. Bailey

concerning language choice in the plurilingual context of Timor-Leste, where four languages are commonly shared by students and teachers; the ways in which an English learner is marginalized in group work in a ninth-grade physics lab with inadequate attention to helping her develop needed communicative strategies; how local policy actors, including teachers, administrators, parents, and members of the community, challenged state policy and established a dual language immersion program; and the ways in which a dual language immersion program in a rural part of the US is described and evaluated through the media of newspapers and television.

The first chapter, by Trent Newman, "Policy and Practicality in Timorese Higher Education: Lessons From Lecturers in Development-related Disciplines," reports on the views of lecturers in three higher education institutions in Timor-Leste (also known as East Timor) as they respond to competing institutional, national, and global policy issues. Individual interviews and focus groups were conducted with these lecturers from petroleum studies, agriculture, tourism, and community development studies. The data surfaced a number of challenges in working with plurilingual students who are likely to have experienced some of their learning through Tetun (the national lingua franca), Portuguese (the official and former colonial language), Indonesian (the former official language under Indonesian rule), and possibly some local languages (Quinn, 2013), as well as technical and discipline-specific English. Lecturers, based on the contexts for their own graduate education, have varied competence in teaching through Portuguese, Indonesian, or English. Newman records "diverse mixings in plurilingual and translanguaging teaching and learning practices" by both lecturers and students (Newman, this volume, p. 121). Students' plurilingualism is viewed by lecturers as a resource (in that both students and lecturers can move fluidly among the languages) as well as a problem (in students' inadequate competence in technical or disciplinary vocabulary in individual languages). Drawing on the views of García and Flores (2012) and Hornberger (2002), Newman finds a "localized devaluing of linguistic repertoires that students bring to the classroom" and "a monoglossic bias in how academic transformation is conceived" (Stroud & Kerfoot, 2013, p. 400, as cited in Newman, this volume, p. 122).

Sarah Braden and MaryAnn Christison, in "The Absence of Language-focused Teacher Education Policy in U.S. K12 Contexts: Insights From Language Socialization Research in a Ninth-Grade Physics Classroom," also focus on a discipline other than language. By applying "Braden's (2016) descriptions of three prominent classroom identities—(1) the science expert, (2), the good student, and (3) the good assistant"—they investigate "the linguistic practices" (Braden & Christison, this volume, p. 131) of six ninth-grade students of varying linguistic and cultural backgrounds as they participate in physics laboratory classes in a school in the western United States. Although there "no national policies that govern the teaching of science" in the US (Braden & Christison, this volume, p. 131), a 2011 framework for science education recommends that teachers of

Introduction **11**

science, technology, engineering, and mathematics (the STEM fields) be prepared to accommodate learners of diverse language backgrounds and English proficiency levels in their classes. However, few science teachers have any specific training in the ways in which language and language socialization operate in science classrooms. Nor is there an explicit policy requiring science teachers to engage in specific training to "effectively respond to the language demands facing" English learners as they engage in the practices of science (Braden & Christison, this volume, p. 131). This situation relegates the student with the least English proficiency (Sofia, the focal student in this study) to the role of "good assistant" or "good student," despite the fact that she exhibits the capability of taking on the role of "the science expert" (Braden & Christison, this volume, p. 134).

Laura Hamman, in "Bilingualism for All?: Interrogating Language and Equity in Dual Language Immersion in Wisconsin," describes the role of local stakeholders and agents—"nonauthorized policy actors" (Levinson, Sutton, & Winstead, 2009, p. 768)—in influencing policy from the ground up. As Hamman describes the situation, local "teachers, administrators, parents, and community members . . . approached the school board with the aim of establishing a dual language charter school" (Hamman, this volume, p. 142) for K–5 children. The goal was to enable English-speaking children to learn Spanish and Spanish-speaking children to learn English. This dual immersion model implemented in Lakeville seems to stand in contrast to the official policy of the state, which authorizes "fundamental courses" being "taught in the pupil's non-English language to support the understanding of concepts" with "the ultimate objective [being] to provide a proficiency . . . in the English language in order that the pupil will be able to participate fully in a society whose language is English" (Wisconsin Statutes, 2009–2010, 115.95(5)). Drawing upon Ruiz's (1984) three orientations to language policy (as a problem, as a resource, and as a right), Hamman finds that state policies view bilingualism as a problem to be remedied by a transitional bilingual model, reflecting a subtractive view of bilingualism (Lambert, 1975); local media and policy view bilingualism as an educational and economic resource; but the Lakeville community predominantly view it as a right because, for many participants, "achieving social justice was the primary reason for founding the school" (Hamman, this volume, p. 146). As Hamman makes clear, this program demonstrates "the power of local policy actors to foster more equitable educational models" (this volume, p. 142).

Crissa Stephens, in "Media Discourses of Language Policy and the 'New' Latino Diaspora in Iowa," also discusses policy related to dual language immersion, but this time with a focus on how the media represented the program. Similar to the Wisconsin case discussed by Hamman, Stephens reports that official language policies in Iowa are more closely related to "monoglossic language ideologies (where English monolingualism is seen as the norm) than to heteroglossic ideologies (where bilingualism is seen as the norm)" (Stephens, this volume, p. 155). However, whereas state policy identifies English proficiency "as the main goal of language programs" (Stephens, this volume, p. 155), it also lists bilingualism

12 JoAnn (Jodi) Crandall and Kathleen M. Bailey

and biliteracy as goals of bilingual education programs, making it possible for this first dual language immersion program in West Liberty, Iowa, to be developed. As was the case in Hamman's research context, the goal here was for "both English- and Spanish-speaking students [to] learn language and content through bilingual instruction" (Stephens, this volume, p. 155). Although Stephens points out that "bilingual education is often portrayed unfavorably in media coverage" (Stephens, this volume, p. 154), her analysis of local, regional, and state newspapers and a transcript of a radio show about the bilingual program in West Liberty found that the media reports of the views of community members and educators were "overwhelmingly positive," with only one article expressing "a monoglossic language ideology" (Stephens, this volume, p. 157). The media also report that similar programs are being established in other Iowa school districts.

These four chapters provide the views of diverse stakeholders—administrators, teachers, students, parents, community members, the media—on educational language policy, responding to and often contesting the official language policy regarding the medium of instruction (as in Timor-Leste) or even the design of educational programs (as in the case of Wisconsin and Iowa). One chapter deals with a context in which there is no official policy to require science teachers with English learners to have specific language-related training, with negative consequences for an English learner trying to participate in a physics lab class. All of these chapters reveal the complexities of agreeing upon and implementing language education policy.

Part 4: Identity and Individual and "Invisible" Language Policy and Planning

The final part of the volume focuses on identity and individual and invisible language policy. It includes reports of four studies conducted in diverse contexts, all of which reflect the significance of social and economic factors, as well as family language policies, on identity and individual language use. These largely invisible language policies are made visible through interviews and observations with the participants (girls in an afterschool book club; boys interacting with technology in Canada; administrators and teachers in Paraguay; and government officials and linguists, as well as primary, junior high, and high school teachers in Jamaica). Family language policy plays an important role in these studies, providing interesting additions to a relatively recent focus in educational language policy (e.g., King, Fogle, & Logan-Terry, 2008; Spolsky, 2012).

First, Yu-Chi Wang, in "Rethinking Culturally and Linguistically Diverse Students' Perceptions of Family Language Policies and Identities in an American Afterschool Program," reports on her three-year experience working with a group of culturally diverse fourth- to sixth- grade girls in an afterschool book club. Some of the girls were nonnative speakers of English, and Wang focuses on three of these participants. In the book club, these young women had opportunities to explore and express their identities as they read and discussed literature that addressed multicultural themes. In her study, Wang focuses on the ways in which language choices and social identity "are influenced by language policies inside and outside" the home (this volume, p. 169). As Wang notes, parental attitudes toward multilingualism and language maintenance—invisible family language planning—play an important role in these young girls' constructions of multilingual identities and the ways they are positioned by others. However, it is only through these girls' discourse that we learn about their positive perspectives toward their multilingual identities, as well as about negative episodes (such as being made fun of because of having an accent) related to their use of their heritage languages. Wang concludes her discussion by stressing the need for "safe and comfortable environments outside formal school settings [such as this afterschool book club] for students to discuss questions about multilingual and multicultural practices . . . [and] to exercise their agency to resist unfavorable language policies that are shaped by inside and outside of school settings" (this volume, p. 179).

The next chapter in this part, "Digital Literacy, Language Learning, and Educational Policy in British Columbia," by Ron Darvin, also explores invisible family language policy in the online practices of two young Filipino boys whose families had immigrated to Canada. The author contrasts the activities of these two secondary school students to problematize the concept of the "*digital native*" (Prensky, 2001, p. 1): "an individual who was born after the widespread adoption of digital technology" (Techopedia, 2017, para. 1). These two boys were comparable in the sense that they came from the same country, were the same age, spoke the same first language, and were immigrants to British Columbia. However, their families' educational and socioeconomic situations, as well as the boys' educational experiences, created the contexts for extremely different access to and uses of technology. One boy, who attends private school and speaks English at home, spends several hours at night using the computer to complete schoolwork, take an online course, and connect through Facebook. The other boy, who attends public school and speaks Filipino at home, relies on an iPad, primarily to play digital games and post his anime images on Facebook, and has to go to the library when an older sibling needs to use the only desktop computer in the home. As Darvin explains, the two boys not only live in very different socioeconomic and educational worlds; they also differ in the ways in which they envision possible futures (Norton, 2013). Darvin concludes that "policy makers need to be aware that technology choices have social and economic implications, privileging some and marginalizing others" (Darvin, this volume, p. 190). They also need "to design new curricula and reimagine pedagogy that addresses the specific needs of a digital age" (this volume, p. 182) perhaps the greatest challenge of language education in the 21st century (Darvin & Norton, 2015).

The next two chapters focus on issues of language and identity. The first, "Small Stories of/in Changing Times in Paraguay: A Resource for Identity Work in Language Policy Appropriation," by Katherine S. Mortimer, describes

14 JoAnn (Jodi) Crandall and Kathleen M. Bailey

Paraguayan people's views of individuals speaking Guarani in Paraguay. Historically, the official language and the language of education in Paraguay was the colonial language, Spanish, whereas Guarani, the national, Indigenous language spoken by the majority of Paraguayans (and important in national identity), was prohibited in education. However, in 1992, a major change in language education policy mandated Spanish-Guarani bilingual education, with all children required to learn Guarani and to learn *in* Guarani, as well as to learn Spanish and learn *in* Spanish. At the time of the study, a generation of school children had learned in the new system; however, their parents had learned under the earlier language policy, when Guarani was not accepted. As a result, many adult Paraguayans, including teachers, do not speak Guarani (or do not speak it well). This study is part of a larger ethnographic project that examined Guarani identities portrayed in policy texts, talk about policy, and classroom practices (Mortimer, 2012). In it, Mortimer focuses on the social attitudes toward speaking Guarani and the social identity of a Guarani speaker. Here she uses a prominent theme from the larger study of the "*guarango*," an individual who is seen as uneducated and ignorant, as a means of eliciting attitudes toward Guarani by urban Spanish-dominant speakers and rural Guarani-dominant speakers. Mortimer's study illustrates "how policy positions speakers and how speakers position themselves in relation to policy" (Mortimer, this volume, p. 194).

Shondel Nero's chapter, "Challenges of Language Education Policy Development and Implementation in Creole-speaking Contexts: The Case of Jamaica," also explores issues of identity as they relate to the speaking and teaching of Jamaican Creole. Her study reports on part of a larger ethnographic study (Nero, 2014) of language education policy in Jamaica, a former British colony. As in other Creole contexts, the European language, English, is "privileged," whereas the Creole is generally "stigmatized." There is also "sharp social stratification and a strong association between language and social class where proficiency in the European language is linked to high social class and academic achievement. Conversely, Creole-dominant speech is associated with low social status and academic underachievement" (Nero, this volume, p. 206). In this study, Nero focuses on a draft bilingual policy promoting the oral use of Jamaican Creole (JC) in early and secondary grades while students develop literacy in Standard Jamaican English (SJE). The policy was a compromise between the Ministry of Education (who wanted to promote literacy in SJE) and the linguists from the University of West Indies (who sought recognition of JC as a language). However, the compromise policy was never ratified by the Parliament because legislators could not accept the idea that Jamaica is a bilingual country—i.e., that both JC and SJE should be accorded the status of languages. Nero elicited teachers' understandings of the 'invisible' policy, their attitudes toward JC, and the differences in their approaches to teaching language and literacy in a primary school in the capital, a primary and junior high school in a suburb, and a traditional high school in the capital. She found that teachers generally understood the purpose of the policy was for

Introduction **15**

children to acquire SJE, but their views and uses of JC differed widely, to some degree depending on the socioeconomic status of the students and the academic standing of the school.

These four chapters provide a variety of contexts in which to consider identity and individual or family language planning. The young girls in Wang's study of the afterschool book club expressed pride in their multilingual identities, but their uses of their heritage languages differed, depending on family perspectives. In Darvin's research, socioeconomic and educational differences in the family, as well as language and computer use at home, had a strong impact on the ways in which the two "digital natives" used technology and how they viewed its effect on their futures. The change in bilingual policy in Paraguay, mandating the use of both Spanish and Guarani after decades of prohibition of the use of Guarani, presented a challenge to Paraguayan identity by urban, Spanish-speaking teachers, as did the stereotype of the *guarango* to rural, Guarani-dominant teachers, but both were able to adjust their discourse to express Guarani/Paraguayan identity. In Jamaica, differences in the socioeconomic status of teachers and the educational status of the schools in which they taught were reflected in both teachers' attitudes and their uses of Jamaican Creole.

Epilogue

As G. Richard Tucker notes in his "Summary and Concluding Observations," the chapters in this volume demonstrate that "we live in a time of enormous economic, political, and social change and development—a time in which the role of languages and the ability to communicate effectively to diverse stakeholders has become increasingly important" (Tucker, this volume, p. 219). Tucker reviews the four parts of the volume, and the individual contributions, and then ends by identifying three "relatively neglected areas" of language policy: the evolving uses of digital technology in language education, the preservation of indigenous languages, and the need to ensure that classroom teachers are adequately prepared to teach English learners, especially in STEM (science, technology, engineering, and mathematics) fields. He also endorses the view of recent publications that consider language education as a "persistent national need" (Tucker, this volume, p. 224) in a global and multilingual 21st century.

Concluding Comments

As the chapters in this collection richly illustrate, "the field of language planning and policy (LPP) provides a rich array of research opportunities for applied linguists and social scientists" (Ricento & Hornberger, 1996, p. 401). As Ricento (2009) notes, "Language policy debates are always about more than language" (p. 8). It is influenced by social, economic, and political factors, as well as ideologies and discourses (Johnson & Johnson, 2015), and those factors are constantly being

16 JoAnn (Jodi) Crandall and Kathleen M. Bailey

affected and influence changes in perspectives and implementation of the policies. As these chapters demonstrate, "educational language policy and its analysis are of major significance for the individual, for group vitality, for national identities, and international relations" (Phillipson & Skutnabb-Kangas, 2009, p. 27).

References

Abraham, R., & Plakans, B. S. (1988). Evaluating a screening/training program for NNS teaching assistants. *TESOL Quarterly*, *22*, 505–508.

Bailey, K. M. (1984). The "foreign TA problem." In K. M. Bailey, F. Pialorsi, & J. Zukowski/ Faust (Eds.), *Foreign teaching assistants in U.S. universities* (pp. 3–15). Washington, DC: National Association for Foreign Student Affairs (NAFSA).

Baldauf, R. B. (2006). Rearticulating the case for micro language planning in a language ecology context. *Current Issues in Language Planning*, 7(2–3), 147–170.

Braden, S. K. (2016). *Scientific inquiry as social and linguistic practice: Language socialization pathways in a ninth-grade physics class* (Unpublished doctoral dissertation). University of Utah, Salt Lake City, Utah.

Briggs, S., & Hofer, B. (1991). Undergraduate perceptions of ITA effectiveness. In J. D. Nyquist, R. D. Abbott, D. H. Wulff, & J. Sprague (Eds.), *Preparing the professionals of tomorrow to teach* (pp. 435–445). Dubuque, IA: Kendall-Hunt.

Byrd, P., & Constantinides, J. C. (1988). FTA training programs: Searching for appropriate teaching styles. *English for Specific Purposes*, 7, 123–129.

Clyne, M. (2001). Micro language policy as a barometer of change. In R. L. Cooper, E. Shohamy, & J. Walters (Eds.), *New perspectives and issues in educational language policy: A festschrift for Bernard Dov Spolsky* (pp. 211–234). Philadelphia, PA: Benjamins.

Cooper, R. L., Shohamy, E., & Walters, J. (Eds.). (2001). *New perspectives and issues in educational language policy: A festschrift for Bernard Dov Spolsky*. Philadelphia, PA: John Benjamins.

Coulmas, F. (2005). Changing language regimes in globalizing environments. *International Journal of the Sociology of Language, 175/176*, 3–15.

Council of Europe. (2001). *Common European framework of reference for languages*. Strasbourg, France: Council of Europe Publishing.

Council of Europe. (2007). *Guide for the development of language education policies in Europe: From linguistic diversity to plurilingual education*. Strasbourg, France: Council of Europe Publishing.

Curdt-Christiansen, X. L. (2009). Invisible and visible language planning: Ideological factors in the family language policy of Chinese immigrant families in Quebec. *Language Policy, 8*(4), 351–375.

Darvin, R., & Norton, B. (2015). Identity and a model of investment in applied linguistics. *Annual Review of Applied Linguistics, 35*, 36–56.

Freire, P. (1970). *Pedagogy of the oppressed*. New York, NY: Continuum Publishing Company.

García, O., & Flores, N. (2012). Multilingual pedagogies. In M. Martin-Jones, A. Blackledge, & A. M. Creese (Eds.), *The Routledge handbook of multilingualism* (pp. 232–246). London, UK: Routledge.

García, O., & Menken, K. (2010). Stirring the onion: Educators and the dynamics of language education policies (looking ahead). In K. Menken & O. García (Eds.), *Negotiating language policies in schools: Educators as policy makers* (pp. 249–261). New York, NY: Routledge.

Hamid, M. O., Zhu, L., & Baldauf, R. B. (2014). Norms and varieties of English and TESOL teacher agency. *Australian Journal of Teacher Education, 39*(10), 77–95.

Hashimoto, K. (2009). Cultivating "Japanese who can use English": Problems and contradictions in government policy. *Asian Studies Review, 33*(1), 21–42.

Hinofotis, F. B., & Bailey, K. M. (1981). American undergraduates' reactions to the communication skills of foreign teaching assistants. In J. C. Fisher, M. A. Clark, & J. Schachter (Eds.), *On TESOL '80, building bridges: Research and practice in teaching English as a second language* (pp. 120–136). Washington, DC: TESOL.

Hinofotis, F. B., Bailey, K. M., & Stern, S. L. (1981). Assessing the oral proficiency of prospective foreign teaching assistants: Instrument development. In A. Palmer, P. Groot, & G. Trosper, (Eds.), *The construct validation of tests of communicative competence* (pp. 106–126). Washington, DC: TESOL.

Hornberger, N. H. (1997). Language planning from the bottom up. In N. H. Hornberger (Ed.), *Indigenous literacies in the Americas: Language planning from the bottom up* (pp. 357–366). Hawthorne, NY: Mouton de Gruyter.

Hornberger, N. H. (2002). Multilingual language policies and the continua of biliteracy: An ecological approach. *Language Policy, 1*(1), 27–51.

Hornberger, N. H., & Johnson, D. C. (2007). Slicing the onion ethnographically: Layers and spaces in multilingual language education policy and practice. *TESOL Quarterly, 41*(3), 509–532.

Johnson, D. C., & Johnson, E. J. (2015). Power and agency in language policy appropriation. *Language Policy, 14*(3), 221–243.

King, K. A., & Fogle, L. W. (2013). Family language policy and bilingual parenting. *Language Teaching, 46*(2), 1–13.

King, K. A., Fogle, L. W., & Logan-Terry, A. (2008). Family language policy. *Language and Linguistics Compass, 2*(5), 907–922.

King, L. (2017). *The impact of multilingualism on global education and language learning.* Cambridge, UK: Cambridge English Language Assessment.

Kling, J. (2016). Content teachers engaged in English-medium instruction in Denmark. In J. A. Crandall & M. A. Christison (Eds.), *Teacher education and professional development in TESOL: Global perspectives* (pp. 224–239). New York, NY: Routledge/TIRF.

Lambert, W. E. (1975). Culture and language as factors in learning and education. In A. Wolfgang (Ed.), *Education of immigrant students: Issues and answers* (pp. 55–83). Toronto, Canada: Ontario Institute for Studies in Education.

Landis, D., Umolu, J., & Mancha, S. (2010). The power of language experience for cross-cultural reading and writing. *The Reading Teacher, 63*, 580–589.

Levinson, B. A. U., Sutton, M., & Winstead, T. (2009). Education policy as a practice of power theoretical tools, ethnographic methods, democratic options. *Educational Policy, 23*(6), 767–795.

McCarty, T. (2011). Introducing ethnography and language policy. In T. McCarty (Ed.), *Ethnography and language policy* (pp. 1–28). New York, NY: Routledge.

Menken, K., & García O. (Eds.). (2010). *Negotiating language policies in schools: Teachers as policymakers.* New York, NY: Routledge.

Mortimer, K. S. (2012). *The Guarani speaker in Paraguayan bilingual education policy: Language policy as metapragmatic discourse* (Unpublished doctoral dissertation). University of Pennsylvania, Philadelphia, Pennsylvania.

Nero, S. (2014). De facto language education policy through teachers' attitudes and practices: A critical ethnographic study in three Jamaican schools. *Language Policy, 13*(3), 221–242.

18 JoAnn (Jodi) Crandall and Kathleen M. Bailey

Norton, B. (2013). *Identity and language learning: Extending the conversation* (2nd ed.). Bristol, UK: Multilingual Matters.

Park, J., & Pawan, F. (2016). Korean professors' pedagogical efforts and professional development needs in English-medium instruction. In J A. Crandall & M. A. Christison (Eds.), *Teacher education and professional development in TESOL: Global perspectives* (pp. 193–204). New York, NY: Routledge/TIRF.

Pearson, P. (2014). Policy without a plan: English as a medium of instruction in Rwanda. *Current Issues in Language Planning, 15*(1), 39–56.

Pettitt, N. (2017). *Social positioning in refugee women's education: A linguistic ethnography of one classroom* (Unpublished doctoral dissertation). Georgia State University, Atlanta, Georgia.

Phillips, D., & Ochs, K. (2004). Researching policy borrowing: Some methodological challenges in comparative education. *British Educational Research Journal, 30*(6), 773–784.

Phillipson, R., & Skutnabb-Kangas, T. (2009). The politics and policies of language and language teaching. In M. H. Long & C. J. Doughty (Eds.), *The handbook of language teaching* (pp. 26–41). Chichester, UK: Wiley-Blackwell.

Plüddemann, P. (2015). Unlocking the grid: Language-in-education policy realisation in post-apartheid South Africa. *Language and Education, 29*(3), 186–199.

Prensky, M. (2001). Digital natives, digital immigrants part 1. *On the Horizon, 9*(5), 1–6.

Quinn, M. (2013). Talking to learn in Timorese classrooms. *Language, Culture and Curriculum, 26*(2), 179–196.

Ricento, T. (2009). Theoretical perspectives in language policy: An overview. In T. Ricento (Ed.), *An introduction to language policy: Theory and method* (pp. 3–9). Hoboken, NJ: John Wiley & Sons.

Ricento, T. K., & Hornberger, N. H. (1996). Unpeeling the onion: Language planning and policy and the ELT professional. *TESOL Quarterly, 30*(3), 401–427.

Ruiz, R. (1984). Orientations in language planning. *NABE: The Journal for the National Association for Bilingual Education, 8*(2), 15–34.

Shohamy, E. (2006). *Language policy: Hidden agendas and new approaches*. New York, NY: Routledge.

Shor, I., & Freire, P. (1987). *A pedagogy for liberation: Dialogues on transforming education with Ira Shor and Paulo Freire*. New York, NY: Bergin & Garvey.

Spener, D. (1992). *The Freirean approach to adult education*. Washington, DC: Center for Applied Linguistics.

Spolsky, B. (2012). Family language policy—the critical domain. *Journal of Multilingual and Multicultural Development, 33*(1), 3–11.

Steiner-Khamsi, G. (2014). Cross-national policy borrowing: Understanding reception and translation. *Asia Pacific Journal of Education, 34*(2), 153–167.

Stroud, C., & Kerfoot, C. (2013). Towards rethinking multilingualism and language policy for academic literacies. *Linguistics and Education, 24*(4), 396–405.

Techopedia (2017). *Digital natives*. Retrieved July 28, 2017 from www.techopedia.com/definition/28094/digital-native

Wiley, T. G. (2000). Continuity and change in the function of language ideologies in the United States. In T. K. Ricento (Ed.), *Ideology, politics and language policies: Focus on English* (pp. 135–152). Amsterdam, The Netherlands: John Benjamins.

Wiley, T. G., & García, O. (2016). Language policy and planning in language education: Legacies, consequences, and possibilities. *The Modern Language Journal, 100*(S1), 48–63.

Wisconsin Statutes. (2009–2010). *Chapter 115, subchapter VII, bilingual-bicultural education, 115.95–115.996*. Retrieved July 6, 2017 from https://docs.legis.wisconsin.gov/statutes/statutes/115/VII/

Zacharias, N. T. (2013). Navigating through the English-medium-of-instruction policy: Voices from the field. *Current Issues in Language Planning, 14*(1), 93–108.

PART 1

The Teacher as Language Planner and Policy Maker

2

WHITHER MOTHER TONGUE (IN) EDUCATION?

An Ethnographic Study of Language Policy in Rural Primary Schools in Pakistan

Aziz U. Khan

This chapter reports on narrative ethnographic research that explored how two teachers viewed and put into practice the recently introduced language-in-education policy of the learners' mother tongue as the medium of instruction in one rural primary school in northwest Pakistan. Although substantial theoretical and empirical literature documents the effectiveness of mother tongue as the medium of instruction during the early years of education, the findings of this study indicate otherwise.

Issues That Motivated the Research

A common thread running through the language-in-education policies of most of the former colonized states is the dominance of colonial language(s) to this day. The situation in postcolonial Pakistan is no different. Success, opportunity, employment, upward mobility, and power are all associated with proficiency in English. It is a common belief that to be educated is to speak English and that the earlier English is introduced as a subject and medium of instruction, the better it is for the child's education (Rahman, 2004). Urdu, a second language for the majority, has its own proponents as a subject and medium of instruction at primary-level schooling. The experiences in other countries, however, indicate that instruction in a second or foreign language inhibits creativity and cognitive development, results in subtractive bilingualism, and leads to teacher-centered methods (Brock-Utne, 2005, in the context of Tanzania), routinized teacher-dominated performances (Arthur, 1996, in Botswana), safe language practices (Martin, 2005, in Malaysia), safe talk (Chick, 1996, in South Africa), codeswitching (Bunyi, 2005, in Kenya), and poor educational results (Rao, 2013, in India). Primary-level education in the mother tongue is, therefore, considered as the logical choice worldwide to ensure that learning is both meaningful and effective. The basic motivation behind this study, therefore, was to explore how the mother tongue is viewed and used in primary schools in rural Pakistan.

The motivation for this study also emanates from the conception of the nature of language policy as an onion. Ricento and Hornberger (1996) unpeeled the onion to carry out a bottom-up review of the layers that constitute the language policy whole. Hornberger and Johnson (2007) then sliced the onion ethnographically to reveal the agentive spaces in which actors at the local level (such as teachers) implement, negotiate, or resist policy initiatives. García and Menken (2010), however, believe that it is time to look at the ways teachers stir the onion through enacting language policies in classrooms, bearing in mind a myriad of contextual factors. A study of teachers' stories and actions, they believe, enables an understanding of language policies "as moment-to-moment, dynamic performances" (p. 259). A call for such research inspired me to analyze the innermost layer of the onion (that which contains teachers), slicing it ethnographically to explore whether and how teachers stir the onion and negotiate policies according to the local situations with which they have to contend.

Context of the Research

The norm in the government sector in Pakistan is to allocate less than 2% of the gross national product for education each year, one of the lowest percentages in the world. The result is weak institutional capacity at both the central and local levels, which is evidenced in the highly fragmented, segregated, and anomalous nature of the education system, in terms of both type and media of schooling. Despite the mushrooming growth of English-medium private schools, it is the Urdu- (and in some cases vernacular-) medium government schools which mostly cater to the underprivileged rural children. Both the Constitution of Pakistan and the National Education Policy, while leaving the decision concerning medium of instruction to respective provinces, advise teaching English (the only official language), Urdu (the only national language), and one regional language as subjects in primary-level schooling (Government of Pakistan, 1973, 2009). English and Urdu are, therefore, taught as subjects across all types of schools, whereas regional languages are largely ignored.

Pashto is the mother tongue of the Pashtun, who constitute a majority of the population in the Khyber Pakhtunkhwa province. The previous ethno-nationalist government (2008–2013) reintroduced Pashto as a compulsory subject in the government schools across the province, with some schools also employing it as a medium of instruction. Due to power and politics associated with language policy and planning (LPP) in multilingual Pakistan, little cognizance was taken of how the policy was to translate into teachers' perceptions and practices.

Teachers, being classroom practitioners, are at the heart of language policy (Ricento & Hornberger, 1996), as classrooms are the actual sites where language policies are enacted (García & Menken, 2010). It is teachers who decide inside a classroom whether to religiously put the macro-level language-in-education policies into practice or to use the language(s) that they themselves deem appropriate for ensuring optimum learning on the part of students. Their language perceptions and practices can give a clear indication of the problems with language-in-education policy formulated at the macro-level. This study explores Pakistani rural primary school teachers' language perceptions, preferences, and practices and the implications these factors hold for the macro-level language-in-education policy.

Research Questions Addressed

This study investigated language policy as viewed and practiced by teachers at the micro-level. It, therefore, sought answers to the following research questions:

1. How do Pashtun rural primary school teachers perceive their (and their students') mother tongue Pashto as a language?
2. Do they prefer Pashto's inclusion as a subject and/or medium of instruction in primary-level education?
3. How and to what extent do they put into practice a mother tongue (in) education policy?

Research Methods

This narrative ethnographic research has been conceptualized by drawing on a constructivist-interpretive paradigm (Lincoln, Lynham, & Guba, 2011). Narrative research is increasingly being considered an established tool for studying aspects of teachers' personal and professional lives (Barkhuizen, 2011). In addition, ethnography of language policy (Hornberger & Johnson, 2007)—a 21st-century approach to researching LPP (Johnson & Ricento, 2013)—emphasizes the centrality of teachers' language perceptions and practices (Valdiviezo, 2013) in understanding how policies are viewed, appropriated, and implemented (García & Menken, 2010). Use of ethnographic instruments thus enables a thick description of the context of the teachers' narratives and helps make their practices explicit in all their contextuality and variability. The use of narrative inquiry in combination with ethnography, therefore, helped bring richness, depth, and complexity to my study.

Data Collection

For the larger study, I selected three primary schools that were located in the same rural area in Khyber Pakhtunkhwa, with each following a different language (English, Urdu, and Pashto) as the medium of instruction. The Pashto-medium government primary school, the focus of this chapter, is located in a small village in Khyber Pakhtunkhwa province. The six subjects taught at the school are English, Urdu, Pashto, mathematics, science, and Islamic studies. All the textbooks except those of Urdu and English are written in Pashto. There are two male teachers employed at the school.

Shamroz (a pseudonym) has been serving as a primary school teacher for the last 24 years. Selected on the basis of a one-year Primary Teaching Certificate (PTC) qualification, he has since attained an MA in (Urdu) and an MEd degree through distance education. Angaar (also a pseudonym), the only other teacher at the school, holds a BA and a BEd and has been teaching at the school since his appointment in 2004. I interviewed each of the two teachers eight times during a period of 12 weeks that I was in the field, each interview lasting one hour on average. I also observed and audio-recorded eight lessons taught by each teacher to be able to obtain the best understanding of their language practices. Other data collection instruments included participant journal entries, field notes, and policy documents.

Data Analysis Procedures Used

Because I conducted all the interviews in the participants' (and my) native language, Pashto, I translated and transcribed the interview data and had it cross-checked by a fellow Pashto-speaking PhD student for accuracy and consistency. I then organized and analyzed the data using NVivo10, assigning labels, coding the data, and categorizing the related codes into sequential themes to get a fuller picture of the teachers' language-related experiences.

Findings and Discussion

Teachers' General Perceptions Concerning Pashto

Both the teachers portray themselves as proud Pashtuns and exhibit a deep love for their mother tongue. For Angaar, Pashto is the best of all languages because it is "an old, sweet and rich language." Shamroz, equally proud of Pashto, expressed his love for the language with a famous Pashto couplet:

وايي اغيـــــار چې د دوزخ ژبــه ده
خه به جنت ته د پښـــتو ســـره خم

[The rivals name it as the language of hell,
But I will go to heaven with Pashto only.]

He went on to interpret the couplet, saying that the poet does not take Pashto merely as a language in this couplet.

> Pashto is not only a language; it is also a way of life. When somebody does something dishonorable, he is said to have no Pashto in him. Pashto

in this sense is a particular way in which a Pashtun should lead life, and is called *Pashtunwali*. In fact, every letter of the word *Pashtun* (پښتون) stands for a quality, like *Pay* پ for *Patt* پت (Respect), *Sheen* ش for *Shegarha* شیګره (Welfare), *Thay* ت for *Toora* توره (Bravery), *Wow* و for *Wafa* وفا (Loyalty), and *Noon* ن for *Nang* ننګ (Honor). So the word *Pashtun* does not merely mean a Pashto-speaking person; it means much more.

(Interview, 4, 1: 9–15)

The participants thus view Pashto not only as a language, but also as a specific code of life based on certain qualities which the Pashtuns feel proud of (Shackle, 2007). However, as much as they may love their mother tongue, they also devalue Pashto in terms of its practical or worldly utility. Shamroz contends that "an MA Pashto person is laughed at; he is considered no better than an illiterate person" (Interview, 7, 2: 15–16). Similarly, Angaar said:

Pashto does not have any importance. Even if you do MA in Pashto, you cannot get any benefit out of it. Those who do MA in English are in superiority complex, as they consider all others dumb, knowing nothing. On the contrary, those who do MA in Pashto are in inferiority complex, because people do not take them seriously.

(Interview, 4, 6: 25–29)

Thus, whereas the participants have great love and pride for their mother tongue, they doubt its instrumental value. Rahman (2004) blames this perceived devaluation of indigenous languages on ineffective state language policies in Pakistan, which merely pay lip service to the local languages while promoting English and Urdu. Other studies carried out in Pakistan also report that the populace perceives their mother tongues to be useful only for in-group communication, with no significant value in the pragmatic sense (e.g., Khan, 2014; Mahboob, 2002).

Teachers' Preferences Concerning Pashto in Education

Whereas the participants show their attachment to their mother tongue, the aspirations they have for their students to occupy positions of power and the lure of English have a detrimental effect on their view of the value of Pashto in education. They believe that students already know how to speak Pashto; therefore, it does not need to be taught as a language. As Shamroz expressed it:

To me, knowledge of a new language, may it be Urdu, English, or Arabic, is good for students, because it is beneficial to them. But we already know Pashto, so we must learn other languages instead of wasting learners' time on Pashto.

(Interview, 6, 9: 10–12)

28   Aziz U. Khan

Angaar expressed a similar view:

> I believe that as things stand at the moment, Pashto should not be taught as a subject in schools. . . . We have to make choices, and the choice of Urdu and English is the better one.
>
> *(Interview, 5, 1: 6–13)*

Both the participants viewed the policy of Pashto as the medium of instruction as ineffective and a step in the wrong direction. Shamroz, for instance, believes that "the change in medium to Pashto means a step backwards" (Interview 6, 7: 18–19). Angaar holds a similar opinion:

> I am not saying that we should forget Pashto, but I think it is not the language that students need at the moment. . . . If they learn and speak Pashto both in school and at home, where is the improvement?
>
> *(Interview, 6, 2: 3–10)*

A related theme concerns the difficulties teachers and students face in reading and writing the language. The teachers came up with three main reasons for this view:

- The vocabulary and pronunciation of the standard Pashto used in textbooks is quite different from the regional variety used in the area.
- Some recent changes in Pashto orthography have made the language all the more complicated.
- Most of the teachers did not study Pashto as a subject when they were students, and they have not had any training in teaching it as a subject or medium.

The participants' Pashto perceptions seem quite relevant to what Alexander (2003) refers to as the "static maintenance syndrome," a state where:

> people begin to accept as "natural" the supposed inferiority of their own languages and adopt an approach that is determined by considerations that are related only to the market and social status value of the set of languages in their multilingual societies.
>
> *(p. 15)*

Conforming to Alexander's diagnosis, whereas the teachers value their mother tongue, Pashto, they perceive it as inherently incapable of attaining the capacity, status, and prestige of more powerful languages like English or Urdu.

Teachers' Practices Concerning Pashto

School and classroom observations revealed a pervasive use of the local variety of Pashto, but its use was mainly limited to classroom management. The teachers used vernacular Pashto to show their authority and to grab students' attention, to discipline them, and to ensure that the students remained attentive. However, the use of the local variety of Pashto for instructional purposes was infrequent, if not rare. Mostly regardless of what subject they taught, the teachers simply read from the textbook (written in standard Pashto) and the students repeated after them. Even though the standard Pashto of the textbooks included vocabulary items not in use in the local variety, the teachers provided few explanations of the textbook content or new vocabulary. It, therefore, seemed next to impossible for these rural-area students to understand concepts in subjects like science through mere reading and memorization.

The teachers also used the local Pashto variety to give task-related instructions such as telling the students to open to a certain page of a textbook, to copy from the blackboard into notebooks, or to memorize a particular lesson. For instance, Shamroz, while doing question number two in the exercise section of one of the lessons in the Islamic studies book, gave the following instructions to Year-Five students. Please note that the mechanical way in which the teacher used the question–answer section canceled out any potential benefits of using the mother tongue:

T: *Reads the question in standard Pashto from the textbook:*
Explain the difference between miserliness and squandering.
Switches to the local Pashto variety:
This answer has been given in the beginning (of the lesson). Look at the third line.
Reads four lines in standard Pashto from the textbook. Then starts speaking in local Pashto variety:
These four lines are its answer. OK, now write it down in your notebooks.
Memorize it at home. I will ask about it tomorrow.
Then don't stand with open mouth and say, "I don't know."

(Observation, 7, p. 3)

The teacher's emphasis was on having students write down answers to questions in notebooks so that they could memorize them later and reproduce them in exams. He seemed to care little about the fact that the students might not have understood what these concepts actually meant. The mother-tongue medium-of-instruction policy imposed by the provincial government thus seems to have little relevance to the situation on the ground.

English at this supposedly Pashto-medium school was invariably translated into Urdu rather than Pashto. In the following excerpt, for instance, Angaar writes a story entitled 'Greedy Dog' on the blackboard while teaching Year-Five students. He then reads the story from the blackboard and asks (using Pashto) about the Urdu meaning of the word *mouth*. (Please note that of the words in different script, the shaded ones are in Urdu and the unshaded ones in Pashto.)

T: The dog thought that another dog had a piece of meat in his mouth.
معنه څه دی؟ mouth [What is the meaning of mouth?]

30 Aziz U. Khan

Students remain silent. Teacher asks every single student one by one, but none comes up
*   with the correct answer. He then hits every student twice on their hands with a stick.*

T: ما درته پرون ویېلی وو چه دا ده مِنه په شان لیکلی کیګی خو ده موں په شان وېیلي کیګی

[I told you yesterday it is written like *manna* but is pronounced as *moo*.]

بیاچه درنه هیر نه شی خه؟

[Don't forget it again, OK?]

(Observation, 3, p. 2)

After the teacher left, I asked the students about the meaning of the word *mouth*;
all of them came up with a choral answer, saying 'منہ'—the Urdu word for *mouth*.
Ironically, upon my inquiry, not a single one of the 13 Year-Five students knew
the meaning of *mouth* in their mother tongue.

The findings pertaining to the teachers' language practices indicate that their
language (in) teaching practices were in large part inconsistent with or different
from the macro-level policy prescriptions, especially with regard to the medium
of instruction followed at the school. Specifically, the findings revealed that macro-
level policy decisions regarding the medium of instruction had little relevance to
how the teachers actually employed languages for teaching and learning at the
micro-level in their rural primary schools. Considering the substantial evidence
for the effectiveness of mother-tongue schooling in primary-level education (see,
for example, Benson, 2008; Kirkpatrick, 2011; Walter & Benson, 2012), one would
expect Pashto-medium instruction in a Pashtun-dominated rural society to be
more effective compared to schooling in the second language, Urdu, or the foreign
language, English. However, the findings of this study indicate that the mother-
tongue medium-of-instruction policy appears to have led to less-than-desired
outcomes. Transition into Pashto-medium education seemed based on the sup-
position that, because it is the mother tongue of both teachers and students in the
area, there was no need for teachers' language-specific training or refresher courses.
Context insensitivity in the policy implied lack of both adequate standard Pashto
proficiency and sufficient methodological awareness on the part of the teachers.
They faced difficulties in writing the language due to its complex orthography,
understanding some of the standard Pashto vocabulary, and coping with dialectal
differences in the language of the textbook and that spoken in the area.

By implication, whereas the decisions regarding language (in) teaching and
learning were taken at the macro-level, no grounded planning was visible. Policy implementation was left entirely in the hands of teachers without equipping
them with sufficient skills and resources—other than a textbook. The teachers,
therefore, continued to *reproduce the past* through teaching the way they taught
before Pashto was introduced as the medium of instruction. They relied heavily
on the textbook, regardless of the subject they taught or the language in which
they taught it. Being the only tangible resource at their disposal, a textbook was
"like a holy book" (Interview 3, 2: 23) (Shamroz) for them. They considered it a
necessity to teach by the book (Richards, 1993) and could not "imagine a class

Whither Mother Tongue (in) Education? **31**

without it" (Nunan, 1999, p. 98). The top-down policy decisions thus implied disempowerment of teachers, with the result that the teachers adhered to traditional language teaching methods and developed a disempowered belief in their roles, leading them to become servants of translation-based, textbook-dependent, and *Urduized* methods rather than proactive and reflective practitioners. Macro-level policy appears to have either overlooked or failed to predict the problems teachers faced in implementing the policy. In essence, it was a "policy without a plan" (Pearson, 2014, p. 51).

The teachers thus had no other alternative but to assume agency to appropriate and adjust the imposed policy in a way they thought best, although they viewed it as inherently ineffective. Regardless of its effectiveness, however, the teachers' agency—which could be referred to as 'imposed agency' because it was necessitated by the lack of grounded policy actions—made them the final arbiters of the language-in-education policy and its implementation. Taking note of and responding to this agency—an agency devoid of purpose—is a key issue for policy makers to consider.

Implications for Policy, Practice, and Future Research

The findings of this study indicate the complexity of language-in-education policy as practiced in rural northwest Pakistan and raise significant questions and a number of implications for Pakistani language-in-education policy and planning, particularly in the Khyber Pakhtunkhwa province. Considering the fluidity inherent in the current National Education Policy (Government of Pakistan, 2009), the choice of an appropriate medium of instruction is a complex decision. The teachers' perceptions, preferences, and practices regarding Pashto give clear evidence that introducing Pashto in schools without sufficient grounded planning has not worked, at least for these and some other teachers who were part of the extended study. Macro planners, therefore, need to realize that the mere introduction of a language or a change in medium of instruction is not enough; the whole language ecology in the area needs to be taken into account, or the policy, no matter how well-intentioned, may not result in effective implementation (Canagarajah, 2005; García & Menken, 2010).

The study gives an indication of the desperate need for more contextualized and rural-specific LPP research in order to make sense of the underprivileged people's understanding of the role of languages in education in their local settings. The government currently in power in Khyber Pakhtunkhwa has introduced English as medium of instruction in all government schools across the province. It would be interesting to investigate how teachers view this new shift in policy and whether any systematic planning has been carried out in this regard.

More importantly, the findings in this study allude to the multiple identities that the teachers revealed as they coped with the tensions, adjusted to the local realities, and enacted their agency in implementing a policy without a plan.

32 Aziz U. Khan

Future studies could, therefore, analyze the interplay between the teachers' multiple identities and their agency as a way of illuminating their language-related stories, actions, and experiences, and the implications these factors hold for language policy and planning.

References

Alexander, N. (2003). *An ordinary country*. New York, NY: Berghahn Books.

Arthur, J. (1996). Code switching and collusion: Classroom interaction in Botswana primary schools. *Linguistics in Education, 8,* 17–33.

Barkhuizen, G. (2011). Narrative knowledging in TESOL. *TESOL Quarterly, 45*(3), 391–414.

Benson, C. (2008). Summary overview: Mother tongue-based education in multi-lingual contexts. In C. Haddad (Ed.), *Improving the quality of mother tongue-based literacy and learning: Case studies from Asia, Africa and South America* (pp. 2–11). Bangkok, Thailand: UNESCO.

Brock-Utne, B. (2005). Language-in-education policies and practices in Africa with a special focus on Tanzania and South Africa: Insights from research in progress. In A. Lin & P. Martin (Eds.), *Decolonisation, globalisation: Language-in-education* (pp. 175–195). Clevedon, UK: Multilingual Matters.

Bunyi, G. W. (2005). Language classroom practices in Kenya. In A. M. Y. Lin & P. M. Martin (Eds.), *Decolonisation, globalisation: Language-in-education policy and practice* (pp. 131–152). Clevedon, UK: Multilingual Matters.

Canagarajah, S. (2005). Introduction. In S. Canagarajah (Ed.), *Reclaiming the local in policy and practice* (pp. xiii–xxx). Mahwah, NJ: Lawrence Erlbaum.

Chick, K. (1996). Safe-talk: Collusion in apartheid education. In H. Coleman (Ed.), *Society and the language classroom* (pp. 21–39). Cambridge, UK: Cambridge University Press.

García, O., & Menken, K. (2010). Stirring the onion: Educators and the dynamics of language education policies (looking ahead). In K. Menken & O. García (Eds.), *Negotiating language policies in schools: Educators as policymakers* (pp. 249–268). New York, NY: Routledge.

Government of Pakistan. (1973). *Constitution of Pakistan.* Islamabad, Pakistan: Ministry of Law.

Government of Pakistan. (2009). *National education policy.* Islamabad, Pakistan: Ministry of Education.

Hornberger, N. H., & Johnson, D. C. (2007). Slicing the onion ethnographically: Layers and spaces in multilingual language education policy and practice. *TESOL Quarterly, 41*(3), 509–532.

Johnson, D. C., & Ricento, T. K. (2013). Conceptual and theoretical perspectives in language planning and policy: Situating the ethnography of language policy. *International Journal of the Sociology of Language, 219,* 7–21. doi:10.1515/ijsl-2013–0002.

Khan, A. (2014). *A study of the language attitudes and practices in the context of two elite English-medium schools in Pakistan.* (Unpublished doctoral thesis). University of Auckland, New Zealand.

Kirkpatrick, A. (2011). English as a medium of instruction in Asian education (from primary to tertiary): Implications for local languages and local scholarship. *Applied Linguistics Review, 2,* 99–120. doi:10.1515/9783110239331.99.

Lincoln, Y. S., Lynham, S. A., & Guba, E. G. (2011). Paradigmatic controversies, contradictions, and emerging confluences, revisited. In N. K. Denzin & Y. S. Lincoln (Eds.), *The Sage handbook of qualitative research* (4th ed.) (pp. 97–128). Thousand Oaks, CA: Sage.

Mahboob, A. (2002). "No English, no future!": Language policy in Pakistan. In S. G. Obeng & B. Hartford (Eds.), *Political independence with linguistic servitude: The politics about languages in the developing world* (pp. 15–39). New York, NY: Nova Science.

Martin, P. (2005). "Safe" language practices in two rural schools in Malaysia: Tensions between policy and practice. In A. M. Y. Lin & P. W. Martin (Eds.), *Decolonisation, globalisation: Language-in-education policy and practice* (pp. 74–97). Clevedon, UK: Multilingual Matters.

Nunan, D. (1999). *Second language teaching and learning*. Boston, MA: Heinle & Heinle.

Pearson, P. (2014). Policy without a plan: English as a medium of instruction in Rwanda. *Current Issues in Language Planning, 15*(1), 39–56. doi:10.1080/14664208.2013.857286.

Rahman, T. (2004). *Denizens of alien worlds: A study of education, inequality and polarization in Pakistan*. Oxford, UK: Oxford University Press.

Rao, G. (2013). The English-only myth: Multilingual education in India. *Language Problems & Language Planning, 37*(3), 271–279. doi:10.1075/lplp.37.3.04rao.

Ricento, T. K., & Hornberger, N. (1996). Unpeeling the onion: Language planning and policy and the ELT professional. *TESOL Quarterly, 30*(3), 401–427.

Richards, J. C. (1993). Beyond the textbook: The role of commercial materials in language teaching. *RELC Journal, 24*(1), 1–14.

Shackle, C. (2007). Pakistan. In A. Simpson (Ed.), *Language and national identity in Asia* (pp. 1–30). Oxford, UK: Oxford University Press.

Valdiviezo, L. A. (2013). Vertical and horizontal approaches to ethnography of language policy in Peru. *International Journal of the Sociology of Language, 219*, 23–46.

Walter, S. L., & Benson, C. (2012). Language policy and medium of instruction in formal education. In B. Spolsky (Ed.), *The Cambridge handbook of language policy* (pp. 278–300). Cambridge, UK: Cambridge University Press.

3

AGENTIC RESPONSES TO COMMUNICATIVE LANGUAGE TEACHING IN LANGUAGE POLICY

An Example of Vietnamese English Primary Teachers

Duc Manh Le

In many Asian countries, efforts at globalization have placed the goals of achieving English communicative competence at the forefront because a good command of English is considered a key resource (Baldauf, Kaplan, & Kamwangamalu, 2010) or a national asset (Adamson, 2001). Consequently, many governments in Asia, including Vietnam, have introduced new language policies that lower the starting age of English learning to Grade 3. These policies are based on the "assumption on the part of the governments and ministries of education that when it comes to learning a foreign language, younger is better" (Nunan, 2003, p. 605). Given the new language policies, teaching ideologies and pedagogies in different regions have been shifted from "the grammar-centered into the communicative approach" (Kirkpatrick & Bui, 2016, p. 10), in which communicative competence is set as an ultimate goal. Whereas current research mostly addresses the constraints that English teachers might encounter in relation to the language policy implementation (Kırgöz, 2008; Li & Baldauf, 2011; Nishino, 2008), very few studies explore teacher agency in response to the policy. This chapter aims to investigate the agency of English primary teachers in under-resourced and prescribed conditions, where their powers are presumably greatly constrained by the policy enactment.

Issues That Motivated the Research

The calls for research on the micro-level from language policy scholars and the paucity of seminal literature on teacher agency are two main motivations for this study. Each of these issues will be discussed in turn.

First, language policy is considered multi-layered, due to the involvement of different actors at multiple levels, including the macro-, meso-, and micro-levels (Baldauf, 2006; Johnson & Johnson, 2015). Traditionally, the focus of language policy studies was at the macro-level and overlooked micro-level issues. Therefore, contemporary studies mostly focus on top-down policies and analyze written policies (Kaplan & Baldauf, 1997; Ricento & Hornberger, 1996; Spolsky, 2004), but undervalue the roles of practitioners who are at the grassroots level (Menken & García, 2010). However, it has recently been argued that macro-level language policy and planning is not sufficient to bring about the desired changes in the language education of a nation (Liddicoat & Baldauf 2008). This change in perspective has reshaped the conventional view of language policy and planning at the macro-level and led to a focus on the micro context, in which teacher roles are to be emphasized (Baldauf, 2006; Hamid & Nguyen, 2016; Menken & García, 2010).

Second, regarding implementation, schools are seen as sites of implementation and contestation of language policy (Cooper, 1989; Corson, 1999). Teachers are "the final arbiters of language policy implementation" (Menken & García, 2010, p. 1) and act as "central agents in language policy development" (Baldauf, 2006, p. 154). They also have power to act as mediators between the policy and the pupils, classroom practices, and texts (Martin, 1999). In this sense, "individual agency, particularly at the micro-level—and the agency of teachers in particular—has started to receive important consideration" (Hamid & Nguyen, 2016, p. 31). However, current research on teacher agency seems to be slanted. In the limited literature, teacher agency has been examined in either the literacy context (Ollerhead, 2010) or English as a foreign language (EFL) tertiary or college contexts (Hamid, Zhu, & Baldauf, 2014; Kaewnuch, 2008; Lee, 2011; Yang, 2012; Zacharias, 2013), rather than primary EFL contexts. The dearth of current studies on teacher agency leads to the need for further investigation of the topic.

Although the concept of agency has recently gained increased research interest in the field of language policy and planning, the construct is acknowledged to be elusive (Emirbayer & Mische, 1998), slippery (Hitlin & Elder, 2007), and difficult to define (Biesta & Tedder, 2006). It depends on "the epistemological roots and goals of scholars who employ it" (Hitlin & Elder, 2007, p. 170). In this study, *teacher agency* is defined as the capacity of actors to "critically shape their responses to problematic situations" (Biesta & Tedder, 2006, p. 11).

Context of the Research

This study was conducted in Vietnam, where the educational hierarchy is centralized and top down. The impact of regional and global integration has propelled the government to initiate a new language policy entitled "Teaching Foreign Languages in the National Education System 2008–2020" (commonly known as NFLP 2020, Project 2020, or Decree 1400). The introduction of NFLP 2020 clearly indicates the Vietnamese government's strong commitment and political will to promote good communicative competence within labor forces for the international and regional markets (Le, 2015; Nguyen, 2011). The overarching goal of NFLP 2020 explicitly stipulates that most young Vietnamese graduates will possess a good command of a foreign language in order to communicate effectively for different purposes, as stated in the following:

> [B]y 2020, most young Vietnamese graduates of professional secondary schools, colleges and universities will have a good command of a foreign language which enables them to independently and confidently communicate, study and work in a multilingual and multicultural environment of integration; to turn foreign languages into a strength of Vietnamese to serve national industrialization and modernization.
>
> *(Decree1400, 2008, p. 1)*

To achieve this goal, the policy has lowered the starting age for learning English to Grade 3, rather than from Grade 6, as it had been conventionally implemented. As a result, English is a compulsory subject in the mainstream curriculum from primary to university level. The policy also mandates a communicative language teaching approach as the pedagogical backbone and is intended to promote an innovative curriculum in the national education system. This study is located within the primary education level by examining how the policy is responded to from teachers' perspectives.

Research Questions Addressed

This qualitative study was guided by two research questions as follows:

1. What major challenges do English primary teachers encounter when they implement communicative approaches?
2. Do they respond as agents to these challenges? If so, how?

Research Methods

Data Collection

A group of six Vietnamese primary teachers of English were purposively selected as participants. The teachers' names were replaced by Teacher 1, Teacher 2, . . . and Teacher 6. The selection criteria included their teaching experience, professional training experience, availability, and commitment to the study. These criteria meant that the selected participants were familiar with the language policy implementation. The qualitative accounts were derived from semi-structured interviews over a four-month period. With the teachers' consent, all the interviews were audio-recorded and then transcribed verbatim.

Data Analysis Procedures Used

The data analysis followed Saldaña's (2015) guides on qualitative coding procedures. More specifically, the process was as follows: First, I read, and reread the data many times (without any coding) to get familiar with them. Second, I read the data and broke them down into fragments (i.e., phrases, sentences, statements, or paragraphs) under two categories: teaching constraints and teachers' agentic responses. Third, I reread these fragments and labeled each with temporary indexes such as *professional support, teaching contents,* or *resources.* Afterwards, I reconsidered all the labels and then grouped them into themes. Finally, I constantly compared and contrasted these themes for the final outputs.

Findings and Discussion

From the analysis of the qualitative accounts, four emergent themes arose: (1) insufficient professional support, (2) overloaded teaching contents, (3) limited teaching resources, and (4) constrained classroom settings.

Insufficient Professional Support

The interview accounts showed that the teachers lamented the lack of sufficient professional training on how to teach communicatively. Not all teachers had equal opportunities to take part in professional training workshops due to the limited budgets for these activities. Even when teachers had professional development opportunities, they did not feel confident with communicative teaching because the training content was so general and was beyond their specific needs.

> I found training workshops not really helpful to my teaching. These workshops did not help me to understand and address the nature of the problem that I was concerned. What trainers provided was so general, unsystematic, and somewhat impractical to my work.
>
> *(Teacher 5)*

To compensate for this insufficient support, teachers sought diverse resources to promote their professional learning, including past experiences, veteran colleagues, student observations, online sources, and teacher guide materials, as indicated in the following excerpts:

> I observed my students and noted that they remembered and imitated what I had said to them very well. Therefore, I would take advantage of this.
>
> *(Teacher 2)*

> The teacher's book provided me with suggestions of teaching techniques when I made lesson plans. It also gave me examples of warm-up activities, and provided me with standard teaching procedures.
>
> *(Teacher 1)*

38 Duc Manh Le

> I often visited some websites for English primary teachers when I prepared the lesson.
>
> *(Teacher 5)*

It was noted that teachers' active professional learning derived from their responsibilities of teaching children and their desires to be professional teachers.

> I transited my teaching career from junior high school. Therefore, I needed to find the ways to accomplish my teaching responsibilities as a primary teacher. I knew that I myself had to find the ways.
>
> *(Teacher 1)*

This category revealed that sufficient professional training was not provided to the teachers when they implemented the policy. Instead, teachers themselves looked for opportunities to improve their professionalism. Their motives were driven by their professional needs and responsibilities.

Overloaded and Inappropriate Teaching Contents

Textbooks were used as teaching materials. However, all of the teachers complained that the teaching content was overloaded and sometimes inappropriate for the children:

> The vocabulary volume was overloaded and its contents were sometimes inappropriate for the daily communication.
>
> *(Teacher 3)*

> Pictures were sometimes not vivid and child-friendly. They seemed to be used for adults.
>
> *(Teacher 2)*

Teachers noted that they were mandated to teach all of the textbook content. If they were caught missing any tasks, they would be going against the regulations and their teaching practices might be graded as "unsuccessful," "wrong," or "misled" by their job inspectors or supervisors.

However, the analysis of interviews revealed that, in their daily teaching practices, the teachers flexibly utilized the textbook content. Whereas they still covered all the items in the textbooks, they prioritized them and focused more on what they thought would be useful for their students. They would quickly go through teaching items that they believed were not appropriate or not important to make time for their prioritized sections. The data analysis also showed that the teachers sought ways to adapt the material (i.e., through addition, deletion, modification, simplification, or reordering of teaching contents):

Agentic Responses to Language Teaching · 39

> If I found tasks or pictures not as good to my students as I thought, I would add or replace them with external resources.
>
> *(Teacher 1)*

> The writing activity was difficult for my students. Therefore, I decided to modify it by making some changes in the inputs.
>
> *(Teacher 4)*

Teachers adapted the textbook because they wanted to benefit students' learning and interests, to reduce teachers' burn-out, and to deal with time constraints.

> I should understand children and do my best to seek appropriate teaching methods to work with my students. Only this could help me reduce the work stress and regain my energy at work. I expected to have an exciting and stress-free working day.
>
> *(Teacher 1)*

In summary, the teachers admitted that they were mandated to cover all the textbook contents and that their practices were supervised by the inspectors. However, the data showed that teachers flexibly used the course book because of its overloaded and irrelevant content.

Limited Teaching Resources

Although the policy explicitly showed that teachers were to be sufficiently equipped with teaching resources such as flashcards, pictures, teaching software, CD players, and realia to teach communicatively, in the interviews, teachers revealed that they received very few provisions:

> We did not receive any supports for the new curriculum: no pictures and no CDs. We had to buy equipment and other resources by ourselves.
>
> *(Teacher 1)*

> My school did not provide anything except a teacher book. The principal said that I needed to get other teaching equipment by myself.
>
> *(Teacher 2)*

Under such constrained conditions, rather than waiting for the provision of materials, the teachers decided to use their own money to buy necessary teaching resources. For example, despite her low salary, one teacher responded, "Finally, I myself bought a CD player" (Teacher 1). In addition, teachers themselves actively sought online resources for pictures, video clips, and songs, although this search was very time-consuming.

I had to spend a lot of time seeking the online materials, downloading them, and watching them to see if they were appropriate for the lesson. It often took me an hour or more to get the desired materials for a 35-minute lesson. Obviously, it was time-consuming.

(Teacher 2)

When asked what motivated them to seek out these activities, the interviewed teachers responded that these resources made the lesson more appealing to their students' interests and excitement: "I try to use external resources for each lesson because I believe that my children will get more excited and interested with the lesson and I will teach them much better" (Teacher 3). In addition, they spent time collecting teaching materials because they found them necessary to their practice. For instance, one teacher made the following comment:

I knew that it really cost me a lot of money to buy external resources. But I still loved to spend money on this because it was necessary for my teaching. Without external pictures, I might not teach well.

(Teacher 2)

Teacher 2 also confessed in an interview, "Honestly, I was passionate for seeking external teaching resources. However, I was not sure how long my passion for it might last." A closer look at Teacher 2's response indicated that although this teacher was proactive in seeking teaching resources for the class, the length of her passion was not certain.

Constrained Language Classroom Settings

Another constraint was the teaching facilities. All the teachers indicated that they did not have a classroom specially designed for language teaching purposes. Instead, they had to share the room with teachers of other subjects. These rooms were not well sound-proofed, the seats were set in rows, and free spaces were very narrow. Therefore, teachers tended to encounter obstacles to their routine teaching practices:

If I had a private room, I would conduct the lesson better. I would let my students go around the class and interview three other classmates at random.

(Teacher 1)

The data revealed that teachers still decided to conduct diverse activities for their children even though they might get complaints from other subject teachers about the disruptions. In these circumstances, teachers responded differently to their colleagues' complaints. For example, when they conducted noisy activities in the class, they expected that their colleagues would sympathize with what they were doing.

> I did not know what to do. I only smiled. This subject required me to teach such a way. I hoped subject teachers could understand that.
>
> *(Teacher 2)*

> I know making noises was a problem. But I begged my colleagues for their empathy. This activity required students to read in chorus.
>
> *(Teacher 3)*

Teachers also believed that their students loved to work in groups or partake in fun or physical movement activities. However, these activities required large and flexible spaces. In this sense, teachers satisfied their students' needs by making use of the rigid and set-in-stone seats and flexibly designed group activities to promote their students' involvement.

> I let the students who sat next to each other work in pairs and in groups. In this way, they did not need to move around the class that might cause chaos or disruptions.
>
> *(Teacher 1)*

This theme highlighted the constrained teaching spaces for teachers to manage the classrooms. However, teachers responded to these barriers in different ways because they believed that their children needed interactive activities.

Discussion

This study provides evidence that teachers exercised their agency when they were mandated by the policy makers to implement communicative activities in under-resourced and constrained conditions. In order to accomplish their responsibilities, teachers actively sought solutions to address the challenges created by the government-mandated language policy from various sources. Teachers took active roles in responding to the policies. In other words, rather than consider them as passive policy recipients or teaching technicians, the study demonstrates that these teachers had the capacity to act as agents. They performed their agentic teaching practices, given the existing classroom conditions and realities. This evidence supports the view in the literature that teachers are a crucial segment in language policy implementation.

In this study, the teachers had the capacity to act as agents of their own free will rather than from input from the top levels, such as policy makers and educational managers. This finding demonstrates that teachers exercise their agency as

42 Duc Manh Le

a consequence of "policy dumping at the macro level" (Hamid & Nguyen, 2016, p. 26). To put it simply, this kind of agency germinates because policy makers or educational managers dump the policy down to teachers for implementation without providing them with mandated conditions, such as sufficient professional training and teaching resources for effective policy enactment. Therefore, the teachers exercise their agency in response to the language policy because of their teaching passion and their goals and for their students' benefits.

It is also noted that teacher agency in this study is ephemeral and fragile. It is subjected to micro politics including students', principals', and teachers' motivations. In other words, these vulnerabilities enable or constrain the extent to which teachers exercise their capacity as agents in response to the policy. In addition, the findings of vulnerabilities further support what Stritikus (2003) identified as factors that govern teachers' teaching practices, including the local school context, as well as teachers' beliefs and assumptions. The capital and resources that teachers use to operate their agency are to draw from their own knowledge, experience, and understandings (Menken & García, 2010), their language ideologies, and their professional backgrounds (Varghese, 2008). In this sense, teacher agency is historically and culturally situated.

Implications for Policy, Practice, and Future Research

The study has some implications for future policy and practices and for future related research. In terms of the policy level, top-down policy makers should be aware that teachers themselves have the capacity to act as agents in response to language policies. Freeman (1996) states:

> Teachers have considerable autonomy in their implementation of high-level decisions, which leaves room for significant variation in the way they put the plan into practice on the classroom level. . . . Considering teachers and administrators as planners allows an understanding of how practitioners potentially shape the language plan from the bottom up.
>
> *(p. 560)*

Given this view, rather than forcibly imposing the policy on teachers for implementation, policy makers should encourage and emphasize teachers' roles and get them involved in the processes of policy construction, negotiation, and renegotiation. Policy makers should also be aware of the need to empower and provide teachers with sufficient professional support and resources when the policy is transferred and translated into classrooms.

Regarding the pedagogical level, Shohamy (2003) argues that language policies are not acts, but simply static and dead policy documents, which must be translated into practice by the enacting of agency. At the classroom level, teachers are considered direct policy implementers whose agency is to be exercised.

However, to promote the effective operation of teacher agency, teachers should be liberated and provided with sufficient support in terms of professional training, administration, and resources. Teachers should also be provided space to exercise their agency and capabilities.

Finally, this study puts forward some implications for future studies on teacher agency. Although teacher agency has received more attention recently, the concept is still under-examined and under-theorized. As teachers' agency is contextually bound, dynamic, relational, multi-faceted, and ongoing (Edwards, 2005; Priestley, Edwards, Priestley, & Miller, 2012), it needs further investigation from different theoretical perspectives or approaches. These could include culturally figured worlds (Holland, Lachicotte, Skinner, & Cain, 1998), positioning theory (Harré & Van Langenhove, 1998), and sociocultural theory (Lantolf, 2000).

In conclusion, this study has highlighted how teachers exercise their agency in response to communicative teaching mandated by language policy in centralized educational contexts. It has also discussed teacher agency when the policy is implemented in the classrooms. This study further suggests some implications for teacher agency in relation to policy making, pedagogical practices, and future research directions.

References

Adamson, B. (2001). English with Chinese characteristics: China's new curriculum. *Asia Pacific Journal of Education, 21*(2), 19–33. doi:10.1080/02188791.2001.10600192.

Baldauf, R. B. (2006). Rearticulating the case for micro language planning in a language ecology context. *Current Issues in Language Planning, 7*(2–3), 147–170.

Baldauf, R. B., Kaplan, R. B., & Kamwangamalu, N. (2010). Language planning and its problems. *Current Issues in Language Planning, 11*(4), 430–438. doi:10.1080/14664208. 2010.550099

Biesta, G., & Tedder, M. (2006). *How is agency possible? Towards an ecological understanding of agency-as-achievement* (Learning lives: Learning, identity, and agency in the life course No. 5). Exeter, UK: The Learning Project.

Cooper, R. L. (1989). *Language planning and social change.* Cambridge, UK: Cambridge University Press.

Corson, D. (1999). *Language policy in schools: A resource for teachers and administrators.* Mahwah, NJ: Lawrence Erlbaum Associates.

Decree1400. (2008). *Quyết định về việc phê duyệt Đề án "Dạy và học ngoại ngữ trong hệ thống giáo dục quốc dân giai đoạn 2008–2020"—1400/QĐ-TTg ngày 30/9/2008* [The approval of the project "Teaching and learning foreign languages in the national education system, 2008–2020"]. Hanoi: The NFLP 2020 Retrieved May 6, 2017 from http://dean2020.edu.vn/vi/laws/detail/Quyet-dinh-ve-viec-phe-duyet-De-an-Day-va-hoc-ngoai-ngu-trong-he-thong-giao-duc-quoc-dan-giai-doan-2008–2020–1400-QD-TTg-ngay-30-9-2008-8/

Edwards, A. (2005). Relational agency: Learning to be a resourceful practitioner. *International Journal of Educational Research, 43*(3), 168–182.

Emirbayer, M., & Mische, A. (1998). What is agency? *American Journal of Sociology, 103*(4), 962–1023.

Freeman, R. D. (1996). Dual-language planning at Oyster bilingual school: "It's much more than language." *TESOL Quarterly, 30*(3), 557–582.

Hamid, M. O., & Nguyen, H. T. M. (2016). Globalisation, English language policy, and teacher agency: Focus on Asia. *The International Educational Journal: Comparative Perspectives, 15*(1), 26–44.

Hamid, M. O., Zhu, L., & Baldauf, R. B. (2014). Norms and varieties of English and TESOL teacher agency. *Australian Journal of Teacher Education, 39*(10), 77–95.

Harré, R., & Van Langenhove, L. (1998). *Positioning theory: Moral contexts of international action.* Oxford, UK: Blackwell Publishers.

Hitlin, S., & Elder, G. H. (2007). Time, self, and the curiously abstract concept of agency. *Sociological Theory, 25*(2), 170–191.

Holland, D., Lachicotte Jr., W., Skinner, D., & Cain, C. (1998). *Identity and agency in cultural worlds.* Cambridge, MA: Harvard University Press.

Johnson, D. C., & Johnson, E. J. (2015). Power and agency in language policy appropriation. *Language Policy, 14*(3), 221–243.

Kaewnuch, S. (2008). *Teaching agency and power as social: Creating transformative subjects in the clashes of modernity and postmodernity in Thai EFL writing classrooms.* (Unpublished doctoral dissertation). Illinois State University, USA.

Kaplan, R. B., & Baldauf, R. B. (1997). *Language planning from practice to theory.* Clevedon, UK: Multilingual Matters.

Kırkgöz, Y. (2008). A case study of teachers' implementation of curriculum innovation in English language teaching in Turkish primary education. *Teaching and Teacher Education, 24*(7), 1859–1875.

Kirkpatrick, R., & Bui, T. T. N. (2016). Introduction: The challenges for English education policies in Asia. In R. Kirkpatrick (Ed.), *English language education policy in Asia* (pp. 1–25). Zurich, Switzerland: Springer.

Lantolf, J. P. (2000). *Sociocultural theory and second language learning.* Oxford, UK: Oxford University Press.

Le, V. C. (2015). English language education innovation for the Vietnamese secondary school: The Project 2020. In B. Spolsky & K. Sung (Eds.), *Secondary school English education in Asia: From policy to practice* (pp. 182–200). New York, NY: Routledge.

Lee, Y. C. (2011). *Agency, identity, and English learning in a Taiwanese college EFL classroom* (Unpublished doctoral dissertation). Indiana University, Bloomington, USA.

Li, M., & Baldauf, R. B. (2011). Beyond the curriculum: A Chinese example of issues constraining effective English language teaching. *TESOL Quarterly, 45*(4), 793–803.

Liddicoat, A. J., & Baldauf, R. B. (2008). *Language planning in local contexts: Agents, contexts and interactions.* Clevedon, UK: Multilingual Matters.

Martin, P. W. (1999). Close encounters of a bilingual kind: Interactional practices in the primary classroom in Brunei. *International Journal of Educational Development, 19*(2), 127–140. doi:10.1016/S0738-0593(98)00057-1.

Menken, K., & García, O. (2010). Introduction. In K. Menken & O. García (Eds.), *Negotiating language policies in schools: Educators as policymakers* (pp. 1–10). New York, NY: Routledge.

Nguyen, H. T. M. (2011). Primary English language education policy in Vietnam: Insights from implementation. *Current Issues in Language Planning, 12*(2), 225–249.

Nishino, T. (2008). Japanese secondary school teachers' beliefs and practices regarding communicative language teaching: An exploratory survey. *JALT Journal, 30*(1), 27–50.

Nunan, D. (2003). The impact of English as a global language on educational policies and practices in the Asia-Pacific region. *TESOL Quarterly, 37*(4), 589–613.

Ollerhead, S. (2010). Teacher agency and policy response in the adult ESL literacy classroom. *TESOL Quarterly, 44*(3), 606–618.

Priestley, M., Edwards, R., Priestley, A., & Miller, K. (2012). Teacher agency in curriculum making: Agents of change and spaces for manoeuvre. *Curriculum Inquiry, 42*(2), 191–214.

Ricento, T. K., & Hornberger, N. H. (1996). Unpeeling the onion: Language planning and policy and the ELT professional. *TESOL Quarterly, 30*(3), 401–427.

Saldaña, J. (2015). *The coding manual for qualitative researchers.* London, UK: Sage.

Shohamy, E. (2003). Implications of language education policies for language study in schools and universities. *Modern Language Journal, 87,* 278–286.

Spolsky, B. (2004). *Language policy.* Cambridge, UK: Cambridge University Press.

Stritikus, T. T. (2003). The interrelationship of beliefs, context, and learning: The case of a teacher reacting to language policy. *Journal of Language, Identity and Education, 2*(1), 29–52.

Varghese, M. M. (2008). Using cultural models to unravel how bilingual teachers enact language policies. *Language and Education, 22*(5), 289–306.

Yang, H. (2012). *Chinese teacher agency in implementing English as Foreign Language (EFL) curriculum reform: An activity theory perspective* (Unpublished doctoral dissertation). University of New South Wales, Sydney, Australia.

Zacharias, N. T. (2013). Navigating through the English-medium-of-instruction policy: Voices from the field. *Current Issues in Language Planning, 14*(1), 93–108. doi:10.1080/14664208.2013.782797

4

EXAMINING BRAZILIAN FOREIGN LANGUAGE POLICY AND ITS APPLICATION IN AN EFL UNIVERSITY PROGRAM

Teacher Perspectives on Plurilingualism

Angelica Galante

Linguistic and cultural diversity has become the norm in many societies worldwide, including Brazil. With over 250 immigrant and indigenous languages (IBGE, 2010), Brazil's diverse mix goes beyond language to influence culture. It is common for Brazilians to have social, educational, and professional relationships with people from different ethnic and cultural backgrounds, although exchanges are mainly in Portuguese, the country's official language. Similar to other non-English-speaking countries, the most popular foreign language for business and academia in Brazil is English, which is not surprising given its high status as a global international language. Unfortunately, many Brazilians are unable to have basic conversational exchanges in English despite approximately seven years of studying it as a foreign language in school. With only 5.1% of the population over 16 years old having some knowledge of English (British Council, 2014), many adults look to private sector language institutes.

In fact, private sector English as a foreign language (EFL) institutes are an industry in Brazil. Courses are generally costly and accessible only to the financially privileged. They are marketed with culturally attractive components alluding to America or Britain. For example, a prominent language school uses British decorations and imagery, such as the Union Jack and Big Ben. Instructors may even fabricate a British accent to appear more "authentic." As a former English coordinator in one Brazilian language institute, I often heard comments from prospective students such as "I want to learn American English" and "I don't want that teacher because she has a Brazilian accent." The overall picture of the EFL industry in Brazil limits pedagogy to American and British cultures (Galante, 2015) and is incongruent with the diverse Brazilian landscape.

Ironically, many of these institutes make use of the Common European Framework of Reference (CEFR; Council of Europe, 2001) in establishing their standards for both language assessment and pedagogy. The CEFR considers plurilingualism, which fosters linguistic and cultural diversity, to be an essential component of language learning; similarly, Brazilian language policies value linguistic and cultural pluralism in foreign language education. However, research shows that language teachers find implementing plurilingualism in the classroom challenging, even when local language policies support it (Abiria, Early, & Kendrick, 2013; Ellis, 2013; Pauwels, 2014; Pinho & Andrade, 2009). Thus, investigating EFL teachers' perceptions of the implementation of plurilingualism is important, particularly in Brazil, a country in which plurilingualism has been underinvestigated. This qualitative study examines the extent to which the linguistic and cultural diversity represented in Brazilian foreign language policies aligns with the concept of plurilingualism (Council of Europe, 2001, 2007). It then investigates EFL teachers' perspectives ($N = 8$) on the inclusion of plurilingualism in one language program at a university in Brasília.

Issues That Motivated the Research

Foreign language teaching is integral to the Brazilian education system in elementary and secondary schools. Two important educational policies provide guidelines for the teaching of a foreign language: Lei de Diretrizes e Bases (Law of Guidelines and Bases; henceforth LDB) and Parâmetros Curriculares Nacionais (National Curricular Parameters; henceforth PCNs). The LDB, which is aimed at assuring fundamental laws and rights surrounding educational standards at the federal level, incorporated the teaching of a foreign language in 1986 (Paiva, 2003). The PCNs provide comprehensive information at the state level about curriculum orientations on several subjects, including foreign language instruction, from Grades 5 to 8 (Ministério da Educação, 1998) and through secondary school (Ministério da Educação, 2000). At a macro-level, the LDB mandates a foreign language in the school curriculum, and state authorities can choose the foreign language that best represents the needs of their population. At a micro-level, the PCNs allow school authorities to determine which foreign language to include in the curriculum based on the needs of the community. For example, a school located near the Brazil-Paraguay border might choose Spanish. However, despite sharing borders with seven Spanish-speaking countries, Brazil's most popular foreign language is English.

Language pedagogy that moves away from monolingualism and embraces linguistic and cultural diversity in the English class has been advocated for years (Cook, 1999, 2015; Cummins, 2007; Moore & Marshall, 2016; Piccardo, 2013), and plurilingualism has been gaining special attention in applied linguistics and teaching English to speakers of other languages (TESOL) (Kubota, 2014; Taylor & Snoddon, 2013). Plurilingualism is not a method but an approach to teaching languages that harnesses the use of students' knowledge of other languages, dialects, and cultures (Coste, Moore, & Zarate, 2009; Council of Europe, 2001, 2007;

48 Angelica Galante

Piccardo, 2013). In a plurilingual class, teachers encourage the use of students' entire linguistic and cultural repertoire to learn a new language (Coste et al., 2009), facilitating the transfer of linguistic and cultural competence (García & Sylvan, 2011; Piccardo, 2013). In addition, plurilingualism acknowledges partial proficiency as normal, removing the pressure of having to be fully proficient in many languages. This approach aims at facilitating language learners' integration in linguistically and culturally diverse settings, enhancing democratic citizenship (Council of Europe, 2007).

Similar to the CEFR, the PCNs state that any foreign language should be taught in relation to the local and global landscape, suggesting a focus on "the multilingual and multicultural world in which one lives" (Ministério da Educação, 1998, p. 66, my translation). The words *pluri* and *plural* are present in the document in many instances, yet in contradictory ways. One contradiction is that the concept of plurilingualism is considered by the PCNs as "the acceptance and existence of different languages and the promotion of teaching several languages" (Ministério da Educação, 1998, p. 22), which is a limited view of plurilingualism. Whereas the CEFR also states that plurilingualism includes appreciation of different languages and the use of plurilingual repertoires to learn new languages, plurilingualism is not necessarily related to the teaching of several languages. It is possible that in some contexts, plurilingual education can include the teaching of multiple languages in mainstream education, but it is important to note that plurilingual education mainly refers to the existence of languages in one person's repertoire and how connections among languages can aid in new language learning. Thus, plurilingualism should be seen as context-specific, meaning that the use of more or fewer languages/dialects is dependent on local demands (Galante, forthcoming; Piccardo, forthcoming).

Another contradiction refers to the justification offered by the PCNs that reading skills in a foreign language are more important than oral skills because "only a small portion of the population has the opportunity to use a foreign language as a tool for oral communication in and outside of the country" (Ministério da Educação, 1998, p. 20). This is a simplistic justification for the exclusion of a focus on oral communication when developing oral proficiency in English is a main goal among Brazilians (British Council, 2014). Because of the lack of provision of oral communication skills in mainstream foreign language education, many adult Brazilians enroll in private English courses.

Contradictions aside, the PCNs include elements that align well with the concept of plurilingualism. Similar to policies encouraging plurilingualism in countries such as Uganda (Abiria et al., 2013), Germany (Göbel & Vieluf, 2014), the UK (Pauwels, 2014), and Portugal (Pinho & Andrade, 2009), the PCNs situate linguistic and cultural plurality at the core of foreign language teaching (Ministério da Educação, 1998). The PCNs are centered on questions of cultural plurality, variations in language and cultural values, local and global citizenship, linguistic and cultural hegemony, political and social structures, and cognitive and metacognitive abilities. Critical *conscientization*, a term coined by Brazilian educator Paulo Freire (1978), is integral to foreign language teaching, according to the PCNs, in that students are expected to be aware of and question power structures related to language and culture.

Plurilingualism facilitates openness to learning new languages and cultures beyond the target language (Moore & Gajo, 2009), as well as the development of cultural empathy (Dewaele & van Oudenhoven, 2009). However, despite support from policies, practical application remains a challenge (Abiria et al., 2013; Pauwels, 2014; Pinho & Andrade, 2009). Research shows that many language teachers ignore their students' diverse backgrounds, thus limiting students' use of multiple languages and cultures while learning a new one (Ellis, 2013). Similarly, teachers find it challenging to accommodate the changing student language profiles due to globalization and immigration, and linguistic diversity is therefore generally not taken into consideration (Pauwels, 2014).

Context of the Research

The study took place in a language program provided at a federal university in Brasília. This program differs from those of private language institutes as it offers courses in many languages, including German, Esperanto, Chinese, and Hebrew. Given the demand for English instruction in Brazil (British Council 2014), English courses in this university are the most popular.

Research Question Addressed

Preparing language students to integrate into the diverse national and global linguistic and cultural landscapes is crucial (Grommes & Hu, 2014), and this research is well positioned in the context of Brazil. To expand on previous studies (Ellis, 2013; Pauwels, 2014), this chapter addresses key issues of language and cultural diversity suggested by the PCNs and the CEFR by investigating how EFL teachers perceive the inclusion of plurilingualism in their practice. Thus, the overarching research question examined in this chapter is as follows: What are Brazilian university EFL teachers' perceptions of the inclusion of plurilingualism in their own pedagogy?

Research Methods

Data Collection

This study used semi-structured interviews to investigate EFL teachers' perceptions of their own pedagogy and whether it included elements of linguistic and cultural diversity. Eight EFL teachers participated in the study (five females and three males), ranging from 22 to 59 years old, with the average age being

50 Angelica Galante

35.9 years. At the time of data collection, they all lived in Brasília, although most were born elsewhere. Seven were Brazilian, and one was a Spanish-speaking person from Spain who had been living in Brazil for approximately a year. The Spanish participant was an English teacher who also taught German and Spanish. None were native speakers of English, and all made use of the textbook series *English File* (Oxford University Press) in their classes. Their experience teaching English ranged from 4 to 30 years (averaging 14.3 years). They all reported being fully proficient in both English and Portuguese, with five participants reporting proficiency in at least one other language.

The interview followed typical social science standards, using the same questions and maintaining consistency across participants (Patton, 2014). It posed three main questions: (1) Can you explain the approach you use when teaching English? (2) Can you talk about the inclusion of knowledge of other languages and cultures in your English class? (3) What are some challenges and benefits for including knowledge of other languages and/or varieties and other cultures in your English class? All participants elaborated on their answers, and follow-up questions were used when responses needed clarification.

Data Analysis Procedures Used

Data analysis procedures typical of qualitative research (Patton, 2014) were used. First, I transcribed the interviews verbatim. Second, I read the data multiple times and used a color-coding system to identify significant themes that emerged. Finally, I grouped the themes across participants, according to each interview question, and identified major categories. Data irrelevant to the overarching research question were excluded from analysis.

Findings and Discussion

When asked about the approach used in their classes, over half the participants ($N = 5$) reported a concern with linguistic aspects of English teaching, including reading, listening, and grammar, with a focus on oral communication. As one stated, "We focus on the four skills, right? But I try to really focus on speaking because most students want to learn how to speak English" (Participant 2). Although students enrolled in this EFL program had had several years of English instruction in mainstream education, they were unable to develop their speaking skills and thus needed a focus on oral communication (Cf. British Council, 2014). Interestingly, linguistic and cultural diversity as suggested by the PCNs and plurilingualism as suggested by the CEFR were not mentioned when the first interview question was asked.

Monolingual ideologies in the EFL class emerged as another theme. Two participants reported refraining from using Portuguese (students' L1) in the classroom. One said its use was "not allowed" (Participant 3), except when students

Examining Brazilian Foreign Language **51**

had questions that could not be clarified in English, and alluded to this being somewhat taboo: "It's not so intelligent to use this. It's a delicate thing." Another participant reported, "I don't like to use Portuguese. I teach more with the Direct Method." Whereas it seems the English-only policy is not necessarily mandated by program administrators, these teachers felt constrained, possibly due to the historical dominance of monolingual ideologies in ELT (Cook, 1999, 2015; Cummins, 2007).

A shift from linguistic to social aspects of the language emerged when the second question (related to the inclusion of knowledge of other languages and cultures in the classroom) was asked. All participants reacted positively and stressed the importance of plurality. Although the integration of knowledge of other cultures was highlighted, three English teachers placed particular focus on American and British cultures, a trend that has been previously identified in Brazil (Galante, 2015): "If I learned something new about a culture, for example, the United States, I speak a little about it" (Participant 4). One participant also spoke of linguistic diversity within the same language and power attributed to certain dialects as a concern: "It's not only English from the United States or French from France that are most important. They are more influential but there are others which are not as visible" (Participant 5). These accounts indicate that some participants may have a plurilingual orientation to EFL teaching, but American and British cultures can still dominate their pedagogy, perhaps in part due to the dominance of these varieties in both Brazil and in EFL textbooks.

The last interview question asked about challenges and benefits of including the knowledge of other cultures and languages in the EFL classroom. Three major benefits were identified: (1) connections among languages and cultures facilitating the learning of new ones; (2) open-mindedness and respect toward other languages and cultures; and (3) development of critical global citizens.

The first benefit is well defined by two participants who said, "The benefit is that you're actually working on the basis of your students' prior knowledge" (Participant 7), and "when you know another language it becomes easier to learn a third language, a fourth language. The teacher should use other languages to call attention to similarities and differences" (Participant 2). Participants reported that many of their students had previous knowledge of other languages and cultures due to travel, personal heritage, or other language courses taken in the same university program; thus, building on this repertoire was highly valued. This view aligns well with the concept of plurilingualism in that the linguistic resources one has can aid in new language learning (García & Sylvan, 2011; Piccardo, 2013).

The second perceived benefit relates to fostering open-mindedness and respect toward languages and cultures in general. Besides the dominant British and American cultures, participants reported making comparisons to other cultures such as Mexican, Egyptian, and Japanese. They pointed out that "knowing other cultures is opening your mind to new words, to new challenges" (Participant 8) and that "people can always profit from opening their minds of the fact that people

52 Angelica Galante

are different, languages are different, cultures are different, and not judge" (Participant 2). These results accord well with previous literature identifying open-mindedness as a feature of plurilinguals (Dewaele & van Oudenhoven, 2009).

The third benefit includes the concept of global community, which is cited in the CEFR as integral to plurilingualism (Council of Europe, 2007) and also in the PCNs, but with a critical perspective highlighted. Two participants clearly stated that diversity in the EFL program prepares students to develop a "global mentality" (Participant 1) and that inter-connectedness via news and media contributes to teaching English in a "globalized situation" (Participant 6). In addition, given that this EFL program was located in a prestigious federal university, it attracted highly educated instructors and students who possibly analyze textbooks and other class materials from a critical and global perspective, as pointed out by one participant:

> Today we were learning about sleeping problems and they have statistics but we thought "are they talking about America, Southern hemisphere?" Because normally the research is in England, they say a lawyer sleeps 7.9 hours a day. The book doesn't say where, you know? And then one student said "is it talking about Brazilian people? Europeans? Americans? Who is it about?" So we started to discuss this kind of culture, of Anglophonic countries to be the top and colonize the other ones.
>
> *(Participant 8)*

The notion of colonization due to the influence of dominant Anglo cultures in textbooks and in Brazilian society was questioned and challenged by this participant and her students. This result is important as it adds a critical take to plurilingualism, which aligns with the process of *conscientization* suggested by the PCNs, even though this process is not clearly stated in the CEFR.

In contrast, challenges related to the inclusion of other languages and cultures in the EFL program were identified, with three main themes reported: (1) amount of L1 use in the EFL classroom, (2) limits to teachers' and students' knowledge of other languages and cultures, and (3) teachers' lack of preparedness to address diversity. Most EFL students in Brazilian language programs spend limited time in the classroom (approximately three hours a week), and some participants felt the use of the L1 in the classroom should be limited or avoided, as two participants indicated: "If you are using a lot of Portuguese, then it's not good" (Participant 8) and "if you don't use the Direct Method, just English, sometimes the student finish the advanced course but the person don't get to speak" (Participant 4). Ensuring students have enough practice in the target language is a valid concern. Plurilingualism encourages the use of the L1, but this use should be seen as context-specific (Galante, forthcoming; Piccardo, forthcoming). In English-speaking countries with a high intake of immigrants (e.g., Canada, the UK), English classrooms are typically multilingual, and the use of the students' L1 can provide beneficial practice in both the L1 and the L2. In contrast, most EFL students in Brazil speak Portuguese as an L1 and have ample opportunities to use their L1 outside the classroom.

Furthermore, three participants perceived that the lack of knowledge of other languages and cultures can place teachers and students at a disadvantage, or even exclude them from classroom interactions. For instance, Participant 7 said:

> There's this problem with people who don't speak other languages. They feel pushed aside like they are not at the same level as the others are. I try not to point it out so much so these people don't feel offended.

Participant 5 noted, "Even if I have knowledge of more than two languages, I don't have the same mastery among all of them." Participant 6 added, "The challenge is the students that don't see it as a helpful tool, the student feels that that is a waste of time and they are like, 'Uh, we should speak English here.'"

A main issue is that even if plurilingualism is encouraged in EFL education in Brazil, some students might have monolingual orientations and demand that only English be used. Another concern is teachers' lack of preparedness to address linguistic and cultural diversity, as indicated by two participants: "I have difficulty in preparing what I'm going to give them . . . it's more work . . . I have to do more research" (Participant 5) and "I didn't write on my notebook this kind of question about cultures . . . this kind of discussion . . . they emerge" (Participant 8). This situation can be a result of textbooks with little or no inclusion of themes around diversity, leaving teachers to do extra research and rely on other materials or on their own previous knowledge.

Implications for Policy, Practice, and Future Research

This chapter has explored the extent to which Brazilian foreign language policies align with the concept of plurilingualism. Both the PCNs and the CEFR value linguistic and cultural diversity. Individual plurilingualism is encouraged by the CEFR, but this is not a concern in the PCNs. Whereas the PCNs place a focus on reading abilities in a foreign language and view plurilingualism as the teaching of multiple languages in the school curriculum, the CEFR focuses on all the skills (reading, writing, speaking, and listening) and views plurilingualism in a holistic way that relates to individual repertoires. In addition, a critical perspective, with elements of *conscientization*, is integral to the PCNs but is not clear in the CEFR, except for a simple mention of democratic citizenship.

Results from this qualitative study with EFL teachers in a university language program in Brazil suggest that the linguistic and cultural plurality proposed by the PCNs and the CEFR is highly valued. Together, the teachers suggest that plurilingualism is seen as beneficial for language learning. Equally important is the inclusion of cultures that are not necessarily particular to the English language.

54 Angelica Galante

Additionally, the teachers perceive that critical analysis of language and culture is crucial in preparing Brazilian EFL students for a diverse national and global landscape.

Finally, echoing previous research (Ellis, 2013; Pauwels, 2014), participants perceive the practical implementation of plurilingualism as a challenge, despite recognizing its importance. Plurilingualism as supported by language policy does not seem to be sufficient. It would be beneficial if the process of *conscientization* about language dominance, power, colonization, etc. was included in language policies, particularly the CEFR, given its heavy influence on foreign language guidelines in many countries. In addition, many EFL teachers rely on textbooks, and these need to include critical topics on plurilingualism and to move away from monolingual/monocultural orientations. This inclusion would benefit EFL education and best support the needs of linguistically and culturally diverse learners, particularly, but not exclusively, in the Brazilian context.

References

Abiria, D. M., Early, M., & Kendrick, M. (2013). Plurilingual pedagogical practices in a policy-constrained context: A northern Uganda case study. *TESOL Quarterly, 47*(3), 567–590.

British Council. (2014). *Demandas de aprendizagem de inglês no Brasil: Elaborado com exclusividade para o British council pelo instituto de Pesquisa data popular.* São Paulo, Brazil: British Council. Retrieved April 18, 2017 from www.britishcouncil.org.br/sites/default/files/demandas_de_aprendizagempesquisacompleta.pdf

Cook, V. (1999). Going beyond the native speaker in language teaching. *TESOL Quarterly, 33*, 185–209.

Cook, V. (2015). Where is the native speaker now? *TESOL Quarterly, 50*(1), 186–189.

Coste, D., Moore, D., & Zarate, G. (2009). *Plurilingual and pluricultural competence: Studies towards a common European framework of reference for language learning and teaching.* Strasbourg, France: Council of Europe Publishing. Retrieved April 18, 2017 from www.coe.int/t/dg4/linguistic/Source/SourcePublications/CompetencePlurilingue09web_en.pdf

Council of Europe. (2001). *Common European framework of reference for languages.* Strasbourg, France: Council of Europe Publishing. Retrieved April 18, 2017 from www.coe.int/t/dg4/linguistic/source/framework_en.pdf

Council of Europe. (2007). *Guide for the development of language education policies in Europe: From linguistic diversity to plurilingual education.* Strasbourg, France: Council of Europe Publishing. Retrieved April 18, 2017 from www.coe.int/t/dg4/linguistic/Guide_niveau3_EN.asp#TopOfPage

Cummins, J. (2007). Rethinking monolingual instructional strategies in multilingual classrooms. *Canadian Journal of Applied Linguistics, 10*(2), 221–240.

Dewaele, J-M., & van Oudenhoven J. P. (2009). The effect of multilingualism/multiculturalism on personality: No gain without pain for Third Culture Kids? *International Journal of Multilingualism, 6*(4), 443–459.

Ellis, E. (2013). The ESL teacher as plurilingual: An Australian perspective. *TESOL Quarterly, 47*(3), 446–471.

Freire, P. (1978). *Pedagogy of the oppressed.* New York, NY: Continuum.

Galante, A. (2015). Intercultural communicative competence in English language teaching: Towards validation of student identity. *Brazilian English Language Teaching Journal, 6*(1), 29–39.

Galante, A. (forthcoming). Plurilingualism and TESOL in two Canadian postsecondary institutions: Towards context-specific perspectives. In S. Lau & S. Stille (Eds.), *Plurilingual pedagogies: Critical and creative endeavors for equitable language (in) education.* Toronto, Canada: Springer.

García, O., & Sylvan, C. (2011). Pedagogies and practices in multilingual classrooms: Singularities in pluralities. *Modern Language Journal, 95,* 385–400.

Göbel, K., & Vieluf, S. (2014). The effects of language transfer as a resource in instruction. In P. Grommes & A. Hu (Eds.), *Plurilingual education. Policies—practices—language development* (pp. 181–198). Philadelphia, PA: John Benjamins.

Grommes, P., & Hu, A. (2014). Introduction. In P. Grommes & A. Hu (Eds.), *Plurilingual education. Policies—practices—language development* (pp. 1–12). Philadelphia, PA: John Benjamins.

IBGE. (2010). *Censo demográfico. Características gerais dos indígenas.* Retrieved April 18, 2017 from ftp://ftp.ibge.gov.br/Censos/Censo_Demografico_2010/Caracteristicas_Gerais_dos_Indigenas/pdf/Publicacao_completa.pdf

Kubota, R. (2014). The multi/plural turn, postcolonial theory, and neoliberal multiculturalism: Complicities and implications for applied linguistics. *Applied Linguistics, 37*(4), 1–22.

Ministério da Educação. (1998). *Parâmetros curriculares nacionais: Terceiro e quarto ciclos do ensino fundamental, língua estrangeira.* Brasília, Brasil: MEC. Retrieved April 18, 2017 from http://portal.mec.gov.br/seb/arquivos/pdf/pcn_estrangeira.pdf

Ministério da Educação. (2000). *Parâmetros curriculares nacionas: Ensino médio. Parte II—Linguagens, códigos e suas tecnologias.* Brasília, Brasil: MEC. Retrieved April 18, 2017 from http://portal.mec.gov.br/seb/arquivos/pdf/14_24.pdf

Moore, D., & Gajo, L. (2009). French voices on plurilingualism and pluriculturalism: Theory, significance and perspectives. *International Journal of Multiculturalism, 6*(2), 137–153.

Moore, D., & Marshall, S. (2016). Plurilingualism amid the panoply of lingualisms: Addressing critiques and misconceptions in education. *International Journal of Multilingualism,* doi:10.1080/14790718.2016.1253699

Paiva, V. L. M. O. (2003). A LDB e a legislação vigente sobre o ensino e a formação de professor de língua inglesa. In C. M. T. Stevens & M. J. C. Cunha (Eds.), *Caminhos e colheitas: Ensino e pesquisa na área de inglês no Brasil* (pp. 53–84). Brasília, Brazil: UnB.

Patton, M. Q. (2014). *Qualitative analysis and interpretation. Qualitative research & evaluation methods. Integrating theory and practice* (4th ed.). Thousand Oaks, CA: Sage Publications.

Pauwels, A. (2014). The teaching of languages at university in the context of super-diversity. *International Journal of Multilingualism, 11*(3), 307–319.

Piccardo, E. (2013). Plurilingualism and curriculum design: Towards a synergic vision. *TESOL Quarterly, 47*(3), 600–614.

Piccardo, E. (forthcoming). Plurilingualism: Vision, conceptualization and practices. In P. P. Trifonas & T. Aravossitas (Eds.), *International handbook on research and practice in heritage language education.* Toronto, Canada: Springer.

Pinho, A. S., & Andrade, A. I. (2009). Plurilingual awareness and intercomprehension in the professional knowledge and identity development of language student teachers. *International Journal of Multilingualism, 6*(3), 313–329.

Taylor, S. K., & Snoddon, K. (2013). Plurilingualism in TESOL: Promising controversies. *TESOL Quarterly, 47*(3), 439–445.

5

REFUGEE WOMEN IN THE UNITED STATES WRITING THEMSELVES INTO NEW COMMUNITY SPACES

Nicole Pettitt

Today, 60 million individuals are classified as refugees—more than at any time since World War II (United Nations High Commissioner for Refugees, 2015). In the US, where English is the implicit official language, programs for adult English for speakers of other languages (ESOL) are a principal site where new-comers learn to negotiate the complex language and literacy tasks of life in their new communities. From communicating with healthcare workers to negotiating a raise in English, newcomers are continually learning what is expected of them linguistically and culturally. ESOL classrooms, then, are a window into "specific efforts to modify or influence (language) practices" of refugees in the US (Spolsky, 2004, p. 5). This chapter investigates such efforts within one adult ESOL classroom embedded within a family literacy program for refugee women and children.

Issues That Motivated the Research

Women who have migrated between countries may experience tension between multiple, competing, and gendered duties (Menard-Warwick, 2009; Norton, 2012), which can constrain their access to classroom language learning (Muro & Mein, 2010). Family literacy programs have attempted to facilitate women's educational access by providing childcare, transportation, and flexible scheduling (Cuban & Hayes, 1996). However, family literacy programming has been criticized both for foregrounding children's education and for operating with gendered discourses of "mother-as-literacy-worker" (Griffith & Smith, 2005). These discourses place undue responsibility for children's school performance on mothers, discounting the effects of myriad historical, political, and economic factors on school performance, poverty, and unemployment (Anderson, Anderson, Friedrich, & Kim,

2010; Dudley-Marling, 2009; Hendrix, 1999; Luttrell, 1996; Taylor, 1993). Participatory teaching methods that reposition women at the center of their learning have the potential to challenge such deficit orientations (Hutchison, 2001). In this chapter, I examine the mediational practices of one teacher who took up one participatory approach in an ESOL classroom for refugee women.

Context of the Research

The research site for this study, Refugee Education Center (REC), was an ESOL family literacy program in the southeastern US for refugee women and their children (ages 0–5). Over 150 women were enrolled, each bringing from one to three children to school. Both mother and child registered together, as the school's goals included preparing children for kindergarten and making ESOL available to women who needed childcare in order to attend. REC, similar to the Kenan family literacy model (Wasik & Hermann, 2004), offered five levels of English for women (pre-literacy to intermediate); early childhood classes for the women's children; facilitated literacy activities for mothers and children together; and special presentations for women (e.g., children's health). Although REC had no written language policy, administrators and teachers promoted multilingualism (e.g., advising mothers to use languages other than English with children; encouraging women to use full linguistic repertoires during class).

The focal classroom was REC's beginning adult ESOL class, taught by "Joy," a woman in her early 30s with an elementary teaching license, a master's degree in applied linguistics, and over 10 years' teaching experience. (Note: All names are pseudonyms.) Learners identified with eight ethnolinguistic or national backgrounds: Burmese, Karen, Karenni, Kunama, Mandingo, Pashai, South Sudanese, and Tigrinya. Half self-identified as bi/multilingual; one-third reported interruptions in their formal, school-based learning. Most had arrived in the US within the previous 18 months, some a month before beginning school. Average daily attendance in this class was 12 students.

At the time of my data collection, REC was a young program gaining its curricular bearings; it had not yet adopted standards, level descriptors, or standardized assessments for adult programming. To guide adult instruction, administrators and teachers created checklists of topics to address (e.g., shopping, emergencies). Additionally, administrators expected adult teachers to integrate early childhood content, provided by the early childhood coordinator (e.g., shapes, animals). REC's primary public funder supplied the adult ESOL textbook series *Side by Side* (Molinsky & Bliss, 2001), expecting teachers would utilize it for instruction; most teachers at REC declined. Whereas most of Joy's colleagues created materials for classroom use themselves, Joy opted for core texts co-created with learners using the Language Experience Approach. Joy's choice to eschew the funder-provided text in favor of texts produced collaboratively with learners demonstrates one way that teachers engage in language planning: as mediators of instruction.

58   Nicole Pettitt

This chapter examines the language and literacy practices surrounding the Language Experience Approach in Joy's classroom (see the following). Her role as "de facto [classroom-level] planner and policy maker" (McCarty, 2011, p. 15) was interesting as she prioritized curriculum and instruction within incomplete administrative priorities. Spolsky (2009) notes that undertaking studies of language (and literacy) practices is particularly appropriate and necessary when written policies are not in place, as was the case at REC.

Research Question Addressed

The data and analyses presented in this chapter are drawn from a larger ethnographic study of Joy's class. Here, I zero in on one classroom practice, the Language Experience Approach (LEA). In doing so, I ask what are the "patterns of valued practices" (Wohlwend, 2009, p. 70) surrounding LEA in Joy's classroom?

Research Methods

Data Collection

Data for the broader study were collected in two phases. Phase one consisted of participant observation in Joy's class, October 2014 through May 2015, during class meetings: Monday, Wednesday, and Friday, 9 to 11:30 a.m. During class, my role included assisting Joy and the learners, who began calling me "teacher." Collection methods included field notes, classroom audio and video recordings, photographs, and classroom and school artifacts (e.g., copies of student work, etc.). I also conducted semi-structured audio-recorded interviews with Joy and REC's lead administrator. Phase two consisted of additional semi-structured interviews with Joy and three focal students from her classroom, conducted between September 2015 and October 2016.

Data Analysis Procedures Used

Data for this chapter are drawn from phase-one data collection, which adopted Mediated Discourse Analysis (MDA; Scollon, 2001). MDA takes up the Vygotskyan concept of mediation, which holds that "humans do not act directly on the world but rely, instead, on tools and labor activity [i.e., mediational means], which allows us to change the world, and with it, the circumstances under which we live in the world" (Lantolf, 2000, p. 1). Mediational means may include tools, signs, language, and more expert others such as teachers and classmates (Lantolf, 2000; Vygotsky, 1978). Wohlwend (2009) offers a framework of filters for MDA, one of which is "observing social scenes and practices" and patterns within these contexts (p. 70). For this chapter, I returned to data previously coded for LEA to identify "where, when, and with whom participants carry out regular practices with mediational means to manage artifacts and identity texts" (Wohlwend, 2009, p. 71).

Findings and Discussion

Grounded in principles of participatory literacy, the Language Experience Approach "incorporates students' retellings of home and community events to create reading materials for instructional purposes . . . and written transcriptions about these events for use in reading and writing instruction" (Landis, Umolu, & Mancha, 2010, p. 580). Key to this approach is the mediating role of scribe, enacted by the teacher or a more advanced learner (Mace, 2002); this role is illustrated in more detail in the following. (For more information about LEA, see Landis, Umolu, & Mancha, 2010; Woodin, 2008; Wurr, 2002).

In Joy's class, "community events" included class field trips to community sites (e.g., a library, museums, historical sites, etc.), volunteering as a class at an elementary school, and more. The creation of LEA stories based on those experiences followed a formulaic, yet flexible, five-step structure shown in Appendix A. In the following section, I briefly describe and demonstrate each step with data from a focal event—an educational visit from local firefighters to REC—giving special attention to Joy's mediation at each step. Finally, I present three patterns of valued practices demonstrated through this analysis.

Step 1: Preparation for Experience

In step one, Joy announced and prepared learners for an upcoming learning experience in the surrounding community and/or with community members. Common preparations included looking at pictures or exploring short informational texts together. In the focal event for this chapter, Joy prepared the class for a visit from local firefighters by conducting a read-aloud from the children's book, *What Happens at a Fire House?* (Pohl, 2006). In the following data excerpt Joy sets up the read-aloud. (Transcription conventions appear in Appendix B.)

JOY: So right now your babies are all downstairs looking at the fire truck.
S10: Yeah.
JOY: And then (administrator's name) will come and say, "Oka:y mommies YOU can go look at the fire truck." Uh-hu:h. So I brought some books? That we can look at about the fire truck together. Um you know what I think? S3, S4, S10 can I take your table? I wanna take it. (Pushes tables into a U shape.) It's okay I will. (Waves off help moving tables.)
(five turns later)
JOY: Okay come come come. (Moves her chair from desk at side of classroom to opening of U-shape and sits with book, motions for women to pull their chairs toward new table arrangement, looks at complete rearrangement.)

60 Nicole Pettitt

> I don't know. I'm gonna try it. See if it works. Okay I'm going to tell you about the fire truck so when we go downstairs we'll be ready.
>
> *(audio recording and field notes, March 11, 2015)*

Although the use of children's materials in adult education is contested, Joy's choice for this read-aloud was in line with administrative expectations that her instruction include content and materials from the school's concurrent early childhood programming. By choosing a children's book for the activity and rearranging the classroom to mirror a common layout during elementary school read-alouds, Joy blurred the lines between practices that are traditionally taken up in classrooms for adults versus for children. (No data were collected in REC's early childhood program, so it is unknown whether this text was also read there.)

Step 2: Community-based Experiences

Next, as the class moved into community spaces, Joy drew the learners' attention to images, words, and artifacts that appeared in texts they had previously reviewed together, which is demonstrated by the following field note recorded after the firefighters' visit.

> As they [firefighters] were talking, Joy would point at things and repeat what they said but more slowly. Or sometimes she would ask a question that their stories had just answered, which made them repeat like, "So that's the hose? Look, students, just like in the book. How much water does it carry? Wow!"
>
> *(field notes, March 11, 2015)*

This excerpt shows how Joy mediated the firefighters' presentation by taking up the subject position of learner in order to teach. That is, voicing a learner position (e.g., "So that's the hose?") was a means to model which information she felt was most important. However, others present at the event may have interpreted Joy's mediation differently, perhaps as blurring the lines between teacher and learner as she voiced her questions.

Step 3: Generating and Recording Learner Language

Upon returning to the classroom, Joy engaged learners in generating oral language to recount their experience. As learners provided words and phrases, Joy expanded them into sentences as she wrote them on the white board. The following data excerpt briefly demonstrates this process.

JOY: Okay okay okay. What did we see. What on the fire truck.
(Simultaneously talking, noise from hall)

JOY: (closes door to hall) What were they wearing.

STUDENT: Clothes for the fire.

JOY: Yeah what kind of clothes.

S8: Hat

JOY: Mhm yeah (begins writing *hat* on white board)

S3: Everyone fire truck picture

JOY: (still writing *hat*) Yeah, S3 you're you're saying good things. Helmet. (writes *helmet*) What is this? (shows picture of firefighter from her phone)

S8: Jacket

JOY: Yeah jacket good (writes *jacket*)

STUDENT: Shoes shoes boots=

JOY: =Boo::ts very good (writes *boots*) and what's on his back (reaches to tap on her upper back)

S8: Oxygen

JOY: Oxyge::n very good (writing *oxygen*) Okay S3 what did you say? What did we see?

S3: Everyone everyone take everyone fire truck take picture (laughing)

JOY: Ye::s (laughing) everyo:ne (writes *everyone took pictures with the fire truck*) Let's see did he tell us anything do you remember ANYthing he SAID?

(Students speaking quietly.)

JOY: Do you remember anything the fireman said?

AISA: Yeah yeah

JOY: What did he say if there's a fire what should you do. What did he say.

AISA: If a fire=

JOY: =yeah

AISA: uh outsi walk out outside=

JOY: = ye::s=

AISA: =and close the door.

JOY: YE:S (claps hands together) WOO::: very GOO:D (gives Aisa a 'high five')

(audio recording and field notes, March 11, 2015)

Here, Joy mediated learners' production of language through questions (lines 1, 5, etc.), a photograph (line 10), gesture (lines 14–15), encouragement (lines 26–31), and positive evaluations (lines 12, 14, 17, 31). Recording learners' language on the board at the front of the room legitimized their contributions and communicated what kinds of language was desired. Joy's mediation, then, not only supported learners in producing language for this story, but also guided and shaped what language was produced (e.g., lines 13–14, 17–19, 28–33).

Step 4: Reviewing and Planning for Writing

When Joy and the learners were finished sharing details about their experience, Joy engaged the class in chorally reading what she had written, using a stick as a

62 Nicole Pettitt

pointer. As the class read aloud, Joy numbered each sentence, thus planning the order in which she would re-write them in Step 5. For the story generated from the firefighters' visit, Joy decided she was satisfied with the event order and syntax she had chosen as she recorded learners' contributions, stating, "I think I like it how it is" (audio recording, March 11, 2015). In other words, Joy's choices at this step mediated the final story structure. The final text of the LEA firefighter story thus read as follows:

> We saw a fire truck. The fireman wore a helmet, jacket, boots, and oxygen. The fireman said, "If a fire, take children go outside. Close the door. Call 911." We saw a long hose. There is 500 gallons inside the truck. We saw a water gun that can break a window and shoot water into the burning building.

Step 5: Drafting and Publishing

Here, Joy and the learners took up different tasks. Joy wrote a final draft of the LEA story on a piece of butcher paper, signifying it was published by taping it to the back classroom wall, where all LEA stories were posted together. The learners copied a first draft of the story into their notebooks and received feedback from Joy and me—mainly spelling and English print conventions, as many women were beginning to read and write for the first time in their lives (e.g., forming and orienting letters, writing left to right, putting spaces between words, using capital letters and punctuation). As learners became familiar with the kinds of revisions Joy sought, she asked them to check their own work first.

Once Joy and a learner agreed that the first draft had been copied correctly into her notebook, the learner wrote a final draft on a half sheet of 8.5 x 11 paper and made an accompanying illustration. Learners published their final drafts by pasting the half sheets into books they had previously made by hand with cardboard, fabric, string, construction paper, and glue. The class-generated LEA stories, and the handmade books they appeared in served as core texts for Joy's class. Joy had clear standards for what was worthy of being included in learners' books: "It needed to be neat and legible and usually have a picture that went along with it" (interview, November 13, 2015). In these steps, then, Joy's mediation centered on writing as process and product, with a focus on what makes a text worthy of publishing.

Patterns of Valued Practice

In this section, I briefly focus on only three patterns of valued practice surrounding the creation of LEA stories in Joy's class, in hopes that readers will make additional inferences pertinent to their own questions and contexts.

Community as Learning (Con)text

In basing the core classroom text on experiences the women shared in community spaces (or with community members, as in the case of the firefighters' visit), Joy demonstrated a value in "diminishing the boundaries between school and place" for language learning (Smith & Sobel, 2014, p. xi). Further, centering class-generated stories (gathered in the students' handmade books) served to ground classroom language and literacy practices in rich, local, concrete experiences connected to specific times and places.

Learner Voice and Positionality

From language used, to story structure, to what is "publishable," Joy's mediation played a major role in shaping the production of LEA stories in her classroom. Yet drawing on learners' oral language (step 3) also positioned the women as legitimate co-creators of classroom texts based on their own experiences, rather than as consumers of texts with which they may identify only abstractly. The LEA stories further served as a record of the women's participation in community spaces and practices that were new to most. In a sense, then, LEA practices in Joy's classroom afforded women a way to use English to "write themselves into" the times and places of their surrounding communities (Trend, 1994, p. 226).

English Prominence

It is unsurprising that English predominated throughout the data shown prior and during the creation of LEA stories in Joy's classroom in general, as this was an ESOL teaching and learning context. What the aforementioned data do not show is that Joy communicated a value in learners' language and literacy repertoires (e.g., using Chinese as a lingua franca with a learner from Burma; encouraging learners to write in other languages, if they knew how; encouraging learners to use home/community languages with children; etc.). Joy's values were in line with REC's language education policy; additionally, the state in which this study was conducted permits the use of languages other than English in TESOL education.

Yet, with one exception, when Joy moved learning outside of REC's walls, the choice of English-dominant spaces prevailed, which is both unremarkable and remarkable. It is unremarkable because the women who came to REC did so in order to expand their language and literacy practices in English. On the other hand, the choice of English-dominant spaces is remarkable because the city in which REC was located was highly multilingual: Over 60% of the population spoke a language(s) other than English at home (U.S. Census Bureau, 2016).

Implications for Policy, Practice, and Future Research

The political landscape for many refugees coming to the US has become more challenging since data were collected for this study. The inauguration and subsequent anti-refugee executive orders of U.S. President Donald Trump in early 2017 have left many in REC's surrounding community feeling uncertain and scared (confidential personal communications, February 14, 2017). Community advocates report that some refugees are afraid to leave home or let their children go to school. Thus, questions surrounding the influence policy makers and practitioners have in the lives of refugee women and their families are particularly salient at the time of this writing.

Hope (2011) notes that refugees may experience social isolation and points to the mitigating role of ESOL family literacy programs. ESOL practitioners, then, do well to follow Joy's lead, grounding curriculum and instruction in experiences of local spaces, "mak[ing] the wall between schools and their communities more permeable and . . . draw[ing] students into a sense of social membership" (Smith & Sobel, 2014, p. 16). With this recommendation, I invite practitioners to move beyond the data presented here, taking up multidirectional relationships between schools and the full spectrum of community spaces that surround them, including non-English-dominant spaces. For instance, engaging learners in planning and leading class experiences in bi/multilingual spaces with which they are familiar legitimizes learners' full linguistic repertoires and positions them as knowledgeable authorities surrounding bi/multilingual community practices. Creating classroom texts that draw on these experiences communicates that bi/multilingual spaces and practices are worthy of inscribing in print and studying. Such texts further permit refugee learners to express their own thoughts about the bi/multilingual practices and community spaces in which they conduct their daily lives, rather than leaving these commentaries solely to researchers. In future studies, then, researchers could partner with practitioners and learners to amplify learner voice in studies that examine linguistic landscapes or bi/multilingual community language and literacy practices (e.g., Hutchison, 2001).

Additional research is also needed to better understand how policies facilitate or impede adult ESOL practitioners taking up curricular innovations. For instance, a lack of explicit policies surrounding language, curriculum, and testing gave REC teachers broad latitude in the classroom, which some teachers found frustrating. However, Joy described the situation as a "big puzzle"; she drew heavily on her elementary training, which she found indispensable to working at REC (interviews, October 30 and December 11, 2014). As is common in many U.S. communities, no local teacher training programs offered formation in teaching emergent reader adults. (Requirements for adult/family literacy ESOL teaching vary widely; in states with little state funding, few full-time positions exist. For a list of adult ESOL teacher requirements by state, please see www.cal.org/caela/esl_resources/briefs/Teacher_Credentialing_Table_RED_MBxls.pdf)

Additionally, some adult/family literacy ESOL teachers may work within greater restrictions on curriculum and instruction than is the case at REC. With this context in mind, researchers should ask what constraints/affordances exist (including teacher preparation and credentialing) and how they shape practitioners' choices.

Although the macro-level language education policy landscape for newcomers to the US is currently uncertain, Joy demonstrates that adult/family literacy ESOL teachers are important mediators of language and education policy at local levels. Joy's encouragement of bi/multilingualism in class and at home countered English-only instructional practices in adult ESOL, and her positioning of learners' experiences at the center of class discourse (via LEA stories) served to resist deficit discourses that prevail in some family literacy programming. Joy's example underscores the importance of resisting growing assimilationist and anti-refugee/anti-immigrant discourses in the US, in favor of language and education policies that complement participatory teaching approaches and center bi/multilingual practices in adult and family literacy ESOL settings.

APPENDIX A

Creation of Story Based on Firefighters' Visit Using Language Experience Approach

Step/ when	Practice	Social scene/where	With whom	Mediational means and identity texts
1	Preparation for community-based experience.	Classroom. Joy sitting in chair at front of room; learners in chairs at tables formed in U.	Joy + learners. Led by Joy.	Children's book: *What Happens at a Fire House?* (Pohl, 2006), wooden pointer, white board, teacher chair, student tables.
2	Shared community-based experience.	REC parking lot.	Joy + learners + local firefighters. Led by firefighters and Joy.	Joy's language (repeating, asking questions) and pointing, fire truck, firefighter tools, uniforms.
3	Generating oral language.	Classroom. Joy at white board; learners at tables.	Joy + learners. Collaborative, led by Joy.	Joy's questions and comments, cell phone photos of firefighters' visit, white board, dry erase marker.
4	Reviewing, preparing for writing.	Classroom. Joy at white board; learners at tables.	Joy + learners. Led by Joy.	White board, wooden pointer.

Step/when	Practice	Social scene/where	With whom	Mediational means and identity texts
5	Drafting and publishing.	Classroom. Learners at tables. Joy in front/rotating to learners' seats. Researcher rotating to learners' seats.	Joy + learners + researcher. Joy, learners, and researcher working together 1:1 or 2:1.	Feedback from Joy and researcher, self-mediation, butcher paper, marker, learner notebooks, pens/pencils, 8.5 x 11 sheets, colored pencils, handmade books.

APPENDIX B

Transcription Conventions

?	rising intonation
.	falling intonation
=	latching (i.e., one utterance immediately following another; no perceivable overlapping/pausing)
:	lengthening
CAPS	louder than surrounding language
""	quoted speech
(xxx)	transcriber notes

References

Anderson, J., Anderson, A., Friedrich, N., & Kim, J. E. (2010). Taking stock of family literacy: Some contemporary perspectives. *Journal of Early Childhood Literacy, 10*, 33–53. doi:10.1177/ 1468798409357387.

Cuban, S., & Hayes, E. (1996). Women in family literacy programs: A gendered perspective. *New Directions for Adult and Continuing Education, 70*, 5–16.

Dudley-Marling, C. (2009). Home-school literacy connections: The perceptions of African American and immigrant ESL parents in two urban communities. *Teachers College Record, 111*, 1713–1752.

Griffith, A., & Smith, D. (2005). *Mothering for schooling.* New York, NY: Routledge.

Hendrix, S. (1999). Family literacy education—panacea or false promise? *Journal of Adolescent & Adult Literacy, 4*, 338–346.

Hope, J. (2011). New insights into family learning for refugees: Bonding, bridging and building transcultural capital. *Literacy, 45*, 91–98.

Hutchison, K. (2001). Gendered readings: Reframing mothers in family literacy. *The Australian Educational Researcher, 28*, 47–61.

Landis, D., Umolu, J., & Mancha, S. (2010). The power of language experience for cross-cultural reading and writing. *The Reading Teacher, 63*, 580–589.

Lantolf, J. P. (Ed.). (2000). *Sociocultural theory and second language learning*. Oxford, UK: Oxford University Press.

Luttrell, W. (1996). Taking care of literacy: One feminist's critique. *Educational Policy, 10*, 342–365.

Mace, J. (2002). *The give and take of writing: Scribes, literacy and everyday life*. Leicester, UK: National Institute of Adult Continuing Education.

McCarty, T. (2011). Introducing ethnography and language policy. In T. McCarty (Ed.), *Ethnography and language policy* (pp. 1–28). New York, NY: Routledge.

Menard-Warwick, J. (2009). *Gendered identities and immigrant language learning*. Bristol, UK: Multilingual Matters.

Molinsky, S., & Bliss, B. (2001). *Side by side* (3rd ed.). Hoboken, NJ: Pearson ELT.

Muro, A., & Mein, E. (2010). Domestic trauma and adult education on the United States-Mexico border. *Adult Basic Education and Literacy Journal, 4*, 140–150.

Norton, B. (2012). *Identity and language learning: Extending the conversation*. Bristol, UK: Multilingual Matters.

Pohl, K. (2006). *What happens at a fire house*. Pleasantville, NY: Weekly Reader Books/ Gareth Stevens Publishing.

Scollon, R. (2001). *Mediated discourse analysis: The nexus of practice*. New York, NY: Routledge.

Smith, G., & Sobel, D. (2014). *Place-and community-based education in schools*. New York, NY: Routledge.

Spolsky, B. (2004). *Language policy*. Cambridge, UK: Cambridge University Press.

Spolsky, B. (2009). *Language management*. Cambridge, UK: Cambridge University Press.

Taylor, D. (1993). Family literacy: Resisting deficit models. *TESOL Quarterly, 27*, 550–553.

Trend, D. (1994). Nationalities, pedagogies, and media. In H. Giroux & P. McLaren (Eds.), *Between borders: Pedagogy and the politics of cultural studies* (pp. 225–241). New York, NY: Routledge.

United Nations High Commissioner for Refugees. (2015, June 18). *Worldwide displacement hits all-time high as war and persecution increase*. Retrieved May 12, 2017 from www.unhcr. org/558193896.html

U.S. Census Bureau. (2016). *2010–2014 American community survey 5-year estimates: Selected social characteristics in the United States*. Retrieved May 12, 2017 from http://factfinder. census.gov/faces/nav/jsf/pages/index.xhtml

Vygotsky, L. S. (1978). *Mind in society*. Cambridge, MA: Harvard University Press.

Wasik, B. H., & Herrmann, S. (2004). Family literacy: History, concepts, services. In B. Wasik (Ed.), *Handbook of family literacy* (pp. 3–22). Mahwah, NJ: Lawrence Erlbaum.

Wohlwend, K. (2009). Mapping multimodal literacy practices through mediated discourse analysis: Identity revision in "What Not To Wear." In K. M. Leander, D. W. Rowe, D. K. Dickinson, M. K. Hundley, R. T. Jiménez, & V. J. Risko (Eds.), *58th yearbook of the National Reading Conference* (pp. 66–81). Oak Creek, WI: National Reading Conference, Inc.

Woodin, T. (2008). "A beginner reader is not a beginner thinker": Student publishing in Britain since the 1970s. *Paedagogica historica, 44*(1–2), 219–232.

Wurr, A. J. (2002). Language experience approach revisited: The use of personal narratives in adult L2 literacy instruction. *The Reading matrix*. Retrieved May 12, 2017 from www.readingmatrix.com/articles/wurr/?collection=col10460/1.13

PART 2

Adoption or Adaptation of Educational Language Policies by/in Institutions

6

POLICY BORROWING IN UNIVERSITY LANGUAGE PLANNING

A Case of Writing Centers in Japan

Tomoyo Okuda

Due to increased pressures of internationalization, universities around the world look to language education models and frameworks with global recognition (Byram & Parmenter, 2012). Focusing on the spread of writing centers in Japan, this paper examines policy borrowing (Steiner-Khamsi, 2014) in language-in-education planning. I focus on how universities in Japan justify the writing center as an innovative facility that can help improve students' English and Japanese writing skills. In the following discussion, all translations from the original Japanese texts are my own.

Issues That Motivated the Research

The writing center is a common student writing support service in American universities. It gained popularity in American universities during the progressive education movement around the 1970s as a non-hierarchical, student-centered environment (Boquet, 1999). Underpinned by Vygotskyian collaborative learning theories and the process writing approach, the writing center pedagogy allows students to discover the writing process collaboratively with their peer tutors (Bruffee, 1984; North, 1984). In the past few decades, the writing center has spread from North America to other parts of the world, as documented by writing center practitioners in Asia (Johnston, Cornwell, & Yoshida, 2008; Tan, 2011), Europe (Bräuer, 2002; Reichelt et al., 2013), Africa (Broekhoff, 2014), the Middle East (Ronesi, 2009), Central America (García-Arroyo & Quintana, 2012), and South America (Carlino, 2012). According to the Writing Center Directory (http://web.stcloudstate.edu/writeplace/wcd/), there are writing centers in 65 countries.

74 Tomoyo Okuda

Multiple educational and social factors have made this global spread possible. First, the writing center's process writing approach is often welcomed as an improvement to existing academic literacy practices and teaching methods. Under the process writing approach (North, 1984), writing center tutors guide writers in the steps of finishing a written product, such as "how to plan, to brainstorm, to ask questions for revision, to rework written text, to add variety to sentence structure, to organize large amounts of material into a research paper, [and] to proofread" (International Writing Center Association, 2017, para. 9). This approach has been highly valued in some English as a foreign language countries (e.g., Japan, Taiwan, Germany, Poland, Hungary) in which teaching writing was not emphasized much in schools or was characterized by teacher-directed, large-size classes and product-oriented teaching approaches (Ertl, 2011; Reichelt et al., 2013).

Writing centers can often be found in international branch campuses of American universities. Because many American universities have campus-wide writing programs and first-year composition classes, writing programs and writing centers are implemented to emulate this education model in off-shore American universities in the Middle East, Europe, and Central America (e.g., Lebanon, UAE, Qatar, Bulgaria, France, Puerto Rico) (García-Arroyo & Quintana, 2012; Ronesi, 2009). It is also common for American university faculty members to collaborate with local staff to establish writing programs and centers (Broekhoff, 2014).

The popularity of writing centers is also enhanced by current trends of neoliberal education reforms characterized by competition, the knowledge economy, and human capital. In this context, some governments identify writing competence as an important communication skill in global businesses (Bollinger, 2016; Gustafsson & Ganobcsik-Williams, 2016). For instance, writing competence is designated as one of the key competencies outlined by the Bologna Reform, a standardized movement in European higher education, and the use of writing center pedagogy is recommended as an effective approach to developing writing competence in both English and the vernacular language (Gustafsson & Ganobcsik-Williams, 2016). In Russia, Bollinger (2016) reports that the Writing and Communication Center at the New Economic School plays a role in fostering business communication skills in English "for Russian students to obtain prestigious positions and contribute to Russia's human development" (p. 33). Because writing is increasingly emphasized as a key competence in the global knowledge economy, writing centers (together with writing programs) may continue to spread.

Context of the Research

In this chapter, I focus on the case of Japan and identify the unique socioeconomic and political factors that allowed writing centers to proliferate. The advent of writing centers in Japan can be traced back to 2004, when several pioneer English writing centers were established (Johnston et al., 2008). As a characteristic

Policy Borrowing in University Language **75**

shared with some other non-English speaking countries, there are writing centers that also assist with writing in the official language, Japanese.

To examine the politics of the transfer of writing center philosophy, the conceptual framework of policy borrowing (or educational transfer) is employed (Phillips & Ochs, 2004; Rappleye, Imoto, & Horiguchi, 2011; Steiner-Khamsi, 2014). Cross-national policy borrowing is a research field in Comparative Education, which studies the political rationales, power dynamics, and consequences of transferring educational systems, models, and concepts across contexts. Policy borrowing is not only a matter of adopting better educational practices, but also involves deeper political and economic interests and motives.

Transfer of educational knowledge not only happens between politicians or governments. Rappleye et al. (2011) contend that due to globalizing forces and independence from the state, institutions such as universities have the autonomy to search for successful models and import them into their systems; writing centers fit this case. Organizations such as the International Writing Center Association (IWCA, 2017) and other regional writing center associations enable practitioners to exchange ideas, bring them back to their own institutions, and implement them.

Research Question Addressed

In this chapter, I attempt to explore the political rationales of the writing center transfer that has occurred in Japan. The following research question will be addressed: How do Japanese universities justify the value of writing centers in their institutional plans?

Research Methods

Data Collection

To address my research question, I analyzed government documents, university writing center webpages, and research articles (i.e., empirical studies and local reports) by writing center practitioners in Japan. These documents were helpful in identifying the social background of the writing center establishment, such as the government's educational agenda and universities' views on the educational value of writing centers. Because several universities received government funding to establish their writing centers, I also obtained their publicly available funding applications.

Data Analysis Procedures Used

Through my analysis, I identified three commonly offered writing center services: (1) Japanese writing consultations for Japanese students (JDS), (2) English writing consultations for Japanese students (ENG), and (3) Japanese writing consultations

76 Tomoyo Okuda

TABLE 6.1 Types of Writing Centers

Type of writing center	Number of writing centers
ENG	9
ENG + JDS + JSL	6
JDS + JSL	5
JDS	3
JSL	3
ENG + JSL	3
ENG + JDS	1
Total	30

for international students (JSL). Some university writing centers offer English and Japanese writing support; some only offer one type of service (e.g., only English or Japanese writing support). Table 6.1 indicates the number of writing centers that offered different types and combinations of writing center services, based on my internet research in 2016. The ENG writing center is the most common type, followed by writing centers with all three types of services. Because the goals, the target language (writing in Japanese or English), and audience of each type of writing center differ and reflect the universities' views toward academic literacy, in the following section, I present my analysis of ENG, JSL, and JDS writing centers, respectively.

Findings and Discussion

Fostering Japanese Who Can Use English (ENG Writing Centers)

Successive Japanese governments have emphasized English as an important subject to teach in schools and have announced various English reform plans throughout the years. ENG writing centers increased around 2003, when the government announced its five-year project to cultivate "Japanese who can use English" (MEXT, 2003). The main goal was to foster students with practical and specialized English skills for the global workplace (MEXT, 2003), with the government-funded universities proposing innovative practices to attain this goal. After this plan was announced, three pioneers of writing centers in Japan—Waseda University, Sophia University, and Osaka Jogakuin University—received Good Practices funding for establishing their writing centers as part of their English-medium Liberal Arts Programs (Osaka Jogakuin University, 2016; Sophia University, 2008; Waseda University, 2005). Because these programs are modeled on American liberal arts colleges that commonly have composition courses and writing centers, the writing center is seen as a necessary piece of liberal arts education to aid students with their English written assignments. For instance, Sophia University and

Osaka Jogakuin University both mention liberal arts, global, and writing communication skills in explaining their writing programs:

> We are training students to be native-like writers so they can effectively utilize their liberal arts knowledge in their global workplaces and in their graduate studies.
>
> *(Sophia University, 2008, p. 2)*

> For this project, we aim to integrate liberal arts education and English education to foster excellent English communication skills for students to actively participate in the globalizing society.
>
> *(Osaka Jogakuin University, 2016, para. 2)*

The strategic connection of competent English writers and the global society aligned well with the government's plan and upheld writing centers as a necessary entity to achieve this goal.

As was the case with these pioneering universities, ENG writing centers are likely to receive funding if they are marketed to implement the government's educational agenda of fostering bilingual workers, researchers, and leaders with high English proficiency. Particularly, English academic writing is increasingly becoming an important skill for Japanese researchers as a means of producing and disseminating their research globally, which is another emergent agenda of the government (Cabinet's Office, 2013). For instance, the University of Tokyo and Nagoya University both established writing centers as a part of their mandatory English curricula for undergraduate students (University of Tokyo) and graduate students (Nagoya University) to learn how to write a research paper in English (Nagoya University Writing Center, n.d.; The University of Tokyo, n.d.). A commonality between these two institutions is that they are two of the leading universities publishing English articles in high-impact journals, especially in science fields. They state that writing skills in general are crucial for fostering researchers' critical thinking skills and logical arguments in research writing (Nagoya University Writing Center, n.d.; The University of Tokyo, n.d.).

For a Quality Undergraduate Education (JDS Writing Center)

A social background that leads to the implementation of JDS writing centers is the so-called open admissions era of universities (*daigaku zen-nyugaku jidai*) (Tsuruta, 2013). Although Japanese universities traditionally administer high-stakes entrance exams, due to the decline in birth rates and decreasing numbers of incoming students, universities have started to administer more lenient exams, such as interview-based exams, to attract students. As a result, it is argued that the lack of a rigorous gate-keeping mechanism led to an influx of incoming students with low Japanese literacy skills and indolent learning attitudes (Iwamoto, 2008).

In order to improve the quality of undergraduate education, the Ministry of Education published guidelines for universities to follow. In the document "Toward the Construction of a Undergraduate Education," the policy articulates a set of skills necessary for students to function well in society upon graduation (MEXT, 2008a), one of which is communication skills. Along with other campus services that the Ministry lists, writing centers are recommended as a way to help foster written communication skills (MEXT, 2008a). After this guideline was publicized, the late 2000s saw an increase in Japanese basic writing programs and JDS writing centers as a space for Japanese literacy development and academic socialization.

Another educational concept promoted by the government which contributed to the spread of writing centers is *active learning*, a concept originating from American higher education. In Japan, active learning was proposed as a measure to transform teacher-directed classrooms and passive learning attitudes of university students (MEXT, 2008a).

Given this interest in active learning, JDS writing centers are not only promoted as improving Japanese writing, but also as increasing study hours and fostering enthusiastic attitudes toward learning (Iwamoto, 2008; Takahashi, 2012). Takahashi (2012) writes about one of the main purposes of the Tsuda College writing center:

> In order to provide a quality undergraduate education, classes are not enough. . . . Thus the writing center collaborating with classes, job hunting activities, and extracurricular activities, will support each student's needs. Through visiting the writing center, students will foster an active attitude and increase studying hours which will lead to a quality undergraduate education.
>
> *(Takahashi, 2012, p. 9)*

In this way, whereas ENG writing centers are justified to foster global human resources, JDS writing centers are justified as a national project to develop responsible Japanese citizens.

As an Internationalization Strategy (JSL Writing Centers)

International student recruitment has become a common internationalization strategy for universities worldwide, and Japan is no exception. According to the Japan Student Services Organization (2017), in 2016, a total of 171,122 international students studied in Japanese higher education institutions, and 91.5% of them came from Asian countries. However, this number is still half of what the Japanese government aims to achieve. In 1983, Prime Minister Nakasone announced a plan to increase the number of international students to 100,000 by the year 2000. This goal was attained in 2003, and in 2008, this goal was increased to 300,000 international students by the year 2020 (MEXT, 2008b). The aim of this second plan is to recruit talented international students who can contribute to the Japanese economy and research fields, in turn enhancing universities' international competitiveness.

However, the insufficient Japanese language proficiency of some international students has continuously been raised as a challenge to universities. In the mid-2000s, a survey of 81 universities conducted by the Ministry of Internal Affairs and Communications reported that universities perceived a decline in the "quality" (*shitsu*) of international students, the major cause being a high number of students with low Japanese language ability who could not follow classroom discussions (Internal Affairs and Communications Ministry, 2005). As has been the case in other countries, international students are often described as a burden when it comes to their language issues (Jenkins & Wingate, 2015).

Given this context, several Japanese universities started writing center consultations for their international students between the late 2000s and early 2010s (e.g., Masamune, 2009; Matsuta, 2011; Taniguchi, 2015). A common rationale reflects the role of writing centers in lessening the burden on instructors to check international students' Japanese writing. As Masamune (2009) comments,

> Since it is hard for teachers to work with students individually on their writing, teachers usually give written feedback. But in this way . . . students did not improve their writing nor even proofread their work before submission. . . . We felt a need for them to learn the process of writing themselves. That is why we felt a need to establish a space for them to learn how to write through one-on-one tutoring with a Japanese tutor.
>
> *(p. 10)*

Similar to Masamune (2009), some writing center practitioners also claim that through the repeated process of talking about writing with a tutor, international students will be able to notice their mistakes and acquire strategies to write papers on their own (Masamune, 2009; Matsuta, 2011). Developing autonomous writers, which is one of the tenets of the writing center (North, 1984), is strategically interpreted as fostering independent writers who learn to write papers by themselves, with minimal help from course instructors.

The writing center has become one of the internationalization strategies to attract more international students for some leading international universities (Ritsumeikan Asia Pacific University, 2012; Senaha, 2011; Waseda, 2012). Waseda University, which had the largest number of international students in 2016 (over 4,000), has continuously received government funding for their writing center services. In their funding application, they wrote about their intentions to hire Chinese students as tutors and offer Chinese writing consultations, to serve the language learning needs of this growing international student population (Waseda University, 2012). Ritsumeikan Asia Pacific University, which had the third largest

80 Tomoyo Okuda

international student enrollment in 2016, also has a writing center for their international students and hires international students to tutor English language learners (Ritsumeikan Asia Pacific University, 2012). These cases show that setting up a writing center for international students is one way to demonstrate the university's readiness to internationalize its campus and accept more international students.

Implications for Policy, Practice, and Future Research

In this chapter, I have demonstrated how writing centers spread not only through writing educators' interests in Western-based pedagogy, but also by selectively borrowing the pedagogical concepts of the writing center to match the Japanese higher education agenda. The ENG writing center was considered beneficial in fostering competent English writers in global research and work. In contrast, the JDS writing center, as a collaborative, peer-learning facility, tied in nicely with fostering responsible and active learners, matching the government's call for raising the quality of undergraduate education. Last, given the pressure to increase international enrollment, writing centers are becoming part of a strategy to help international students become autonomous writers in Japanese and to lessen the burden on instructors. These three types of writing centers are strongly tied to accomplishing the educational goals of the Japanese government. The findings suggest that in all three cases, education models from leading universities (in this case, writing centers from American universities) serve as legitimate resources to solve local institutional issues and to showcase the university's entrepreneurship.

A noteworthy lesson drawn from policy borrowing research is the temporal dimension of policies. Steiner-Khamsi (2014) notes that as policy travels from place to place, is modified, and is held as best practices, it becomes deterritorialized as "everybody's and nobody's reform" (p. 160). This pattern is also occurring in Japan: As many model writing centers are increasing within the country, the idea of the writing center is now circulating amongst Japanese practitioners. It is thus easier for policy makers to reach out to a traveled policy that is so widely accepted, seemingly neutral, and adaptable to everybody's needs. Although there is a writing center philosophy written by IWCA (2017), there is no one-size-fits-all model of writing centers, in terms of tutor profile, language of instruction, location, etc., as writing center practitioners around the world have shown. Because of the flexible educational philosophy, institutions can implement writing centers for all types of reasons.

This chapter suggests that the neoliberal climate of competing for excellence creates a platform for economically driven language planning to take place, in which traveling education models are implemented for the sake of performance, accountability, and raising important numbers. What is important for non–North American universities is to critically examine the impacts of a foreign education policy (e.g., impacts on existing literacy practices, students who might be excluded from the pedagogy, and the possibility of alternative pedagogies). In the case of writing centers, it is noteworthy that some Japanese universities offer proofreading services by professional writing instructors (e.g., Fujishima, Yoshikawa, & Ishikawa, 2004), which have not gained much attention compared to writing centers. Considering inclusive and appropriate writing/academic support for various types of students is a challenging but vital task for Japanese universities in this age of internationalization, globalization, decreasing numbers of incoming students, and ongoing competition among universities.

References

Bollinger, K. M. (2016). Introducing Western writing theory and pedagogy to Russian students: The writing and communication center at the New Economic School. In P. Zemliansky & K. S. Amant (Eds.), *Rethinking post-communist rhetoric: Perspectives on rhetoric, writing, and professional communication in Post-Soviet spaces* (pp. 19–42). Lanham, MD: Rowman & Littlefield.

Boquet, E. H. (1999). "Our little secret": A history of writing centers, pre- to post-open admissions. *College Composition and Communication, 50*(3), 463–482.

Bräuer, G. (2002). Drawing connections across education: The Freiburg writing center model. *Language and Learning Across the Disciplines, 5*(3), 61–80.

Broekhoff, M. (2014). A tale of two writing centers in Namibia: Lessons for us all. *Journal of Academic Writing, 4*(1), 66–78.

Bruffee, K. A. (1984). Peer tutoring and the "conversation of mankind." In G. A. Olson (Ed.), *Writing centers: Theory and administration* (pp. 3–15). Urbana, IL: National Council of Teachers of English.

Byram, M., & Parmenter, L. (Eds.). (2012). *The common European framework of reference: The globalisation of language education policy*. Bristol, UK: Multilingual Matters.

Cabinet's Office. (2013). *University education and global human resource development for the future (Third Proposal)*. Retrieved from www.kantei.go.jp/jp/singi/kyouikusaisei/pdf/dai3_en.pdf

Carlino, P. (2012). Who takes care of writing in Latin American and Spanish universities? In C. Thaiss, P. Carlino, L. Ganobcsik-Williams, & A. Sinha (Eds.), *Writing programs worldwide: Profiles of academic writing in many places* (pp. 485–498). Fort Collins, CO: The WAC Clearinghouse.

Ertl, J. (2011). The role of writing centers: Student learning centers in the United States and their applicability for Japanese universities. *Forum of Language Instructors, 5*, 45–61.

Fujishima, H., Yoshikawa, M., & Ishikawa, M. (2004). The activity and a present condition report of a K.I.T. writing center. *KIT Progress, 9*, 1–35.

García-Arroyo, M., & Quintana, H. E. (2012). The ups and downs of the interdisciplinary writing center of the Interamerican University of Puerto Rico, Metropolitan campus. In C. Thaiss, P. Carlino, L. Ganobcsik-Williams, & A. Sinha (Eds.), *Writing programs worldwide: Profiles of academic writing in many places* (pp. 333–340). Fort Collins, CO: The WAC Clearinghouse.

Gustafsson, M., & Ganobcsik-Williams, L. (2016). Writing centers and the turn toward multilingual and multiliteracy writing tutoring. In K. Hyland & P. Shaw (Eds.), *The Routledge handbook of English for academic purposes* (pp. 517–529). London, UK: Routledge.

Internal Affairs and Communications Ministry. (2005). *Ryuugakusei no ukeire sokushin shisaku ni kansuru seikaku hyōka* [An evaluation of the policies concerning measures to promote the acceptance of foreign students to Japanese universities]. Retrieved August 17, 2016 from www.soumu.go.jp/menu_news/s-news/daijinkanbou/050111_1.pdf

International Writing Center Association. (2017). *Writing center concept.* Retrieved November 30, 2017 from http://writingcenters.org/writing-center-concept-by-muriel-harris/

Iwamoto, T. (2008). Senpai kara Kohai e, shinshi na adobaisu ga ikiru gakushūshien [To seniors to juniors: Academic support through advising]. *Daigaku to Gakusei,* (50), 30–35.

Japan Student Services Organization. (2017). *Heisei 28 nendo gaikokujin ryūgakusei zaiseki jyōkyō chōsa kekka* [International students in 2016]. Retrieved April 3, 2017 from www.jasso.go.jp/about/statistics/intl_student_e/2016/__icsFiles/afieldfile/2017/03/30/data16.pdf

Jenkins, J., & Wingate, U. (2015). Staff and student perceptions of English language policies and practices in "international" universities: A UK case study. *Higher Education Review, 47*(2), 47–73.

Johnston, S., Cornwell, S., & Yoshida, H. (2008). Writing centers in Japan. *Journal of Osaka Jogakuin University, 5,* 181–192.

Masamune, S. (2009). Bunshoryokushien no tame no tiching ashisutanto muke manual soan: Raitingu centa secchini mukete [A teaching manual for teaching assistants]. *Reitaku Daigaku Kiyō, 89,* 109–125.

Matsuta, Y. (2011). Toward the establishment of writing support systems for international students at Kanazawa University. *Forum of Language Instructors, 5,* 27–44.

MEXT. (2003). *"Eigo ga tsukaeru nihonjin" no ikusei no tame no kōdō keikaku* [Developing a strategic plan to cultivate '"Japanese with English abilities"]. Retrieved August 17, 2016 from www.mext.go.jp/b_menu/shingi/chukyo/chukyo3/004/siryo/04031601/005.pdf

MEXT. (2008a). *Gakushikatie kyōku ni mukete* [Reconstructing undergraduate education]. Retrieved August 17, 2016 from www.mext.go.jp/component/b_menu/shingi/toushin/__icsFiles/afieldfile/2013/05/13/1212958_001.pdf

MEXT. (2008b). *Outline of the student exchangement system: Study in Japan and abroad.* Retrieved August 17, 2016 from www.mext.go.jp/a_menu/koutou/ryugaku/081210/001.pdf

Nagoya University Writing Center. (n.d.). *Mei-writing: Department of Academic Writing, Institute of Liberal Arts and Sciences.* Retrieved August 17, 2016 from http://meiwriting.ilas.nagoya-u.ac.jp/

North, S. M. (1984). The idea of a writing center. *College English, 46*(5), 433–446.

Osaka Jogakuin University. (2016). *Kyōiku kenkyū heno torikumi* [Our educational research]. Retrieved August 17, 2016 from www.wilmina.ac.jp/ojc/edu

Phillips, D., & Ochs, K. (2004). Researching policy borrowing: Some methodological challenges in comparative education. *British Educational Research Journal, 30*(6), 773–784.

Rappleye, J., Imoto, Y., & Horiguchi, S. (2011). Towards "thick description" of educational transfer: Understanding a Japanese institution's "import" of European language policy. *Comparative Education, 47*(4), 411–432.

Reichelt, M., Salski, Ł., Andres, J., Lowczowski, E., Majchrzak, O., Molenda, M., . . . Wiśniewska-Steciuk, E. (2013). "A table and two chairs": Starting a writing center in Łódź, Poland. *Journal of Second Language Writing, 22*(3), 277–285.

Ritsumeikan Asia Pacific University. (2012). *Writing center.* Retrieved August 17, 2016 from http://en.apu.ac.jp/academic/page/content0075.html/

Ronesi, L. (2009). Theory in/to practice: Multilingual tutors supporting multilingual peers: A peer-tutor training course in the Arabian Gulf. *Writing Center Journal, 29*(2), 75–94.

Senaha, E. (2011). Writing lab pilot scheme at Hokkaido University: Background, outcome, and future. *Journal of Higher Education and Lifelong Learning, 18*, 11–18.

Sophia University. (2008). *Tokushoku aru daigaku kyoiku shien puroguramu "Nihon to sekai wo musubu kokusaikyōyō no senkuteki torikumi"* [Good Practice Award pioneering international liberal arts education connecting Japan and the world]. Retrieved August 17, 2016 from http://ocw.cc.sophia.ac.jp/?action=lecture_view_main_note&upload_id=572

Steiner-Khamsi, G. (2014). Cross-national policy borrowing: Understanding reception and translation. *Asia Pacific Journal of Education, 34*(2), 153–167.

Takahashi, Y. (2012). Kangae, hyougen shi, hasshin suru chikara wo tsuchikau raitingu/kyariya shien ga saitaku saremashita [Joint project for writing/career support through developing skills to think and express approved by the Ministry of Education]. *Tsuda Today, 85*, 9.

Tan, B. H. (2011). Innovating writing centers and online writing labs outside North America. *Asian EFL Journal, 13*(2), 391–418.

Taniguchi, M. (2015). A needs survey aiming to establish a writing center for international students. *Shizuoka Sangyō Daigaku Jyōhōgakubu Kenkyū Kiyō, 17*, 69–78.

Tsuruta, Y. (2013). The knowledge society and the internationalization of Japanese higher education. *Asia Pacific Journal of Education, 33*(2), 140–155.

The University of Tokyo. (n.d.). *Center for global communication strategies (CGCS) The University of Tokyo*. Retrieved August 17, 2016 from www.cgcs.c.u-tokyo.ac.jp/index.html

Waseda University. (2005). Monbu kagakushō ni yoru "gendaiteki kyōuiku nizu torikumi shien puroguramu" ni saitaku [Waseda accepted for the MEXT Good Practices program]. *Campus now, 5*.

Waseda University. (2012). *Heisei 24 nedo gurōbaru jinzai ikusei suishin jigyō kōsō chōsho* [Institutional Plan for Project for Promotion of Global Human Resources]. Retrieved August 17, 2016 from www.jsps.go.jp/j-gjinzai/data/shinsa/h24/gjinzai_chousho_a08.pdf

7

ECONOMIC MARKETS, ELITE MULTILINGUALISM, AND LANGUAGE POLICY IN NEPALI SCHOOLS

Bal Krishna Sharma

As research on language policies from a globalization perspective has mostly focused on English, we understand very little about the possibilities for other languages to gain the status of an international language. The rapid growth and presence of Chinese worldwide, beyond the national borders of traditionally Chinese-speaking countries, has brought the language into contact with processes that we understand as globalization in today's world. Chinese as a vehicle of cross-cultural communication motivated mainly by economic reasons is promoted and enhanced by global mobilities of people and transnational business and investments. In this chapter, I focus on the role of economic markets, such as business and tourism, in shaping language policies that promote an 'elite' form of multilingualism in Nepali private schools. Among certain groups in Nepal, Chinese is emerging as another global language, alongside English, and has attracted Nepali schools and students for its immediate material value in business and travel. The school policies that promote Chinese as another international language subtly produce counter-narratives of the taken-for-granted role of English as *the* sole international lingua franca. However, these discourses do not replace or weaken the teaching and learning of English. In this chapter, I explore motivations for learning Chinese as an additional bonus to the learners' existing multilingual repertoires.

Issues That Motivated the Research

Ricento and Hornberger's (1996) famous onion metaphor provided a new way of conceptualizing language policy and planning in multiple layers and processes. Their conceptualization recognizes institutions as important agents in formulating and implementing language policy through their action plans to teach a particular language, the standard curricula and tests, and other resources in translating a policy into practice. Schools as institutions exercise language policy power through an array of pedagogical decisions, sometimes reinterpreting and negotiating the dominant state language policies (Menken & García, 2010). When we conceptualize language policy in multiple layers, "it is open to diverse interpretations, both by those who created it, and by those who are expected to appropriate it in practice" (Johnson & Johnson, 2015, p. 223). Language learners are at the bottom of the consuming end and may have little role in shaping the formation of school policies in many contexts. If, however, they do retain agency in making sense of the policy that is enacted upon them, their agency may indirectly influence the policy makers to reconsider their decisions on policy making.

English has long received scholarly attention in terms of how the political-economic conditions of late capitalism and neoliberalism in this era of globalization have impacted language policies enacted in different times and spaces (e.g., Ricento, 2015). Studies that explore the possibilities of languages other than English gaining international status are under-documented (Kobayashi, 2015). Ding and Saunders (2006) highlight this issue in the case of Mandarin Chinese being another candidate for a global language status. It is a matter of further investigation regarding the extent to which this ideology is embraced in language-in-education policies in geo-political contexts where Mandarin Chinese is not a major foreign language. By presenting a case of two elite private schools in Nepal—traditionally a pro-English geo-political context—I discuss how the teaching and learning of Chinese has increasingly become an integral part of language education policy and practice in many private schools in Kathmandu. I also interrogate how language learners make sense of the policy by positioning themselves variously in relation to English vis-à-vis Chinese in their future life trajectories.

Context of the Research

The broader research context of this study is Nepal, where English has historically been *the* dominant foreign language in its educational policies. It was adopted as the only international language in the formal education policy from the beginning of the twentieth century. For example, Giri (2010) writes:

> The schools were modelled on the British education system, which followed the patterns/curricula of the English education system in India. The ELE [English language education] ideology was, thus, imported from British India where the goal of education was to form a class of persons that were English in tastes, in opinions, in morals and intellect. (p. 93)

Now, the reach of English has expanded to people who have had no access to it in the past, mainly through the privatization of school education. The proliferation of private schools has further reinforced the symbolic and economic power of English. Phyak (2016) notes, "The dominant social and educational discourses define the identity of people who send their children to private schools as 'rich,' 'elite,' 'civilized,' and 'more knowledgeable'" (p. 207). Also noticeable in recent years is the number of schools offering courses in Chinese. As the number of Chinese visitors to Nepal is growing, many people see the Chinese language as financially attractive. Moreover, Nepali businessmen's reciprocal ties with their Chinese counterparts and their recurring trips to mainland China have raised the importance of Mandarin Chinese for the purpose of negotiating and accomplishing business transactions. As a result, private schools in Kathmandu have reconsidered their language-in-education policy by introducing Chinese as another international language.

The research sites for this study are two multilingual private schools in Kathmandu: Paradise School and Sunflower Secondary (pseudonyms). These schools can be considered 'elite' in the sense that they are not within the financial access of 'ordinary' Nepali people, but are affordable mostly by the rich and elite. The parents of the students at these schools largely have 'white collar' jobs or run businesses with international connections. These two schools follow English as a medium of instruction from kindergarten. English also functions as a language of communication among the students and teachers within the school premises. These schools have recently introduced a policy starting Chinese as another international language from the fourth grade.

Research Questions Addressed

The general goal of this study is to investigate how the economic market has influenced the language-in-education policy of the elite schools in Nepal. More specifically, in this chapter I attempt to answer the following research questions:

1. What motivated the schools to implement a policy to teach Chinese as an additional international language?
2. How do the language learners make sense of the school policy of teaching Chinese as an international language?
3. How do the learners interpret the school policy in terms of the value of Chinese in relation to English?

In order to answer these research questions, I adopted a qualitative research methodology, which I turn to in the next section.

Research Methods

Data Collection

I collected data from the principals, program coordinators, and Chinese language learners from Paradise School and Sunflower Secondary in 2015. I accessed and recruited 14 and 11 students (ages 14 and 15), respectively, from the schools with the permission of the school principals. I used focused group interviews (Litos-seliti, 2003) because they are effective in eliciting opinions, beliefs, and perceptions around a certain theme related to language learning and use. Moreover, this approach was practical because it enabled me to complete data collection without taking much of the students' class time in school. Ghazali (2014) seems right when he argues that focus group interviews provide the researcher an opportunity to collect candid views through a normal conversation with the participants. Putting the students together in groups of four or five provided a non-threatening environment that allowed them to interact, influence, and get influenced by others as they are in real life (Krueger, 2009). The students chose to be interviewed in English. I audio-recorded the interviews and transcribed them verbatim.

Data Analysis Procedures Used

My noticing in the data was mostly influenced by my research questions, but I also followed an inductive approach (Charmaz, 2014) to take account of any emerging concerns in the data. I analyzed the data drawing insights from discursive positioning. Following Davies and Harré (1990), *discursive positioning* refers to the way interlocuters position themselves and others in an ongoing conversation. By paying attention to the words and discourses that the participants use, I focus on how they position themselves vis-à-vis language policy in their schools and make sense of the policy in relation to their identities as members of some imagined future communities.

Findings and Discussion

Influence of the Economic Market on Chinese Language Policy in Schools

As the number of people traveling to and from mainland China is growing, individuals and institutions in Nepal have realized the importance of Mandarin Chinese for their students. When I interviewed the principals and program coordinators of Paradise School and Sunflower Secondary, they pointed out the instrumental value of Chinese for their students' future employability, business, and education. The following excerpt is from an interview (translated from Nepali) at Sunflower Secondary.

BAL: Why did you implement the policy to teach Chinese in your school?
PRINCIPAL: Many schools in Kathmandu have started teaching Chinese. It increases attraction of the school. Parents have appreciated. Ours is a multilingual school. In addition to English, we only had a German class in the past. But we realized that we need to give options to our kids.

88 Bal Krishna Sharma

COORDINATOR: And most of our students are from family business backgrounds. Nepal's relation with China is getting closer. But Nepali people do not speak Chinese. That is the problem of these kids' parents. We don't want these kids to face the same problem.

BAL: Yes. I noticed this when I talked to the students.

PRINCIPAL: And China is a rising country in the world. It is natural that the school and the students want to learn this. This is an additional wealth that can come in use any time in future.

When asked why the school started Chinese as a second language, both the principal and the program coordinator positioned Chinese in terms of its commodity value in the local economic market. Although the response from the principal clearly points out the importance of English and German, it simultaneously recognizes the pragmatic use of Chinese at a regional level. From a symbolic point of view, Chinese is positioned as the language of the 'rising power.' From a pragmatic perspective, it is considered as the 'problem solver' in business transactions between Nepalis and Chinese. Even when some students might be uncertain about the potential usefulness of Chinese, the language is portrayed as a reservoir of economic benefits in the future. In addition, Chinese is considered as enhancing the symbolic value of the school by 'attracting' more students and by receiving 'appreciation' from the parents. These attractions and appreciations are eventually linked to financial gains that Chinese language instruction potentially offers to private schools in Kathmandu.

Interviews with people involved in policy making show that the two schools implementing Chinese are largely affected by the political-economic ideology of world language education (Ricento, 2015). There is a strong tie between language policy and political economy in these two schools because the policy makers perceive language as a tool for socioeconomic mobility for their students. This perspective to studying language policy helps us understand the status, functions, benefits, and limitations of a language in school contexts where Chinese is taught and learned.

Students from both schools also interpreted their schools' language policies echoing similar sentiments, positioning Chinese as an economically powerful language for their individual lives and for the country's future. Although many students at first told me that they were learning the language because the school offered a course on it, they later were more articulate about their motivations, aspirations, and views, as in the following interview with students from Paradise School. All student names used here are pseudonyms.

BAL: Why are you learning Chinese?

NIMA: Don't know.

BAL: Why are you learning then?

(pause)

NIMA: But I have heard that if we learn it, it can use in future. We can use in tourism. We can talk to Chinese people. We can go to China.

PUSPA: And China is our neighbor, sir. It has products. We buy things that say 'made in China.' Their products are sold everywhere, from branded to third class. Um um I want to read the instructions in Chinese. They assemble iPhone. They do that for other powerful countries like America. We are what to say a little bit less (pause) weak.

The students see several possibilities opening up after learning Chinese: an instrumental tool to communicate with Chinese, a tool for employment in tourism, the symbolic value of Chinese in brand names, and their own stereotyping inferiority in treating Nepal as an economically 'weak' country compared to China.

Another student from Sunflower Secondary, Neeti, also noted a supposedly subordinate economic position of Nepal as a 'not developed' country in the world economy:

> Nepal is not developed in many things, sir. It needs helps from other countries. And now China is more helpful than India. We need more cooperation. Earthquake has destroyed Nepal. Nepal is poor. Many Nepali are poor. And China is a neighboring country. And China can build houses for us, sir. We need to learn their language because we have to talk to them.

Although Neeti's understanding of the usefulness of Chinese is not directly linked to her personal benefits, she sees its value for the country. Neeti positions Nepal and Nepalis as economically 'poor' while simultaneously positioning China as an economically rich and supportive country. When the 7.8 magnitude earthquake hit Nepal in April 2015, thousands of people lost their lives, and several thousands more became homeless. Nepali media broadcasted the news, communicating Nepal's appreciation of the government of China and its people in assisting Nepal for the rescue operations, relief materials, and financial support to build infrastructure. Neeti's response largely represents Nepali people's attitudes toward China and Chinese people at that time.

Some students, however, interpreted their school's language policy as instrumental in achieving their specific goals in life. Rikesh and Rupa from Sunflower Secondary note the growing recognition of China as a destination for business and higher education:

RIKESH: My father is a businessman and I want to help him in future.

BAL: What type of business?

RIKESH: Car accessories?

BAL: Sorry?

RIKESH: Car parts, sir. My father goes to China for business. I want to go with him to China and use Chinese. Sir, in China, people does not understand English very much.

BAL: I see. (pause) And what about you?

RUPA: My aim is to be a doctor, and I have heard that China is a good place for studying medicine. Sir, my teacher also told me that Chinese is used in China. I can speak it with my classmates there. And Chinese people do not speak English, right? I mean most people do not speak.

As Rikesh and Rupa highlight the importance of Chinese, they simultaneously treat Chinese people as non-speakers of English. By posing a question, Rupa doubts the default role of English as a lingua franca in international business transactions involving individuals who do not use English as their first language. Whereas Rikesh seems clearer on the immediate use of Chinese in his life, pointing out that he wants to assist his father in business with Chinese, Rupa develops her understanding based on what she has heard from their teachers and other people: Her goal to pursue medical education in China is possible only if she develops her ability in Chinese. As the responses show, the learners interpret their school's language policy, positioning Chinese as a resource for business, investment, tourism, and development. In other interviews, the learners also highlight the importance of Nepal-China friendship, as well as the importance of Chinese culture, history, food, and lifestyle, movies, and music.

As learners of Chinese, students at Paradise School and Sunflower Secondary positioned themselves variously as members of what Norton (2016) calls "imagined communities" (p. 476), in both local and global contexts. Norton notes that in constructing their identities as present and future members of the imagined communities they want to be part of, learners have a certain level of investment that influences their language and literacy practices and their progress in language learning. The students interviewed positioned themselves as future businesspersons, as travelers to China, and as medical students in Chinese higher education institutions. They reinforce the usefulness of Chinese in their lives, and in so doing they approve of their schools' language policies as catering to their personal and family needs and expectations.

Chinese vis-à-vis English in School Language Policy

As the students at these schools highlighted the instrumental and symbolic value of Chinese for their future lives, they also interpreted the role of English in the schools' policies and in their lives. All the students positioned English in the first place, both at present and in the future. Students treated English as the most powerful language in the world, which has already established itself as a 'global' and 'international' language. The following excerpt is a part of a group interview with students at Paradise School.

BAL: What is the value of English for you then?

PRITI: I give first priority to English, sir.

BAL: Why?

Economic Markets, Elite Multilingualism 91

PRITI: It is an international language.
BAL: What do you mean by that?
PRITI: English is taught in schools in all the countries. People in all countries can use English, sir. But Chinese is not learned in all countries. Only Asian countries.
BAL: Okay. (pause) What about you?
KAMAL: I spoke English since childhood. I learned Chinese from class 6 only. I know English better. (pause) If I have to say "ouch," I can say in English. But not in Chinese. My dad and mom do not speak Chinese but they can speak English, sir.
RAMA: All our teachers speak English. Our social studies and math books are in English. They are not in Chinese. Sir, we also need English to speak in school with teachers and in class.

The students in the interview have an understanding that English is taught in all countries in the world. Priti assumes that Chinese is taught and learned only in countries in Asia. With this geo-political defining criterion, English is positioned as having no boundaries and Chinese as having limitations. These discourses suggest an implication of languages for the learners' potential mobility. As they imagine traveling globally, they see the value of English. Although English is gradually occupying an important role in formal and written communication in Nepal, its role in everyday face-to-face communication is still limited. Such an implication is evident in Rama's response in the previous interview, when she suggests that schools are the key spaces of English use. In private schools, such as the ones in this research, the medium of instruction is English by default. An English-only policy is implemented in communication among the students, and between the students and the teachers, converting school spaces into 'English-speaking zones.' For example, Figure 7.1 exemplifies this conversion.

FIGURE 7.1 Sign Posted on a Classroom Wall at Sunflower Secondary

Giving the first priority to English does not devalue the role of Chinese in Nepal. Whereas the learners position Chinese as second in the hierarchy, they highlight the idea that English-Chinese bilingualism opens up more opportunities for them in the future. Knowledge of English and Chinese, thus, indexes social meanings—about its users, connected with identity and social mobility—in many parts of the world where it is learned as an additional language (Park & Wee, 2012).

The learners consistently noted the need for Nepali people to accommodate Chinese people's communicative requirements because of the supposed lack of English ability in most Chinese people. This view can be seen in the following interview with students at Paradise School.

BAL: Which is more important for you, English or Chinese?

TANKA: English is more important, sir, because when we have to travel (pause) everywhere people speak English. We can go to America and UK. But Chinese is used in China, Japan, Singapore, Tibet, and um maybe in France.

BAL: Also in Malaysia.

TANKA: Okay. (pause) But if we know English and Chinese, this is best. We can do business with Chinese because they do not speak English. They do not speak Nepali.

RITA: If we know English we can become air hostess. All countries have their own languages. But English is common for all. Umm but if we learn Chinese this is also very important. (pause) If the passengers are Chinese, then we want to provide instructions to them in Chinese. Even if we know uneducated type of English—I mean Chinese, we can provide instructions in Chinese.

As the learners articulate their imaginations, assumptions, and understandings of the role of Chinese and English in their lives, in addition to their ability in Nepali and other local indigenous languages, they position themselves as elite multilinguals in the local context. The term *elite multilingualism* (as opposed to *folk* or *indigenous multilingualism*) is used here to refer to the discourses and imaginations that language users and policy makers produce in order to talk about the material value of language skills and competences in the economic market. *Elite multilingualism* is an extension of the term *elite bilingualism* that researchers in other contexts (e.g., Skutnabb-Kangas, 1981) have used to take account of bilingual education in two powerful languages. In the present context, the learners in the two schools become multilingual not because multilingualism is imposed on them, but due to their own and their parents' choice through schooling. This form of multilingualism "represents a definite advantage" (De Mejía, 2002, p. 41) to them. The findings of this study show that English and multilingualism can coexist, taking account of the global forces that have created the current position of English today (Earls, 2016).

This form of multilingualism illustrates the individuals' and schools' status in the society, providing necessary cultural and symbolic capital to the local and

Economic Markets, Elite Multilingualism **93**

global job market and higher studies in the future. As the discourses reflect the value of multilingualism that the learners have deliberately worked for, at the same time they show an important space for dominant languages in school language policy.

Implications for Policy, Practice, and Future Research

The research reported in this chapter has expanded our understanding of how school policies that promote languages other than English are also influenced by recent changes in political-economic conditions around the world. Following Kubota (2014) and others (see, e.g., Kobayashi, 2015), I argue that the hegemonic role of English as unquestionably the only global language of communication can be negotiated by promoting multilingualism, which includes other second languages in addition to English. This observation resonates quite well with Graddol's (2006) claim: "English is no longer the 'only show in town'. Other languages now challenge the dominance of English in some regions" (p. 62). This changing scenario shows a growing awareness among policy makers and language learners that multilingual communicative repertoires are necessary beyond English, in order for institutions and individuals to be successful in the globalizing world (Earls, 2016). This was the case when language learners in Nepal questioned the usefulness of English in international business and tourism with Chinese people.

However, in the formal education sector, the policy that promotes the teaching and learning of Chinese, without the teaching of English, is inadequate as the learners highlight that there is little possibility to develop a globally mobile human capital without a competence in English. Chinese does not replace English, nor is it considered more important, but it is an addition and enrichment to the already existing bilingual and multilingual repertoires of the learners. Introducing a language policy embracing both Chinese and English as powerful international languages by schools in Nepal gives rise to a new linguistic distinction of bilingual commodification (Heller, 2003). In this context, English is positioned as a tool for global mobility and Chinese as a resource for an immediate economic gain at the local level.

It is also my contention that the multilingualism with Chinese, English, and the local official language (in this case Nepali) largely conforms to the ideals of the late capitalist market needs. The policy makers (principals and program coordinators) and the individuals with whom these policies are enacted (learners) see many possibilities opened up by Chinese-English bilingualism. This change also points out another emerging issue with regard to language education and language policy: English-plus multilingualism is predominantly limited to the influential world languages such as Chinese, English, French, Spanish, or German, rendering the local indigenous languages less valuable in terms of their symbolic and economic value for the learners. While not losing a critical stance toward such new forms of stratification, schools as language policy makers should provide

References

Charmaz, K. (2014). *Constructing grounded theory* (2nd ed.). London, UK: Sage.

Davies, B., & Harré, R. (1990). Positioning: The discursive production of selves. *Journal for the Theory of Social Behaviour, 20*(1), 43–63.

De Mejía, A. M. (2002). *Power, prestige, and bilingualism: International perspectives on elite bilingual education.* Clevedon, UK: Multilingual Matters.

Ding, S., & Saunders, R. A. (2006). Talking up China: An analysis of China's rising cultural power and global promotion of the Chinese language. *East Asia, 23*(2), 3–33.

Earls, C. (2016). When English just is not enough: 'Multilingualism with English' in contemporary European higher education. *International Journal of Applied Linguistics, 26*(3), 329–347.

Ghazali, F. A. (2014). A critical overview of designing and conducting focus group interviews in applied linguistics research. *American Journal of Educational Research, 2*(1), 6–12.

Giri, R. A. (2010). Cultural anarchism: The consequences of privileging languages in Nepal. *Journal of Multilingual and Multicultural Development, 31*(1), 87–100.

Graddol, D. (2006). *English next* (Vol. 62). London, UK: British Council.

Heller, M. (2003). Globalization, the new economy, and the commodification of language and identity. *Journal of Sociolinguistics, 7*(4), 473–492.

Johnson, D. C., & Johnson, E. J. (2015). Power and agency in language policy appropriation. *Language Policy, 14*(3), 221–243.

Kobayashi, Y. (2015). Ideological discourses about learning Chinese in pro-English Japan. *International Journal of Applied Linguistics, 25*(3), 329–342.

Krueger, R. (2009). *Focus groups: A practical guide for applied research.* London, UK: Sage Publications.

Kubota, R. (2014). The multi/plural turn, postcolonial theory, and neoliberal multiculturalism: Complicities and implications for applied linguistics. *Applied Linguistics, 37*(4), 1–22.

Litosseliti, L. (2003). *Using focus groups in research.* London, UK: Continuum Publications.

Menken, K., & García, O. (Eds.). (2010). *Negotiating language policies in schools: Educators as policymakers.* New York, NY: Routledge.

Norton, B. (2016). Identity and language learning: Back to the future. *TESOL Quarterly, 50*(2), 475–479.

Park, J. S.-Y., & Wee, L. (2012). *Markets of English: Linguistic capital and language policy in a globalizing world.* New York, NY: Routledge.

Phyak, P. (2016). Local-global tension in ideological construction of English language policy in Nepal. In R. Kirkpatrick (Ed.), *English language education policy in Asia* (pp. 199–217). Cham, Switzerland: Springer International Publishing. DOI 10.1007/978-3-319-22464-0.

Ricento, T. (Ed.). (2015). *Language policy and political economy: English in a global context.* Oxford, UK: Oxford University Press.

Ricento, T. K., & Hornberger, N. H. (1996). Unpeeling the onion: Language planning and policy and the ELT professional. *TESOL Quarterly, 30*(3), 401–427.

Skutnabb-Kangas, T. (1981). *Bilingualism or not: The education of minorities.* Clevedon, UK: Multilingual Matters.

8

LINGUISTIC DIVERSITY AND THE POLITICS OF INTERNATIONAL INCLUSION

Challenges in Integrating International Teaching Assistants at a University in the United States

Nicholas Close Subtirelu

Issues That Motivated the Research

Over the past few decades, universities around the world have increasingly begun to position themselves as international or global institutions. In the United States, one of the ways this trend is evident is the recruitment of students and faculty from other countries. The result has been campuses with greater diversity in terms of national origin, cultural background, and language. Whereas universities are quick to celebrate this fact in their marketing materials, the increased social difference brought about by internationalization is not without its challenges, many of which are yet to be adequately addressed (Dippold, 2015; Jenkins, 2014).

In this chapter, I explore one of these challenges: the integration of international teaching assistants (ITAs). In the United States, ITAs are graduate students who originate from outside the US; most are considered nonnative English speakers. They are assigned instructional duties in exchange for tuition and a small stipend from the university.

Decades of research about ITAs has documented consistent challenges, especially dissatisfaction from students who often argue that their ITAs lack the competence in English necessary to serve as instructors (e.g., Bailey, 1983; Fitch & Morgan, 2003; Plakans, 1997). Consequently, within applied linguistics, extensive work has been undertaken to develop interventions to help ITAs better communicate with their students. These efforts have often been fruitful; for example, many U.S. universities, including the one that is the subject of my case study, began offering ITA preparation courses, often influenced by research in this area. Nonetheless, I argue that, taken as a whole (and with some notable exceptions, e.g., Kang & Rubin, 2009), past research assumes ITAs' Englishes to be the

96 Nicholas Close Subtirelu

primary cause of communication problems between ITAs and students. Consequently, this approach tends to support, whether implicitly or explicitly, policies that seek to increase ITAs' conformity to the norms and expectations of 'standard' U.S. English speakers.

Recognizing that this approach to ITA research and policy does not always represent the sociopolitical ideals of university stakeholders or of researchers, I argue for a critical sociolinguistic approach to ITA-student communication (see Subtirelu, 2017, online access for a more comprehensive discussion). Such an approach posits different means and ends for improved ITA-student communication. In particular, it rejects deficit views of nonnative Englishes, which Jenkins (2014, p. 168) argues are common in ITA research.

This approach, thus, represents ITAs and their students as being engaged in communication across linguistic difference, which potentially requires orientations and competencies unfamiliar to many stakeholders. For example, Canagarajah (2013) argues that communicative success in linguistically diverse spaces is driven not by conformity to static norms, but rather by the efforts of interlocutors who strategically and flexibly engage with each other to arrive at mutual understanding. Hence, the critical sociolinguistic approach to ITA research that I advocate takes strategic efforts made by all interlocutors to communicate across linguistic difference, rather than ITAs' linguistic conformity, as its normative goal.

In doing so, the approach recognizes that power and ideology are often key forces in determining whether interlocutors will share or reject the communicative burden (Lindemann, 2002; Shuck, 2006). For example, in Subtirelu (2017, online access), I analyze a student's narrative which describes how she and her lab partners were unwilling to initiate repair when their ITA apparently did not understand their question. The student reports that she simply feigned satisfaction with the interaction and turned to a different TA to get the information she sought. The student explains that she had grown tired of trying to make herself understood to the ITA. The frustration the student feels is certainly understandable, but I argue that her status as native English speaker grants her the privilege to avoid the sometimes difficult work of communicating across linguistic difference. Furthermore, I take her narrative to reproduce a larger ideology that constructs nonnative English speakers as communicatively incompetent in order to rationalize their exclusion. Thus, my approach stresses the need for research and policy on ITAs to be sensitive to the social hierarchy inherent in the native-nonnative dichotomy and to work to counteract the marginalization of ITAs and other nonnative English speakers.

Context of the Research

This research was carried out at one university in the United States, which I call Shrinking World University (SWU, a pseudonym, as are all names or initials used for people and institutions in this work). SWU is a large public university located in a metropolitan area. Its numerous undergraduate and graduate programs serve a student body that is more racially and linguistically diverse than that of many other universities that have been the site of ITA research (e.g., Iowa State University, Plakans, 1997).

Like many institutions of higher education in the United States and elsewhere (Scott, 2011), SWU is engaged in internationalization, meaning that, among other institutional priorities, it seeks to be globally engaged by, for example, bringing faculty and students from around the world to its campus in order to create a diverse learning space.

My research considers policy related to ITAs across different levels of SWU. Although at other universities discussed in the literature (e.g., University of Southern California, Kaplan, 1989), a central office was often charged with implementing policy related to ITAs, at the time of my research, SWU did not have such an administrative unit, and ITA policy was largely developed and implemented at the department level, often in informal (unwritten) ways. Nonetheless, university-wide requirements stipulated that prospective graduate students demonstrate a threshold level of English proficiency through a standardized test. Thus, my research focused on university-wide policy in addition to policy activity in five academic departments that commonly employ ITAs to teach lower level or laboratory courses: Biology, Computer Science, English, Mathematics, and Physics.

Research Questions Addressed

Informed by the critical sociolinguistic approach I outlined earlier, I focus on SWU's integration of ITAs and specifically what actions the university takes or does not take to ensure that ITAs and students are able to successfully communicate across linguistic difference in the classroom. The analysis and findings I present here represent one part of the larger project (Subtirelu, 2016, 2017, online access). In this chapter, I focus on the following questions:

1. What, if any, institutional support or policies encourage and prepare students to engage successfully in communication across linguistic difference with ITAs?
2. What institutional support or policies assess ITAs' readiness for teaching and prepare them to take on instructional duties? What other effects, intentional or otherwise, do these have on ITAs and their integration into the university?

Research Methods

Data Collection

My qualitative case study of SWU involved an eclectic set of data collection procedures and analytical tools, which is common in ethnographic work on language policy (Johnson, 2013). I gathered print and electronic documents related to

ITA policy or the university's internationalization more generally. I interviewed administrators, ITAs, and their students. I attended events geared toward ITAs at SWU. I also observed classes taught by ITAs and conducted playback sessions with them and with their students to delve deeper into stakeholders' perceptions of classroom communication.

Data Analysis Procedures Used

Although indirectly informed by all the data I collected, the analysis I present in this chapter was developed primarily from the documents I collected and the interviews I conducted with 18 administrators from across SWU and 29 ITAs from the five focal departments. Other findings are or will be reported elsewhere (Subtirelu, 2016, 2017, online access).

One strength of qualitative research is that it can allow unanticipated ideas or perspectives to emerge throughout the research process (Holliday, 2010), particularly when data analysis and collection are "inductive and iterative" (Lichtman, 2012, p. 244), as they were in my project. Hence, my research was not conducted using pre-set, replicable procedures, nor was there a clear transition from the collection to the analysis of data. My analysis was ongoing with the first piece of data I found, and my ongoing interpretations shaped the subsequent information that I sought and collected.

Nonetheless, I approached my analysis systematically. I read and reread transcripts of interviews with stakeholders and coded them to represent emerging themes in my analysis. I compared different stakeholders' accounts of policies to each other and to written documents, searching for discrepancies and attempting to account for these when possible. What I present in the following is a thematic summary of the major challenges that I found SWU faced in integrating ITAs and ensuring they and their students successfully communicated across linguistic difference.

Findings and Discussion

Potential Gaps in Students' "Global Competency"

Like many universities, SWU released a strategic plan intended to identify institutional priorities and serve as one piece of its branding as a globally competitive research university (Gaffikin & Perry, 2009). One of the major goals SWU set for itself in this plan was gaining recognition for "globalizing" through the recruitment of scholars who were "worldwide" academics and the creation of opportunities for students to prepare for a career world characterized by heightened globalization. The plan specified an intention to develop "global competency" among SWU stakeholders, which included both multilingualism and "cultural competencies" (bibliographic information withheld to maintain confidentiality).

SWU's discourse in this area is reminiscent of scholarly work arguing that particular competencies and orientations ensure the success of communication across linguistic difference (e.g., Canagarajah, 2013; Subtirelu & Lindemann, 2016).

Although communication with their ITAs might reasonably be thought of as an opportunity to develop "global competency," I found no evidence of intentional efforts to help students communicate across linguistic difference with their ITAs. Of course, this was not surprising, since only recently have small-scale, pilot interventions for students been reported in the research literature (Kang, Rubin, & Lindemann, 2015; Staples, Kang, & Wittner, 2014).

When I gauged SWU students' interest in interventions that might improve their ability to communicate with ITAs (see Subtirelu & Lindemann, 2016 for suggestions of what these might include), I found mixed responses. When asked whether they would attend a "voluntary workshop," many students said they would not, expressing a preference for spending their time studying course material, which they viewed as the real work of their education, rather than preparing themselves to communicate with ITAs. For example, one student, Faiza, argued that "instead of trying to understand" her ITA, she would rather "use that time . . . to try to understand the material."

Other students welcomed the suggestion, calling it a "cool" or a "great" idea. For example, Dedra expressed interest in the possibility and reasoned that she would like to have "everything in order" before interacting with an ITA, so the experience could "be better for the both of us."

Thus, SWU students appeared to lack institutional support in developing abilities related to successful communication across linguistic difference. Furthermore, such skills were not always valued by students, despite the university's discourse around internationalization and cross-cultural cooperation.

Assessing ITA Readiness: Motivations, Discrepancies, and Concerns

As is common at U.S. universities, prospective ITAs' English proficiency was assessed through standardized tests, like TOEFL®, as a routine part of admission to their graduate programs. Furthermore, it was assessed again using a local test designed to make recommendations of whether incoming international graduate students should take English as a second language (ESL) courses.

Other universities have been reported to require additional testing of prospective ITAs, usually including a teaching simulation, to assess the ability of testees to use English for instructional purposes (e.g., University of California, Los Angeles; University of Florida; and University of North Carolina at Charlotte; Xi, 2007). A test of this type existed at SWU. In it, testees performed two tasks for a panel of raters: a short impromptu presentation, in which they were asked to explain some common classroom materials (e.g., a syllabus), and a longer prepared presentation in which they delivered a lesson. The English Department implemented the current version of this test in the late 2000s to satisfy ESL accreditation requirements which stipulated that faculty "demonstrate excellent proficiency in English."

At the time of my research, this teaching simulation test was only used to assess English Department ITAs. Administrators in other departments pointed to ITAs' satisfactory scores on the local language proficiency test or their completion of required ESL coursework as indications of their linguistic readiness.

Intriguingly, a similar teaching assessment was in place in the Biology Department, where supervisors of one laboratory required that all prospective teaching assistants deliver a lesson and be observed and approved by one of the supervisors. Although the assessment was not specifically geared toward language, the task, which is strikingly similar to the English Department's teaching simulation, clearly required a great deal of linguistic proficiency.

The comparison of the two departments' assessments raises issues about the conceptual separation between teaching competence and language proficiency, an issue that has long been noted in research on ITAs (Bailey, 1985; Hoekje & Williams, 1992). Those involved in language testing at SWU acknowledged this difficult conceptual issue. Describing the purpose of the English Department's test in an interview with me, the local testing coordinator stated that it was not intended "to determine teaching ability, although it's kind of inextricable in a way." At SWU, the inextricable nature of teaching and language was made particularly apparent by different departments' assessment policies, which created potential discrepancies in who was required to demonstrate competence in teaching practice: all TAs (Biology Department) or merely those deemed to be nonnative English speakers (English Department).

Supporting ITAs: Issues of Access and Equity

In addition to assessing ITAs' readiness for teaching, SWU also made possible various forms of support for ITAs before and while they served as instructors. Most of the departments required all TAs to take a course that was designed to prepare them for teaching in the department, but an additional course aimed specifically at ITAs was also offered by the SWU ESL program. The course was similar in nature to those offered at other U.S. universities. It used a popular textbook, *Communicate* (Smith, Meyers, & Burkhalter, 2007), and focused on topics like responding to student questions and the culture of U.S. higher education. Trainees were expected to practice teaching in class and to observe other instructors. The ITAs I interviewed who had taken the course all spoke very positively of the preparation it gave them for teaching. For example, one ITA, YV, said the course was "good for me, mostly in terms of pedagogical, not really in y'know in English." SG reported that she "learned a lot" from the course, notably strategies for dealing with communication difficulties that arise in the classroom.

Despite these positive impressions, the ITA course's enrollment had been low starting from 2000, the first year of available records. Those involved in the ESL program told me that they struggled to enroll enough students to offer the course regularly despite their numerous efforts to advertise and attract students. Of the 29 ITAs I interviewed, only 4 reported that they had taken the course: 2 enrolled voluntarily, and 2 were required to take it by the Mathematics Department, the only department to routinely require the course of some of its ITAs. The local language proficiency test administered to all incoming international graduate students made no recommendations for students to take the ITA preparation course. The score sheet distributed to testees explicitly states "assessment of a student's readiness for a GTA position is not done" through this test.

Lack of awareness of the course may explain some of the low enrollment. Six ITAs I interviewed reported never having heard of the course. However, the more pressing issue appeared to be the lack of incentives (or requirements) to enroll. For example, per recommendation from the local language proficiency test, WM was required to take an ESL speaking course. His ESL instructor recommended that he also take the ITA preparation course. He ultimately chose not to, even though he spoke positively of his ESL course. He reported that he needed to spend his time working on research. Even though many ITAs seemed to feel they could benefit from the additional support, they prioritized other activities that offered greater incentives.

There were also many forms of support at SWU intended to place TAs in positions where they could participate peripherally in instruction. Although it was often not part of formal (written) policy, department administrators often reported that ITAs in particular were assigned these positions or were encouraged to seek out opportunities for peripheral participation in order to give them greater socialization into the discursive practices of U.S. higher education. For example, an administrator in the Biology Department who supervised a teaching laboratory mentioned that ITAs were often paired "with another instructor . . . the first couple of times they try to teach . . . to try to assist them." I observed a similar practice being used in another Biology laboratory where ITAs were more likely than their domestic counterparts to be assigned a more experienced TA as a co-instructor in their first semester.

In another example of practices that assigned different responsibilities to ITAs than to their domestic peers, administrators in the English Department reported that prospective ITAs were often assigned tutoring for ESL classes in their first semester, unlike their domestic counterparts who were usually assigned to teach these same courses. One administrator, JS, reported that the English Department's intention was to ensure that ITAs were "acclimated" to U.S. higher education and that tutoring provided a "good transition," allowing them to learn about the institution before teaching. SW, an ITA in English who was assigned to tutor during his first semester in his PhD program, offered a somewhat different perspective. Although he evaluated his experience positively, he questioned the extent to which tutoring served as effective preparation for teaching at SWU, commenting that, as a tutor, he had neither direct involvement in courses nor any obvious way to gain a complete understanding of them. He suggested that more intentional effort could be made to make tutoring useful socialization for future ITAs. Moreover, before coming to SWU, he had earned a master's degree from a U.S. university and had some experience both tutoring and teaching. He thus reported that he had expected to be assigned to teach in his first semester and was "a bit surprised" when he was instead assigned to tutor. That tutoring is a duty often assigned to new master's students appeared to make SW feel that the department lacked confidence in him, especially relative to his domestic peers.

All five focal departments offered some form of support to ITAs, most of which was offered to all TAs regardless of language status, although they also informally geared additional support toward ITAs. In general, although ITAs appeared to want to increase their comfort and familiarity in communicating with SWU students, they often reported difficulty accessing support when it was available because they were incentivized to invest their time and efforts elsewhere. Furthermore, when departments made attempts to shield them from teaching responsibilities, some ITAs, eager to prove themselves as capable instructors and scholars, were disheartened by what they viewed as the department's apparent lack of confidence in them.

Implications for Policy, Practice, and Future Research

The most urgent need in ITA policy and research at SWU and elsewhere is understanding and addressing students' contributions to ITA-student communication. Although this suggestion has been made for decades (e.g., by Bailey, 1983), it is only recently that any serious efforts have been made to address the imbalance (e.g., Kang et al., 2015; Staples et al., 2014). Subtirelu and Lindemann (2016) review existing literature aimed at helping native speakers better understand nonnative speech and also suggest further directions to help make such proposals more actionable in the future. Overall, our work suggests that students learning to better communicate with ITAs would benefit from an approach that addresses negative attitudes toward nonnative speech, increases familiarity with the sound systems of Englishes other than their own varieties, and explores strategies for dealing with communication difficulty when it arises.

In addition to more theoretical research to increase our ability to help students in these areas, practical and policy-related work is needed to carve out institutional space for these skills and attitudes to be fostered. Whereas some SWU students reported being willing to participate in interventions to help them better communicate with ITAs of their own volition, it is likely that interventions that are purely voluntary would reach very few students and would probably never reach the students that would benefit from them the most. In particular, in my focus groups, those students who reported the most serious problems with ITAs also usually expressed unwillingness to invest in trying to improve their own competencies (Subtirelu, 2017, online access).

There are a few institutional spaces at SWU and other universities where such interventions could be introduced. Students in my focus groups suggested that these issues and skills could be covered as part of an existing course that was required for most first-year students and which was designed to help new students succeed at the university. Similar courses for first-year students are common at other U.S. institutions as well. Another possible space might be first-year composition courses which are required for many students at U.S. universities. Matsuda and Silva (1999) offer fruitful suggestions on incorporating cross-cultural communicative competencies into the composition curriculum.

Assessment and support for ITAs is also an important goal. However, I believe there is a need to reconsider existing practices both in research and policy. For example, teaching simulations are commonly required of ITAs as a way of assessing their control of the linguistic resources specific to teaching. As a comparison of SWU's Biology and English Departments' assessments suggests, such policies are on shaky ground, conceptually, ethically, and perhaps even legally (Brown, Fishman, & Jones, 1990; King, 1998). In particular, at SWU, very similar tasks are used to assess readiness either for all TAs (in the Biology Department) or only for some nonnative English speakers (in the English Department). There is a continued need to find practical solutions so that TAs' readiness can be assessed in a way that is both fair and practical.

Finally, it is important to continue to offer support for ITAs who, at least at SWU, appear to want additional opportunities to practice working with students or observing others doing so. However, the current remedial framing of much of this support means that either it is voluntary and consequently difficult to access, or it is required and potentially sends implicit messages that ITAs do not have the full confidence of the institution. I argue that the most effective way around this issue is to reframe ITA preparation as preparation for communication in linguistically and culturally diverse classrooms, preparation that would be available to or required of all TAs, and to allow it to count toward higher education teaching certification programs (Winter, Turner, Gedye, Nash, & Grant, 2015). Future work will be necessary to explore whether and how courses that build on the ideas of the critical sociolinguistic approach I describe here might be developed and offered.

References

Bailey, K. M. (1983). Foreign teaching assistants at U.S. universities: Problems in interaction and communication. *TESOL Quarterly, 17*(2), 308–310.

Bailey, K. M. (1985). If I had known then what I know now: Performance testing of foreign teaching assistants. In P. Hauptman, R. Leblanc, & M. Wesche (Eds.), *Second language performance testing* (pp. 153–180). Ottawa, Canada: University of Ottawa Press.

Brown, K., Fishman, P., & Jones, N. (1990). Legal and policy issues in the language proficiency assessment of international teaching assistants *IHELG Monographs*. Houston, TX: Institute for Higher Education Law and Governance.

Canagarajah, S. (2013). *Translingual practice: Global Englishes and cosmopolitan relations*. London, UK: Routledge.

Dippold, D. (2015). *Classroom interaction: The internationalised Anglophone university*. London, UK: Palgrave Macmillan.

Fitch, F., & Morgan, S. E. (2003). "Not a lick of English": Constructing the ITA identity through student narratives. *Communication Education, 52*(3/4), 297–310.

Gaffikin, F., & Perry, D. C. (2009). Discourses and strategic visions: The U.S. research university as an institutional manifestation of neoliberalism in a global era. *American Educational Research Journal, 46*(1), 115–144.

Hoekje, B., & Williams, J. (1992). Communicative competence and the dilemma of international teaching assistant education. *TESOL Quarterly, 26*(2), 243–269.

Holliday, A. (2010). Analysing qualitative data. In B. Paltridge & A. Phakiti (Eds.), *Continuum companion to research methods in applied linguistics* (pp. 98–110). London, UK: Continuum.

Jenkins, J. (2014). *English as a lingua franca in the international university: The politics of academic English language policy*. London, UK: Routledge.

Johnson, D. C. (2013). *Language policy*. New York, NY: Palgrave Macmillan.

Kang, O., & Rubin, D. L. (2009). Reverse linguistic stereotyping: Measuring the effect of listener expectations on speech evaluation. *Journal of Language and Social Psychology, 28*(4), 441–456.

Kang, O., Rubin, D., & Lindemann, S. (2015). Mitigating U.S. undergraduates' attitudes toward international teaching assistants. *TESOL Quarterly, 49*(4), 681–706.

Kaplan, R. B. (1989). The life and times of ITA programs. *English for Specific Purposes, 8*(2), 109–124.

King, K. (1998). Mandating English proficiency for college instructors: States' responses to the TA problem. *Vanderbilt Journal of Transnational Law, 31*(1), 203–256.

Lichtman, M. (2012). *Qualitative research in education: A user's guide*. Los Angeles, CA: SAGE.

Lindemann, S. (2002). Listening with an attitude: A model of native-speaker comprehension of non-native speakers in the United States. *Language in Society, 31*(3), 419–441.

Matsuda, P. K., & Silva, T. (1999). Cross-cultural composition: Mediated integration of US and international students. *Composition Studies, 27*(1), 15–30.

Plakans, B. S. (1997). Undergraduates' experiences with and attitudes toward international teaching assistants. *TESOL Quarterly, 31*(1), 95–119.

Scott, P. (2011). The university as a global institution. In R. King, S. Marginson, & R. Naidoo (Eds.), *Handbook on globalization and higher education* (pp. 59–75). Cheltenham, UK: Edward Elgar Publishing.

Shuck, G. (2006). Racializing the non-native English speaker. *Journal of Language, Identity & Education, 5*(4), 259–276.

Smith, J. A., Meyers, C. M., & Burkhalter, A. J. (2007). *Communicate: Strategies for international teaching assistants*. Long Grove, IL: Waveland Press, Inc.

Staples, S., Kang, O., & Wittner, E. (2014). Considering interlocutors in university discourse communities: Impacting U.S. undergraduates' perceptions of ITAs through a structured contact program. *English for Specific Purposes, 35*, 54–65.

Subtirelu, N. C. (2016). *Linguistic diversity and the politics of international inclusion in higher education: A critical sociolinguistic study of international teaching assistants* (Unpublished doctoral dissertation). Georgia State University, Atlanta, GA.

Subtirelu, N. C. (2017). Students' orientations to communication across linguistic difference with international teaching assistants at an internationalizing university in the United States. *Multilingua, 36*(3), 247–280.

Subtirelu, N. C., & Lindemann, S. (2016). Teaching first language speakers to communicate across linguistic difference: Addressing attitudes, comprehension, and strategies. *Applied Linguistics, 37*(6), 765–783.

Winter, J., Turner, R., Gedye, S., Nash, P., & Grant, V. (2015). Graduate teaching assistants: Responding to the challenges of internationalisation. *International Journal for Academic Development, 20*(1), 33–45.

Xi, X. (2007). Validating TOEFL[R] iBT speaking and setting score requirements for ITA screening. *Language Assessment Quarterly, 4*(4), 318–351.

9

OFFICIAL AND REALIZED HIRING POLICY OF ASSISTANT LANGUAGE TEACHERS IN JAPAN

Takahiro Yokoyama

The Council of Local Authorities for International Relations (CLAIR), as a central administrative organization of the Japan Exchange and Teaching Program (JET Program), officially requires an Assistant Language Teacher (ALT) to "be qualified as a language teacher *or* be strongly motivated to take part in the teaching of foreign languages" (CLAIR, 2015, para. 2, emphasis added). In order to understand the local implementation of this broad official hiring policy, this study examined the tertiary qualifications of 101 ALTs—in particular, qualifications related to teaching or English language teaching. Reflecting upon the gap between the official policy in the JET Program and its implementation, the study addresses the extent to which ALTs are 'qualified' to do their jobs in Japanese classrooms.

Issues That Motivated the Research

Team-teaching in English language teaching (ELT) by native-English-speaking teachers (NESTs) and non-NESTs (NNESTs) has gained an increasing level of popularity at a national policy level in many countries (Baniabdelrahman, 2011; Carless, 2006; Liu, 2008; Nurul Islam, 2011). However, team-teaching is "not unproblematic" (Carless, 2006, p. 342). Many NESTs have reportedly experienced communication and classroom management issues, which frustrate both local students and NESTs themselves (Barratt & Kontra, 2000; Christensen, 2014; Han, 2005; Liu, 2008). Communicative language classes that involve NESTs are not always fully integrated within a local curriculum that emphasizes entrance exam preparation (Jeon, 2016). Both local teachers and students often see communicative classes as being "more for fun than for any real academic purpose" (Geluso, 2013, p. 103) and NESTs as entertainers, not as "real teacher[s]" (Falout, 2013, p. 109).

Some people attribute these issues to the lack of formal TESOL teacher training among "unqualified" NESTs (Carless, 2006, p. 329; Christensen, 2014, p. 10; Liu, 2008, p. 104). However, educational backgrounds of NESTs overseas can be extremely diverse, and the types of expertise that distinguish 'qualified' and 'unqualified' teachers can often be ambiguous. Variations can be expected within both TESOL teacher training programs (Christopher, 2005) and the requirement of such training at the national policy level in individual countries (Han, 2005; Jeon, 2016; Liu, 2008). Furthermore, there is often a gap between a national language education policy and the implementation of the policy by local stakeholders (Plüddemann, 2015; Ricento & Hornberger, 1996). Therefore, educational requirements for NEST candidates at the national policy level may not always reflect what they bring to individual classrooms.

In wider contexts of TESOL, the unquestioned idealization of NESTs has been criticized as *native speakerism* (Holliday, 2008). The majority research in this discourse, however, has focused on NNESTs, to discuss "their struggle against unfavorable comparisons with their native speaker counterparts" (Houghton & Rivers, 2013, p. 7). Whereas recent studies have examined political prejudice against NESTs (Geluso, 2013; Kabel, 2009), the educational backgrounds and existing expertise of NESTs have not been adequately studied.

Context of the Research

The JET Program is a national program that the Japanese government has developed to recruit youth from overseas to "promote grass-roots internationalization at the local level" (CLAIR, 2015, para. 2). The majority of the participants in the program are recruited as Assistant Language Teachers to "create a foreign language classroom in which the students, the Japanese teacher of the foreign language (JTE), and the native speaker (ALT) engage in communicative activities" (CLAIR, 2013, p. 42). Over 90% of these ALTs are hired from Kachru's (1992) inner-circle countries, such as the US, the UK, Canada, Australia, and New Zealand (CLAIR, 2015). With no local certification in teaching, these ALTs are contracted to team-teach with locally certified JTEs at one or several schools (CLAIR, 2013).

Whereas the CLAIR administers the JET Program centrally under overall control of the Ministry of Internal Affairs and Communications, the program is also co-administered by two other ministries: the Ministry of Education, Culture, Sports, Science and Technology (MEXT) and the Ministry of Foreign Affairs (MOFA). The MEXT is responsible for providing guidance to local education offices and schools regarding team-teaching practice, whereas the MOFA is charged with recruiting participants through individual embassies and consulate offices overseas (CLAIR, 2015).

The CLAIR outlines academic requirements for ALT candidates in a somewhat inclusive manner. In addition to the completion of a bachelor's degree

108 Takahiro Yokoyama

required for all JET participants, ALT candidates have to be "qualified as a language teacher *or* be strongly motivated to take part in the teaching of foreign languages" (CLAIR, 2015, para. 2, emphasis added). Whereas this particular hiring criterion seems to have some emphasis on second language teaching (SLT), what is considered as 'language teacher qualification' remains unspecified. Further, it appears that 'strong motivation' in SLT may substitute for 'language teacher qualification,' which may diversify the educational backgrounds among ALTs.

The CLAIR also gives an "additional evaluation" specifically to ALT applicants who have "language teaching experience or qualification," "teaching experience or qualification," or "a high level of Japanese ability" (CLAIR, 2015, an additional statement under criterion 17). To date, research on ALTs appears to have focused on their roles during team-teaching (Aline & Hosoda, 2006; Igawa, 2009) or complications involving foreigners working in Japanese schools (Otani, 2007). Little is known, therefore, of how these official hiring criteria, including the stated prioritized expertise (i.e., teaching, ELT, and Japanese), are implemented by individual embassies and consulate offices overseas.

Research Questions Addressed

The study aimed to answer the following research questions:

1. How many ALTs possess a tertiary qualification that relates to teaching or ELT?
2. How proficient are they in Japanese?

Research Methods

Data Collection

Data were drawn from an online survey, which was conducted for another study of the backgrounds and job experiences of various types of ALTs in Japan ($N = 232$). In order to understand ALT backgrounds in the present JET Program, only the data from 101 ALTs who were currently participating in the JET Program were used for the study. Data were collected between February and June 2014 by convenience sampling through organizations such as the Association for Japan Exchange and Teaching.

The study adopted two measurements for a qualification in teaching. First, following the categorization of study majors in the International Standard Classification of Education (UNESCO Institute for Statistics, 2012), the number of participants who completed a tertiary qualification or major in education (i.e., teacher training, curriculum development, assessment/testing) was reported. Second, the number of participants who possessed a qualification that had accredited them for teaching in state or public schools in their home country was also reported.

For Japanese proficiency, both the length of study and self-reported proficiency level were reported. The self-rated proficiency is reportedly as reliable as standardized tests (e.g., Marian, Blumenfeld, & Kaushanskaya, 2007); therefore, it was used as a subjective indication of Japanese proficiency.

Data Analysis Procedures Used

Frequencies are reported for both ALT educational backgrounds and their Japanese learning experience. For a dichotomous comparison of their qualifications in teaching or ELT, the participants were divided into two groups: those who possessed at least one qualification in each respective category (YES), and those who did not possess any qualification in the category (NO). Japanese language backgrounds were examined using four categories in length of study (less than 1 year, 1–3 years, 4–6 years, and 7 years or more) and another four categories in self-rated proficiency (beginner, intermediate, advanced, near-native speaker).

Given the lack of consensus about what constitutes TESOL teacher training, the study adopted a two-stage definition process of qualifications in ELT. First, data were collected broadly on all tertiary qualifications that helped ALTs acquire any skills or knowledge in TESOL, based on their perceptions (TESOL-related studies). Second, individual award names obtained from these TESOL-related studies were visually inspected in order to identify qualifications that appear to have been developed specifically for TESOL teacher training purposes (TESOL certifications). These TESOL certifications were adopted as a proxy measure for 'language teacher qualification' in this study. Most typically, these qualifications had an award name that includes acronyms such as TESOL, TEFL, TESL, or ELT (e.g., MA TESOL, CELTA). A qualification in teacher education or linguistics was not included in this group unless the award name indicated a specific component of training teachers in TESOL (e.g., bachelor's of education with a certificate in TESL).

Findings and Discussion

ALT Qualifications Relating to Teaching or ELT

Table 9.1 summarizes the number of ALTs who possessed a tertiary qualification that relates to teaching and ELT ($N = 101$). Overall, the result corroborates past studies that argued the JET Program is reluctant to hire ALTs with a teaching background (see, e.g., McConnell, 2000). Over 80% of the ALTs in this data set did not possess any qualification in education ($N = 85, 84\%$), or any qualification with an accreditation for local teaching ($N = 86, 85\%$). No evidence was found to suggest that a priority has been given to ALT candidates who possess a tertiary qualification in teaching.

Similarly, the majority did not possess any TESOL certification ($N = 80, 79\%$). Therefore, they were not qualified as language teachers as *qualified* is defined in

110 Takahiro Yokoyama

TABLE 9.1 Teaching or ELT-Related Backgrounds Within ALTs (*N* = 101)

	Education major (% within 101 ALTs)	Local accreditation (% within 101 ALTs)	TESOL certification (% within 101 ALTs)
Yes	16 (16%)	15 (15%)	21 (21%)
No	85 (84%)	86 (85%)	80 (79%)

this study. This finding suggests that the majority of the participants have been selected by somehow demonstrating their strong motivation in SLT. A question remains as to how such a subjective qualification has been assessed during the selection process.

It should be acknowledged that it remains unknown in the study as to how many ALT applicants, including those who were unsuccessful in the selection process, possessed a qualification in teaching or ELT. Therefore, investigating the true picture of the level of priority given to applicants who possess a qualification in these categories remains beyond the scope of the study. Based on the results here, however, despite the emphasis added on the ALT qualifications in (language) teaching within the official hiring criteria, the same level of priority may not have been applied during the selection process at Japanese embassies and consulate offices overseas.

The gap between the official hiring criteria and their implementation may be a result of different objectives of the JET Program expected from each administrative ministry (Hashimoto, 2013; McConnell, 2000). Whereas the Ministry of Education aims to introduce more communicative ELT at local schools, the Ministry of Foreign Affairs reportedly prioritizes enhancing "foreign understanding of Japan ... among young people who were likely to rise to positions of power in their respective countries" (McConnell, 2000, p. 38). This MOFA objective also seems to be represented in the overall goal of the program, which is to "promote grass-roots internationalization at the local level" (CLAIR, 2015, para. 2). Some have argued that the term *internationalization* in Japan is not so much about globalizing or westernizing Japanese citizens at the local level, but promoting Japan's uniqueness and nationalistic values in the international community (Hagerman, 2009; Hashimoto, 2009, 2013). In other words, the JET Program may be seen as a strategic policy to promote "pro-Japan fashion" (McConnell, 2000, p. 38) or "Japaneseness" (Hashimoto, 2009, p. 22) among youth from overseas, in exchange for their presence in local communities (e.g., schools) in Japan.

Over two decades ago, Ricento and Hornberger (1996) used the metaphor of onion peeling to describe how a language education policy is operationalized by many "agents, levels and processes ... [which] permeate and interact with each other in a variety of ways" (p. 402). It appears that the onion indeed exists within the JET Program administration, which has greatly affected how the official hiring criteria have been operationalized by the MOFA through individual embassies and consulate offices overseas. At least from the MOFA perspectives, the JET Program has not represented a national policy that primarily aims to bring a large number of NESTs to Japanese classrooms for the purpose of ELT as the MEXT may have envisaged. This discrepancy in the program objectives may explain the lack of local emphasis on ALT expertise in teaching or ELT during individual selection process overseas.

ALT Proficiency in Japanese Language

Table 9.2 shows a snapshot of the years of learning experiences and self-reported proficiency in Japanese language of the 101 ALTs. Overall, the data seem to indicate that this particular group of ALTs were relatively experienced in Japanese language learning and relatively proficient in the language. Over 20% had studied Japanese for 7 years or longer ($N = 22$, 22%), and in total, 54% had studied Japanese for at least 4 years ($N = 55$). Overall, 30% reported their proficiency as "advanced or above" ($N = 30$), and 75% rated their proficiency at "intermediate or above" ($N = 76$).

Whereas the CLAIR does not specify what is considered as "a high level of Japanese ability" (CLAIR, 2015, an additional statement under criterion 17), the results here clarify the quality of Japanese learning background of ALT applicants. It appears that applicants who have developed their proficiency at the intermediate level or above have been deemed qualified in terms of this specific hiring criterion.

The results also indicate that the official hiring policy and the local implementation of the policy seem to have agreed on this area of ALT expertise. This finding was interesting because the result was in stark contrast to ALT qualifications in

TABLE 9.2 Japanese Language Learning Backgrounds of Current ALTs ($N = 101$)

Category		Counts	% within all participants
Length of Japanese study	None	9	9%
	Less than 1 year	10	10%
	1–3 years	27	27%
	4–6 years	33	32%
	7 years or more	22	22%
	Total	**101**	**100%**
Self-assessed proficiency in Japanese	None	9	9%
	Beginner	16	16%
	Intermediate	46	45%
	Advanced	28	28%
	Near-native	2	2%
	Total	**101**	**100%**

112 Takahiro Yokoyama

teaching and ELT, within which there seemed to be a gap between the stated and realized hiring policy. Also, the JET Program was known to deprioritize applicants who are proficient in Japanese because they are "seen as working against two major purposes of the program: the teaching of English and the introduction of Japanese language and culture to a new generation of foreign youth" (McConnell, 2000, p. 55). Based on the data in the present study, the JET Program no longer seems to have this reluctance to hire ALTs with abilities in Japanese language.

Whereas the exact causes for this shift in emphasis on ALT ability in Japanese remain beyond the scope of the present study, the communication difficulty between ALTs and other stakeholders may have been contributing to the shift. ALTs with little Japanese reportedly felt isolated and stressed when they did not understand school routines (Kobayashi, 2000; Otani, 2007). They also reported difficulties in building rapport with students and with negotiating their specific roles with local teachers who are not always fluent in English (Otani & Tsuido, 2009). English proficiency among Japanese teachers has not been very high, in particular at elementary schools where the MEXT has been actively increasing the amount of ELT as well as ALT involvement (MEXT, 2017). These communication issues may have triggered increasing demands for ALTs who have some abilities in Japanese, which may have changed the priority within the MEXT, the organization responsible for coordinating effective team-teaching between ALTs and JTEs.

The communication difficulties that many ALTs experienced may also have affected the MOFA's priority. In order to promote ALTs' understanding of Japan, their Japanese ability may now be seen not as working against the objective of international exchange, but as being an essential qualification of ALT applicants.

Implications for Policy, Practice, and Future Research

Overall, the results of this study demonstrate that the official hiring policy in the current JET Program (in particular, with regard to educational requirements that relate to teaching, ELT, and Japanese language) are only partially implemented during the individual selection process overseas. The subjective criterion of having 'strong motivation' in foreign language teaching has been used as an alternative qualification for the majority of ALTs who were not qualified as language teachers (CLAIR, 2015, para. 2). Whereas these ALTs may still be deemed 'qualified' (by the MOFA) to participate in the international exchange aspect of the JET Program, whether they are adequately 'qualified' to do their job in Japanese classrooms requires further investigation. According to the CLAIR (2015), ALT duties "typically" include (1) "team-teaching, or assisting with classes taught by JTEs"; (2) "assisting in the preparation of teaching materials"; and (3) "participating in extra-curricular activities with students" (all from CLAIR, 2015, para. 2). Whereas the exact meaning of these "team-teaching" or "assisting" responsibilities remains unspecified in this description, the CLAIR seems to emphasize that ALTs should not be "expected to conduct classes alone, or be the main teacher"

(CLAIR, 2013, p. 42). The result may be that ALTs should not have to be required to possess expertise in ELT and thus to be considered "qualified as a language teacher" (CLAIR, 2015, para. 2).

If ALTs are not engaged in language teaching, but are just participating in an international experience to enhance their understanding of Japan as the MOFA has expected, the present emphasis on academic requirements in teaching or ELT seems to be inconsistent with the expected official roles of ALTs. It is also at odds with the implemented hiring criteria, as evident in ALT academic expertise. ALT applicants should only be required to possess a bachelor's degree, and any statements that prioritize backgrounds in teaching or ELT should not be included in the official hiring criteria.

However, as implied by the term *typically* (CLAIR, 2015, para. 2) in the official role statement, ALTs may also perform more responsible roles. The CLAIR (2013) admits that "despite being given the title assistant, many ALTs are given a great deal of responsibility regarding the curricula and syllabi" (p. 42). Several studies identified gaps between the official ALT roles as stated in the CLAIR (2015) and the roles realized in individual contexts (e.g., Igawa, 2009). Shimizu, Yoshida, Izumi, and Kano (2015), for instance, reported that the majority of ALTs were indeed planning their team-teaching lessons by themselves. The CLAIR (2013) specifically outlines teaching strategies for ALTs to adopt under individual headings, such as "teach all four components of language," "challenge the students to think," "build on past knowledge," "make the lessons relevant," or "speak in your native language as much as possible" (p. 43). These skills are typically discussed as effective language teaching strategies (see, e.g., Richards & Bohlke, 2011), suggesting that the CLAIR indeed expects ALTs to teach English in Japanese classrooms.

Given that realistic roles of ALTs may include more or less teaching of English to Japanese students, ALTs should be required to be qualified as language teachers, and their 'strong motivation' in SLT should only be demonstrated by attainment of such a qualification. However, as discussed earlier, such a rigid academic requirement may not match what the MOFA expects from the JET Program. Indeed, native English speakers who are expected to teach English in the JET Program (or assist someone to do so in team-teaching contexts) should be separated from JET participants who are expected to engage in international experience and enhance their understanding of Japan, both during the hiring process and within role descriptions in the official policy. The current JET Program policy seems to exploit, whether intentionally or not, the confusion between the objectives of ELT and international exchange as a loophole to bring a large number of 'unqualified' language teachers into Japanese classrooms.

At least two issues should be addressed when 'qualified' ALTs are recruited in future practice. The first involves the potential conflict between NESTs and local teachers. Prior to the JET Program, Japan made several attempts to invite TESOL-certified specialists from the US (McConnell, 2000; Tsuido, 2007). These attempts, however, "failed miserably" due to the intense conflict between the

NESTs, who were "wedded to their particular techniques and goals," and local teachers, who "felt threatened" by such a foreign influx (all in McConnell, 2000, p. 41). Because NESTs were primarily hired for professional development purposes for local teachers in these past attempts (Tsuido, 2007), the relationship between ALTs and JTEs in team-teaching may be different now from what it was in the past. Future studies should investigate whether such a tension between ALTs and JTEs regarding their roles during team-teaching indeed exists in the current context, and whether such a tension, if it does exist, is associated with the ALTs' backgrounds in teaching or ELT. If the relationship between ALTs and JTEs is influenced by role negotiation during team-teaching, then it may be best if the CLAIR discontinues the team-teaching policy and develops a new policy that legally allows NESTs to teach independently in Japanese classrooms, particularly for those who are qualified language teachers. This practice may also help NESTs gain status as "real" teachers (Falout, 2013, p. 109), which many ALTs reportedly do not have in the current team-teaching practice.

Second, variations within language teacher qualifications should be considered. To some extent, the present study was able to clarify types of language teacher qualifications as realized by the officials in the present JET Program. At the same time, this chapter has revealed the extreme diversity even within those qualifications, ranging from certificates (e.g., CELTA, Oxford TEFL Certification, Trinity Certificate) to master's degrees (e.g., MAELT, MA in TESOL). Future research should investigate whether and how these existing variations influence the experience and effectiveness of ALTs in Japan (and NESTs in general) in order to understand specific types of language teacher qualifications that are suitable in this particular context.

Finally, the results also suggest that the official priority on ALT applicants with "a high level of Japanese ability" (CLAIR, 2015, an additional statement under criterion 17) was relatively well implemented in the individual selection process. Ability and knowledge in a local language and culture reportedly enhance communication skills and contextual knowledge for second language teachers to teach effectively (Mahboob & Lin, 2016). Such expertise, however, has often been discussed as an advantage of NNESTs (e.g., Moussu & Llurda, 2008). Given that the result of the study shows that many ALTs also have similar abilities, it would be interesting to investigate how such abilities influence their experience in Japan. Future research should investigate the extent to which ALTs' Japanese language proficiency influences various communication issues, as reported earlier. It should also examine whether ALTs who are qualified in this expertise indeed have better work experiences in Japan than those who are not.

References

Aline, D., & Hosoda, Y. (2006). Team teaching participation patterns of homeroom teachers in English activities classes in Japanese public elementary schools. *JALT Journal*, *28*(1), 5–21.

Baniabdelrahman, A. (2011). Effect of team teaching and being the teacher native or non-native on EFL students' English language proficiency. *African Educational Research Journal, 1*(2), 85–95.

Barratt, L., & Kontra, E. (2000). Native English-speaking teachers in cultures other than their own. *TESOL Journal, 9*(3), 19–23.

Carless, D. (2006). Collaborative EFL teaching in primary school. *ELT Journal, 60*(4), 328–335.

Christensen, E. (2014). *On the job teacher training for native English-speaking teachers in South Korean intensive English kindergartens* (Master's thesis). University of San Francisco, San Francisco, CA.

Christopher, V. (Ed.). (2005). *Directory of teacher education programs in TESOL in the United States and Canada, 2005–2007*. Alexandria, VA: Teachers of English to Speakers of Other Languages.

Council of Local Authorities for International Relations (CLAIR). (2013). *ALT handbook*. Retrieved from www.jetprogramme.org/e/current/pubs/alt_hb.html

Council of Local Authorities for International Relations (CLAIR). (2015). *The Japan exchange and teaching programme*. Retrieved from http://jetprogramme.org/en/

Falout, J. (2013). Forming pathways of belonging: Social inclusion for teachers abroad. In S. Houghton & D. Rivers (Eds.), *Native-speakerism in Japan: Intergroup dynamics in foreign language education* (pp. 105–115). Bristol, UK: Multilingual Matters.

Geluso, J. (2013). Negotiating a professional identity: Non-Japanese teachers of English in pre-tertiary education in Japan. In S. Houghton & D. Rivers (Eds.), *Native-speakerism in Japan: Intergroup dynamics in foreign language education* (pp. 132–146). Bristol, UK: Multilingual Matters.

Hagerman, C. (2009). English language policy and practice in Japan. *Osaka Jogakuin College Kiyo Journal, 6*, 47–64.

Han, S. A. (2005). Good teachers know where to scratch when learners feel itchy: Korean learners' views of native-speaking teachers of English. *Australian Journal of Education, 49*(2), 197–213.

Hashimoto, K. (2009). Cultivating "Japanese who can use English": Problems and contradictions in government policy. *Asian Studies Review, 33*(1), 21–42.

Hashimoto, K. (2013). The construction of the 'native speaker' in Japan's educational policies for TEFL. In S. Houghton & D. Rivers (Eds.), *Native-speakerism in Japan: Intergroup dynamics in foreign language education* (pp. 159–168). Bristol, UK: Multilingual Matters.

Holliday, A. (2008). Standards of English and politics of inclusion. *Language Teaching, 41*(1), 119–130. doi:10.1017/S0261444807004776.

Houghton, S., & Rivers, D. (Eds.). (2013). *Native-speakerism in Japan: Intergroup dynamics in foreign language education*. Bristol, UK: Multilingual Matters.

Igawa, K. (2009). EFL teachers' views on team-teaching: In the case of Japanese secondary school teachers. *Shitennouji Daigaku Kiyou, 47*, 145–172.

Jeon, M. (2016). English language education policy and the native-speaking English teacher (NET) scheme in Hong Kong. In R. Kirkpatrick (Ed.), *English language education policy in Asia* (pp. 91–111). Cham, Switzerland: Springer.

Kabel, A. (2009). Native-speakerism, stereotyping and the collusion of applied linguistics. *System, 37*, 12–22. doi:10.1016/j.system.2008.09.004.

Kachru, B. B. (1992). World Englishes: Approaches, issues and resources. *Language Teaching, 25*(1), 1–14. doi:10.1017/S0261444800006583.

Kobayashi, Y. (2000). The problems of "teachers' team" in team teaching and the JET Program. *Inbunka Communication Kenkyu, 3*, 91–109.

Liu, L. (2008). Co-teaching between native and non-native English teachers: An exploration of co-teaching models and strategies in the Chinese primary school context. *Reflections on English Language Teaching*, 7(2), 103–118.

Mahboob, A., & Lin, A. (2016). Using local languages in English language classrooms. In H. Widodo & W. Renandya (Eds.), *English language teaching today: Building a closer link between theory and practice*. New York, NY: Springer International. DOI: 10.1007/978-3-319-38834-2_3.

Marian, V., Blumenfeld, H. K., & Kaushanskaya, M. (2007). The language experience and proficiency questionnaire (LEAP-Q): Assessing language profiles in bilinguals and multilinguals. *Journal of Speech, Language, and Hearing Research*, 50(4), 940–967. doi:10.1044/1092-4388(2007/067)

McConnell, D. L. (2000). *Importing diversity: Inside Japan's JET Program*. Berkeley, CA: University of California Press.

Ministry of Education, Culture, Sports, Science and Technology (MEXT). (2017). *Heisei 28 nendo 'Eigo kyouiku jisshi jyoukyou chousa' no kekka ni tsuite* [Result of English language education report in 2016]. Retrieved November 30, 2017 from www.mext .go.jp/a_menu/kokusai/gaikokugo/1384230.htm

Moussu, L., & Llurda, E. (2008). Non-native English-speaking English language teachers: History and research. *Language Teaching*, 41(3), 315–348. doi:10.1017/S026144480 8005028.

Nurul Islam, M. (2011). Collaboration between native and non-native English-speaking teachers. *Studies in Literature and Language*, 2(1), 33–41.

Otani, M. (2007). Gaikokujin shidou jyoshu (ALT) to nihon no gakkou bukna: Nihonjin kyouin to ALT kanniokeru ibunkayouin [Assistant language teacher (ALT) and Japanese school culture: Intercultural factors between Japanese teachers and ALTs]. *Shimane Daigaku Kyouikugakubu Kiyou*, 41, 105–112.

Otani, M., & Tsuido, K. (2009). A pilot study on utilization of assistant language teachers in foreign language activities at elementary schools: Based on a preliminary questionnaire survey to ALTs. *Shimane Daigaku Kyouikugakubu Kiyou*, 43, 21–29.

Plüddemann, P. (2015). Unlocking the grid: Language-in-education policy realisation in post-apartheid South Africa. *Language and Education*, 29(3), 186–199. http://dx.doi.org/ 10.1080/09500782.2014.994523.

Ricento, T. K., & Hornberger, N. H. (1996). Unpeeling the onion: Language planning and policy and the ELT professional. *TESOL Quarterly*, 30(3), 401–428.

Richards, J. C., & Bohlke, D. (2011). *Creating effective lessons*. New York, NY: Cambridge University Press.

Shimizu, T., Yoshida, K., Izumi, S., & Kano, A. (2015). *Shogakko Chugakko Kotogakko ni okeru ALT no jittai ni kansuru daikibo ankeeto chosa kenkyu chukanhoukokusho* [Interim report of the investigation of current practice of ALT at elementary, junior high schools and senior high schools]. Tokyo, Japan: Sophia University.

Tsuido, K. (2007). A study of English language education reform in Japan: Focusing on the JET Program. *Hiroshima Gaikokugo Kyouiku Kenkyu*, 10, 1–16.

UNESCO Institute for Statistics. (2012). *International standard classification of education 2011*. Retrieved November 30, 2017 from www.uis.unesco.org/Education/DOcuments/ isced-2011-en.pdf

PART 3

Perspectives of Diverse Stakeholders on Educational Language Policy and Planning

10

POLICY AND PRACTICALITY IN TIMORESE HIGHER EDUCATION

Lessons From Lecturers in Development-related Disciplines

Trent Newman

This chapter reports on an empirical study of the policy discourses and other forces impacting East Timorese tertiary educators' conceptualizations of the academic and professional communication skills needed by their plurilingual students. Particular attention is paid to the ways that a variety of competing institutional, national, and global policy discourses enter into the accounts of higher education lecturers in development-related disciplines in Timor-Leste. The data analyzed in this chapter were gathered from interviews and focus groups conducted with lecturers from petroleum studies, agriculture, tourism, and community development studies faculties in three different Timorese higher education institutions. Questions were aimed at eliciting lecturers' descriptions of the communication skills needed by their students for study and work purposes.

Issues That Motivated the Research

Lecturers in higher education institutions in Timor-Leste (also known as East Timor) are faced with a daunting challenge: how to work within a mixture of languages for the academic and professional transformation of their plurilingual students amid a complex and conflicted language policy environment. Timorese students entering tertiary education now are likely to have experienced learning in a mixture of Tetun (the national lingua franca, also spelled *Tetum* when written in English), Indonesian, Portuguese, and possibly some use of local languages (Quinn, 2013). Within individual institutions, teaching and learning happen primarily in Tetun, although there is substantial variation in the loaning of technical and discipline-specific language from Indonesian, Portuguese, and/or English, as well as in the use of teaching and learning resources in these languages. This variation is attributable to differences in lecturers' individual plurilingual

120 Trent Newman

repertoires resulting from differing "educational biographies and social trajectories" (Moore & Gajo, 2009, p. 142).

This complex sociolinguistic context has arisen nationally via a long history of colonial—first Portuguese, then Indonesian—occupation, followed by a succession of shifts in language-in-education policy and planning over the past 15 years since independence (Carneiro, 2014; Taylor-Leech, 2013). Currently, higher education lecturers are under conflicting ideological pressures to choose from among the four co-official and working languages and to adopt monolingual teaching practices, despite the complex and well-entrenched multilingual reality in classrooms. Pressure comes, for example, from the Timorese government and many nationalist voices to abandon the use of Indonesian in tertiary classrooms, although it is the language that most lecturers have been trained in and the language of many teaching and learning resources. There is also pressure to comply with government legislation and education planning documents that prioritize the co-official languages—Portuguese and Tetun—for all post-primary education and emphasize the use of Portuguese for higher education, although relatively few lecturers have studied to tertiary level in Portuguese themselves.

These pressures also play out differently in different disciplines and institutions, each with their own history and relationships with the Timorese government, foreign aid donor countries, and strategic industries. At the national university (the only public higher education institution), an increasing number of lecturers are receiving government-funded scholarships to complete their doctoral degrees in Portugal, as well as in-service Portuguese language training at the university. In contrast, at private institutions, where funding for graduate study for lecturers comes mostly from the institutions themselves, lecturers are being sent mostly to Indonesia to complete their master's degrees because it is the cheapest and most accessible option. At least one private higher education institution has chosen to move to English as the medium of instruction for faculties oriented to strategic industries, notably petroleum studies and tourism. This move is in response to growing demand for English-speaking graduates in these and other national industries, as well as a perception among the institutional leadership that English offers a competitive edge regionally in South East Asia. There are also diverse international pressures, such as those coming from multilateral intergovernmental organizations like the CPLP (Comunidade dos Países de Língua Portuguesa, or Community of Portuguese Language Countries) and ASEAN (Association of Southeast Asian Nations) for the use of Portuguese and English (respectively), and from international aid agencies for even less frequently used languages, such as Spanish in the field of medicine via the Cuban Medical exchange program.

Timorese lecturers are thus caught up in a whirlwind of forces pushing and pulling them in different directions with regard to classroom communication and "practiced language policies" (Bonacina-Pugh, 2012, p. 213). These forces shape lecturers' differing perspectives of the relative values of Tetun, Portuguese, English, and Indonesian (among others) as individual languages for academic and

Policy and Practicality in Timorese **121**

professional purposes in different disciplines, along with these lecturers' views of diverse mixings in plurilingual and translanguaging teaching and learning practices. This whirlwind is occurring at a time when, nationally, the "production" of a highly skilled workforce has been identified as a major priority for the development of the country, specifically in the "strategic industry sectors" of agriculture, petroleum, and tourism/hospitality (RDTL, 2011, p. 23). At the same time, regionally and globally, there is the increasing use of language as "a strategic tool in the construction of international relations in the new global political economy" (Carneiro, 2014, p. 206).

Theoretical Background

As in other postcolonial nation-states, language choices in Timorese higher education are being pushed and pulled by the shifting conditions and demands of decolonization, nation-building, globalization, regional participation, and social and economic development. These conditions produce language ideologies and discourses that are in constant tension and transition, indexing competing hierarchical orders of languages and lingualisms (Johnson, 2011). Bakhtin's (1981) notions of centripetal and centrifugal forces and the dialectical nature of their relationship are particularly useful tools here to understand the origins of the substantial dynamism and flux occurring with language in Timorese society. Language planning efforts by the Timorese government and educational institutions operate as centripetal forces attempting to regulate and centralize all the various manifestations of language in society into standardized and official forms. However, these centralizing efforts must contend with a rich and ever-shifting multiplicity of voices—Bakhtin's (1981) *heteroglossia*—that diversify, decentralize, and complicate by their very existence what constitutes language at any given moment in any particular social context. This perspective brings into sharp focus the significance of individual voices (and, indeed, of individual utterances), particularly those of educators, who are often positioned at the nexus of these conflicting forces.

A study in this context of what Lo Bianco (2005, p. 257) calls "discourse planning" in language policy would seek to understand the processes by which certain language issues are constructed to be 'problems' deserving policy attention, whereas others are neglected or ignored, especially at the micro-level. As Lo Bianco points out, the educational institution is a key location for the analysis of discourse planning because "a great deal of language policy and planning is conducted not at macro social levels but at micro-levels of daily interaction in social contexts" (2005, p. 262). For Canagarajah (2005), it is at the micro-level of individual education institutions that educators must constantly navigate and accommodate tensions between top-down language policy and local sociolinguistic realities, with varying degrees of agency and flexibility of choice. In higher education worldwide, this navigating and accommodating of tensions often means

122 Trent Newman

struggling to find a place for local languages alongside dominant languages, such as English and, in the case of Timor-Leste, also Portuguese and Indonesian.

However, some have argued that the real constraints on the exercise of local agency for multilingual pedagogies in tertiary education lie not so much in the hegemonic domination of English or other colonial languages, but in the localized devaluing of the linguistic repertoires that students bring to the classroom (García & Flores, 2012; Hornberger, 2002) alongside a "monoglossic bias in how academic transformation is conceived" (Stroud & Kerfoot, 2013, p. 400). In recent years, theories of multilingualism have drifted away from conceptualizations of languages as discrete and separable things in favor of views of language and language use as fluid, flexible, intermingling, and ever-changing (Blackledge & Creese, 2010; García, 2009). This shift, in turn, has led to studies into the kinds of creative pedagogic practices that enable and encourage a dynamic plurilingualism as a teaching and learning resource: practices, for example, that take voice, rather than language, as a starting point and that focus on mobility and flexibility within entire linguistic *repertoires*, rather than quantifiable skills within separate language *codes* (Blackledge & Creese, 2010; Moore & Gajo, 2009). In higher education, there is a growing body of evidence that multilingual pedagogies are not only possible, but are in fact preferable for developing the kinds of academic and professional skills needed for the diverse communication demands of today's learning and workplace environments (Blackledge & Creese, 2010; Preece & Martin, 2010). What is less well understood are the forces—namely the discursive and policy forces—that may prevent educators, such as the Timorese lecturers discussed here, from valuing the plurilingual repertoires of their students and from embracing multilingual pedagogies for higher education.

Research Question Addressed

Although this study responded to a number of core research questions, this chapter focuses on just one:

> How do higher education lecturers in development-related disciplines in Timor-Leste conceptualize the academic and professional communication skills needed by their plurilingual students?

It is the findings related to this question that are most germane to my arguments regarding the tensions between policy pressures facing lecturers and the pragmatics of their diverse contexts of multilingual disciplinary teaching and learning. Note that for the purposes of this research the term *development-related disciplines* refers to the three strategic industry sectors identified by the Timorese government in their National Strategic Development Plan 2011–2030 (RDTL, 2011)—agriculture, petroleum, and tourism—along with the discipline of community development studies.

Research Methods

Data Collection

This study drew on a mixture of ethnographic research methods—including focus groups, interviews, and passive classroom observations (with the use of an observation tool)—in order to collect rich and diverse qualitative data from lecturer participants in different disciplinary areas and different institutional settings. Lecturers were recruited from the aforementioned disciplines for participation in the project via direct contact with three Timorese higher education institutions. These were (1) a large public university, which I call 'NU' (National University), and (2) a large private technical institute, which I call 'TI' (Technology Institute), both located in the capital, Dili; and (3) a small, private agriculture institute focused on coffee production, located in the rural district of Ermera, which I call 'CI' (Coffee Institute).

During a three-month visit to Timor-Leste in 2015, I conducted focus group discussions with lecturers by disciplinary area at each of the three institutions. Focus group participants were asked to share their impressions of the communication challenges faced by their students in multilingual study and work contexts particular to their disciplinary area. As much as possible, questions focused on concrete examples and stories of interactions with students, in a conscious attempt to anchor discussion "close to interviewees' real-life worlds" (Codó, 2008, p. 167). Following the focus group interviews, I selected some participants for shorter individual interviews. I asked them to share their individual experiences of teaching in their field in and across multiple languages, to describe their teaching methods and communication strategies in more detail, and to discuss their hopes and expectations of plurilingual graduates in their industries with regard to the future development of Timor-Leste. In this way, the focus groups served both as sources of data in themselves and also as opportunities for the selection of key informants from within the groups.

All interviews and focus group discussions were audio-recorded and were conducted with an interpreter present to assist in communication, unless the participants agreed that an interpreter was not needed and/or requested to hold the interview in English. After this initial phase of data collection, audio recordings of focus groups and interviews were transcribed and coded, with multilingual transcriptions checked and translated by an experienced translator fluent in all the languages used, as well as their various mixings. Following transcription and translation of the first round of data collection, a shorter, return visit to Timor-Leste in February 2017 allowed for follow-up interviews, as well as for checking understandings and interpretations of data with participants. These follow-up interviews enabled greater control by participants over the interpretation process—especially important given the cross-cultural and multilingual nature of this study (Pavlenko & Blackledge, 2004).

124 Trent Newman

Data Analysis Procedures Used

Data gathered from the focus groups and interviews were analyzed via a combination of content and discourse analyses. Content and discourse analyses from transcripts were complemented by analysis of the results of observations of lecturers' teaching methods and communication practices in classrooms and supervised fieldwork settings, as well as relevant institutional and faculty documents (curricula, course outlines, sample teaching resources, sample student assignments, etc.). Data analysis also included intertextual and interdiscursive analysis (Johnson & Ricento, 2013) across the data sets (focus groups, interviews, observations, documents) and in relation to national, industry, and institutional language policy documents and discourses. This intertextual and interdiscursive analysis was done in order to examine the multi-layered distribution of implicit and explicit values and ideologies connected to individual languages, monolingualism, and different forms and functions of plurilingualism.

In my analysis, I adapt what Martin-Jones (2007) has called a "critical interpretive approach" to the study of language in education in multilingual settings. That is, an approach that seeks to

> link insights from the close study of the interactional and textual fine-grain of everyday life in educational settings with an account of specific institutional regimes, the wider political economy and the global processes of cultural transformation at work in contemporary society.
>
> *(Martin-Jones, 2007, p. 163)*

I understand lecturers' individual accounts of their students' communication skills both as reflective of the interactional construction of the institutional order and also as embedded in wider social and historical contexts. This means analyzing lecturers' statements with attention to their individual linguistic and educational biographies. I also focus on the implications of the multiple voices—gendered, generational, disciplinary, academic—with which they speak (Bakhtin, 1981).

Findings and Discussion

Plurilingualism as Asset for Communicative Competence Versus Deficit Parallel Monolingualisms

Regarding students' skills conceptualized as communicative competence for understanding classroom instruction, students' plurilingual repertoires are perceived simultaneously and rather paradoxically as both a resource and a problem. Lecturers acknowledge and even participate in the fluid movement back and forth in and between languages characteristic of a plurilingual paradigm (Moore & Gajo,

2009). Yet they also describe students' repertoires as being deficient in technical or disciplinary vocabulary, defined in terms of competence in individual languages. For example, agriculture lecturers despair at the language competency levels of their plurilingual students arriving from secondary school, specifically their competency in scientific Indonesian, even as they describe their own resourceful mixing of languages for classroom communication:

> Students that are now coming from secondary school, their ability, or their knowledge of Indonesian, especially scientific Indonesian, is not yet developed. You see, the materials we use are in Indonesian. It's because of this that we feel we face a big problem: that the communication between us and students, especially scientific communication, is lacking. [So] we try to find a way that they can understand the science. We look for ways in many diverse languages, for example in Indonesian, in English, in Portuguese, in Tetun. Four. If they don't understand when we explain in Indonesian, we try Portuguese. Portuguese they also don't understand well enough. So in order to find a way for them to understand, we might try English. If they can't, we try Tetun. We talk, talk, talk, but they don't understand.
>
> *(Prof. B, Agriculture Faculty, NU; translated from Tetun)*

Note here that while the lecturer is describing her mixing of languages for classroom communication, she speaks of the languages as clearly separate things and of students' ability to understand in terms of their competency in each individual language.

Because most students are strongest in Tetun (out of the four dominant languages), their academic communication skills are also conceptualized via lecturers' perceptions of Tetun as a non-academic language. That is, lecturers' conceptualizations of their students' ability to communicate in tertiary classrooms are filtered through their perceptions of the deficiencies of Tetun as an academic language, as well as their ideologized views of students' plurilingual repertoires as parallel monolingualisms (Heller, 2007). This conceptualization makes the situation appear even more hopeless, with multilingual teaching and learning taking place in and through monolingual mindsets. As one petroleum studies lecturer, Prof. A, explains:

> If they read Indonesian mixed with Tetun, they will be able to receive the knowledge. They understand. But it's difficult for them to write in Indonesian. Because of this, if maybe we force them to write using Tetun, we know that in Tetun there is a lack of technical language. For technical language, you can't write in Tetun because you'll be left short. If you go to English, students' capacity isn't enough. Whether we like it or not, we have to keep using Indonesian for writing.
>
> *(Prof. A, Petroleum Studies, TI; translated from Tetun)*

As this and the preceding comment illustrate, these lecturers tend to view students' ability to understand their teaching, and to reproduce that understanding in writing, in terms of language deficiencies. Deficiencies are perceived in students' prior development of technical and discipline-specific lexicon in any language and/or in terms of perceived deficiencies in Tetun itself as a language. One of the more immediate and problematic consequences of lecturers understanding students' communicative competencies in these ways is that they may come to underestimate their own roles as teachers of disciplinary language, seeing themselves as 'content' and not 'language' teachers. One lecturer with whom I spoke was particularly adamant about this distinction, stating that "my objective is to transfer science, not language" (Prof. J, Agriculture Faculty, NU; translated from Tetun). The danger here, in this lecturer's viewing the transfer of science as somehow separate from language learning, is that the lecturer both excuses himself from and blinds himself to responsibility for students' disciplinary discourse socialization. The possibility of a student mastering a discipline is externalized from the teacher/student relationship and inextricably tied either to a student's capabilities in individual languages or, in the case of Tetun, to the perceived capabilities of the language itself.

The Influence of Institutional Arrangements for Language Instruction

Unfortunately, faculty-based, medium-of-instruction policies and institutional arrangements for language support programs in Timorese higher education institutions can serve to support this problematic view. All tertiary students are required to take at least two semesters each of Portuguese, Tetun, and English in their first year. At TI, students in the petroleum and tourism faculties also take additional English for Specific Purposes (ESP) classes, taught by teachers from the English department, with little or no collaboration with the faculties. These arrangements lead some lecturers to expect, somewhat understandably, that their students should have at least a basic functional literacy in these languages upon arrival in their content classrooms, an expectation that is too easily frustrated:

> My students come to me [with their timetable], they say "I don't know what is this subject." I tell them, "You completed Portuguese 2; you go find out."
> *(Prof. E, Agriculture, NU; English original)*

One of the main reasons that these first-year language programs may be failing to provide students with the communication skills they need to navigate tertiary study is that they tend to focus almost exclusively on vocabulary, spelling, grammar, and orthography, neglecting language for academic purposes. Given that the language programs are also institutionally separated from one another as well as from the other faculties—once again arranging multilingualism as parallel but separated monolingualisms—they also fail to correspond to the mixed, multilingual realities in classrooms. Indonesian is not provided as a compulsory subject anywhere, and there are no general academic skills subjects taught, although Tetun for Study and Work as a course has recently been introduced at TI (Williams-van Klinken, da Silva Ribeiro, & Martins Tilman, 2015). The ESP classes at TI also focus mainly on vocabulary and structures and further contribute to the institutional separation of language instruction from disciplinary expertise.

These arrangements for and approaches to language education at the tertiary level cannot help but shape disciplinary lecturers' views of their students' communication skills, and perhaps also skew their views of their own role in the development of those skills. As another example, the National Institute for Linguistics (INL) at NU claims full responsibility for developing the corpus of Tetun, including technical and scientific vocabulary, which may lead lecturers to doubt their own authority in the coining of new technical or discipline-specific terms in Tetun. Indeed, there are currently no formal processes established for consultation between INL linguists and disciplinary experts on the development of Tetun as an academic and scientific language. There are, however, some lecturers who take the initiative. For example, Prof. M, an agriculture lecturer at NU, sees the process of language development as a collaborative work in progress that requires the input of diverse voices:

> It's not [that] I'm the lecturer, I'm the correct one, or you are the correct one. But I also say that this is interesting—[it] means that we are willing, you know, to develop our language. . . . There may be some experts of the language somewhere, but this is bringing different ideas that you can probably also talk to different people [about].
>
> *(Prof. M, Agriculture, NU; English original)*

Lecturers in Timorese higher education institutions continue to mix languages in teaching and learning and draw on their own and their students' plurilingual repertoires. They do this in the face of diverse institutional, national, and global policy discourses that articulate multilingualism as competing monolingualisms, as well as complicating institutional arrangements for language instruction. Constructive ways forward lie in the conceptualizations and practices of lecturers like Prof. M, who recognize the challenges and constraints that surround them, but determine to see the situation as an opportunity for learning and collaborative language development via interdisciplinary dialogue.

Implications for Policy, Practice, and Future Research

This study has produced information about the attitudes around and manifestations of plurilingualism in Timorese higher education at a turning point in the young nation's history and development. Findings highlight complex educational contextualizations of the relationships among four dominant languages in Timor-ese society—Tetun, Portuguese, Indonesian, and English—for tertiary teaching and learning. They also reveal substantive and far-reaching constraints on the effective mobilization and flexibility of both students' and lecturers' plurilingual repertoires across these languages in processes of disciplinary discourse socialization.

This research comes at a time when the national strategic development plan of Timor-Leste has highlighted the urgent need for a literate, highly skilled work-force (RDTL, 2011). Policy and practice related to workforce development must take account of whether university graduates are learning the communication skills that they need to be job ready. To date, there has been no research con-ducted into how tertiary-level teaching and learning in Timor-Leste is affected by the complex sociolinguistic environment in which it is situated, nor its rela-tionship with competing local and international development agendas. Beyond the Timorese context, there has also been relatively little empirical research con-ducted on plurilingual teaching practices in content-focused tertiary classrooms in multilingual, postcolonial, developing societies. This research contributes to filling these gaps.

Last, and perhaps most practically, with this project I have been able to offer Timorese lecturers unique opportunities for facilitated, professional reflection with peers—specifically on academic and professional communication skills. Lan-guage for study and work purposes is a topic that many content-focused lecturers may not find much time to consider. The focus group discussions on this topic conducted as part of this research highlighted the need for closer consultation and collaboration between language and disciplinary experts. For some lecturers, the discussions may also have stimulated reflection on their own language practices for teaching, perhaps leading to increased self-awareness in their communication with students. Additionally, in acknowledging and valuing the voices, opinions, and practices of the participants, this research emphasizes the inherent worth and localized wisdom of the experiences and perspectives of Timorese tertiary educa-tors, in a context where focus is so often on macro-level policy debates.

References

Bakhtin, M. (1981). *The dialogic imagination: Four essays*. (C. Emerson & M. Holquist, Trans.). Austin, TX: University of Texas Press.

Blackledge, A., & Creese, A. (2010). *Multilingualism: A critical perspective*. London, UK: Continuum.

Bonacina-Pugh, F. (2012). Researching 'practiced language policies': Insights from conver-sation analysis. *Language Policy, 11*(3), 213–234.

Canagarajah, S. (Ed.). (2005). *Reclaiming the local in language policy and practice*. Mahwah, NJ: Lawrence Erlbaum Associates.

Carneiro, A. S. R. (2014). Conflicts around the (de-)construction of legitimate language(s): The situation of Portuguese in the multilingual context of East Timor. In L. P. Moita-Lopes (Ed.), *Global Portuguese: Linguistic ideologies in late modernity* (pp. 204–221). New York, NY: Routledge.

Policy and Practicality in Timorese **129**

Codó, E. (2008). Interviews as sources of data on language contact. In L. Wei & M. Moyer (Eds.), *The Blackwell guide to research methods in bilingualism and multilingualism* (pp. 158–176). Malden, MA: Blackwell Publishing.

García, O. (2009). *Bilingual education in the 21st century: A global perspective*. Chichester, UK: Wiley-Blackwell.

García, O., & Flores, N. (2012). Multilingual pedagogies. In M. Martin-Jones, A. Blackledge & A. M. Creese (Eds.), *The Routledge handbook of multilingualism* (pp. 232–246). London, UK: Routledge.

Heller, M. (2007). Bilingualism as ideology and practice. In M. Heller (Ed.), *Bilingualism: A social approach* (pp. 1–22). London, UK: Palgrave Macmillan.

Hornberger, N. H. (2002). Multilingual language policies and the continua of biliteracy: An ecological approach. *Language Policy, 1*(1), 27–51. doi:10.1023/A:1014548611951.

Johnson, D. C. (2011). Implementational and ideological spaces in bilingual education policy, practice, and research. In F. M. Hult & K. A. King (Eds.), *Educational linguistics in practice: Applying the local globally and the global locally* (pp. 126–139). Bristol, UK: Multilingual Matters.

Johnson, D. C., & Ricento, T. K. (2013). Conceptual and theoretical perspectives in language planning and policy: Situating the ethnography of language policy. *International Journal of the Sociology of Language, 2013*(219), 7–21.

Lo Bianco, J. (2005). Including discourse in language planning. In P. Bruthiau (Ed.), *Directions in applied linguistics* (pp. 255–263). Clevedon, UK: Multilingual Matters.

Martin-Jones, M. (2007). Bilingualism, education, and the regulation of access to language resources. In M. Heller (Ed.), *Bilingualism: A social approach* (pp. 161–182). London, UK: Palgrave Macmillan.

Moore, D., & Gajo, L. (2009). French voices on plurilingualism and pluriculturalism: Theory, significance and perspectives. *International Journal of Multilingualism, 6*(2), 137–153.

Pavlenko, A., & Blackledge, A. (Eds.). (2004). *Negotiation of identities in multilingual contexts*. Clevedon, UK: Multilingual Matters.

Preece, S., & Martin, P. (2010). Imagining higher education as a multilingual space. *Language and Education, 24*(1), 3–8. doi:10.1080/09500780903343070.

Quinn, M. (2013). Talking to learn in Timorese classrooms. *Language, Culture and Curriculum, 26*(2), 179–196.

RDTL [República Democrática de Timor-Leste]. (2011). *Timor-Leste strategic development plan, 2011–2030*. (English version). Retrieved April 4, 2017 from https://sustainabledevelopment.un.org/content/documents/1506Timor-Leste-Strategic-Plan-2011-20301.pdf

Stroud, C., & Kerfoot, C. (2013). Towards rethinking multilingualism and language policy for academic literacies. *Linguistics and Education, 24*(4), 396–405. doi:10.1016/j.linged.2013.09.003.

Taylor-Leech, K. (2013). Finding space for non-dominant languages in education: Language policy and medium of instruction in Timor-Leste 2000–2012. *Current Issues in Language Planning, 14*(1), 109–126.

Williams-van Klinken, C., da Silva Ribeiro, L., & Martins Tilman, C. (2015). *Tetun ba eskola ho servisu*. Dili, Timor-Leste: Dili Institute of Technology.

11

THE ABSENCE OF LANGUAGE-FOCUSED TEACHER EDUCATION POLICY IN U.S. K12 CONTEXTS

Insights From Language Socialization Research in a Ninth-grade Physics Classroom

Sarah Braden and MaryAnn Christison

The number of English learners (ELs) in grades K12 in public schools in the United States is close to five million, which is about one learner in nine, and demographers estimate that in 20 years it is likely be one in four learners (Goldberg, 2008, p. 10). ELs have lower standardized test scores and lower high school graduation rates than their native-English-speaking peers (U.S. Census Bureau, 2011). Furthermore, language minority students, including ELs, are underrepresented in STEM (science, technology, engineering, and mathematics) fields. Equity in access to STEM degrees and professions is a social justice issue that carries economic implications (U.S. Department of Commerce, 2011). As the demographics in the United States change to include more individuals from language minority backgrounds in the workforce (Cohn & Caumont, 2016), it has become imperative to ensure equitable access to STEM careers. Despite the need for science and language education policy that is responsive to the needs of linguistically diverse students, current policy efforts from both science- and language-based perspectives continue to fall short of this goal.

In this chapter, we demonstrate that an inadequate focus on language in the development of STEM expertise leaves even highly qualified teachers ill-prepared to work with ELs. In addition, English as a second language (ESL) endorsement programs that fail to engage mainstream teachers with language socialization issues (i.e., "the process by which individuals acquire the knowledge and practices that enable them to participate effectively in a language community" (Longman, 2008, p. 490) will fall short in helping teachers meet the needs of ELs in science classrooms.

Issues That Motivated the Research

In the United States, there are no national policies regarding the education of science, technology, engineering, and math teachers. Individual states create teacher licensure requirements and have their own processes for developing content standards and administering standardized tests. In the absence of explicit policy on how to educate U.S. science teachers and in the context of teacher accountability through high-stakes testing, content standards have become the guiding principles around which teachers are educated and evaluated. The absence of explicit standards for teaching the language of science means that science teachers are likely underprepared to teach the language of their disciplines.

Although there are no national policies that govern the teaching of science, the National Research Council (NRC) outlined a framework for science education in 2011. Although the NRC framework advocates for teacher performance expectations to be developed based on a knowledge of diverse learners' backgrounds and language proficiency levels, the Next Generation Science Standards (NGSS) (NGSS Lead States, 2013), which are based on the NRC framework, do not contain an explicit language focus. Thus, the use of the NGSS with diverse learners requires that teachers already know how to accommodate ELs in their classrooms. The inclusion of scientific practices (e.g., asking questions, planning and carrying out investigations, constructing explanations) is one of the core dimensions of NGSS. However, the language demands of scientific practices are complex (Lee, Quinn, & Valdés, 2013), and without specific training or attention to the linguistic components of these practices, teachers are not likely to recognize and effectively respond to the language demands facing ELs as they engage in these practices.

Although teachers' knowledge of language is an important factor in improving STEM outcomes for ELs, it is also true that "the school context—its culture and conditions—matters just as much, if not more" (National Research Council, 2011, p. 23). Carlone, Haun-Frank, and Webb (2011) found that for African American and Latina fourth-grade girls, the fact that they were earning good grades on science assessments was not enough for them to identify as "smart science students" (p. 461). In order to help ELs affiliate with science, researchers and teachers must understand how students are positioned socially as they develop the conceptual and linguistic knowledge that is required for success in science classrooms.

The research presented in this chapter analyzes linguistic practices that occurred during inquiry tasks (i.e., tasks that pose questions or problems rather than present a set of facts) in three lab sessions in a ninth-grade physics classroom. To interpret the linguistic practices of the six lab participants, we used Braden's (2016) descriptions of three prominent classroom identities: (1) the science expert, (2) the good student, and (3) the good assistant. According to Braden, students who developed identities as science experts used specific linguistic practices to articulate positions of expertise by issuing directives to their peers, strategically ignoring peer comments, evaluating peer performances, and controlling materials. Those pupils articulating good student positions used similar communicative strategies to those of the science experts, but rather than attending to science content, they focused on ensuring other students followed the teacher's instructions, staying on task, and understanding the actions of the science expert. In contrast, students who developed identities as good assistants participated in lab groups by following their peers' commands, asking for permission from peers before manipulating materials, and abstaining from verbal participation in science content conversations. As we examine the linguistic practices of the participants across the three labs, we focus on Sofia, the EL among the participants, to determine how she was socialized into her role as a good assistant rather than a science expert. We take this stance because in order to help ELs learn language and science content—and to affiliate with science—researchers, policy makers, and teachers must understand the important role that social positioning plays in the development of the conceptual and linguistic knowledge in STEM.

Context of the Research

Science for All Academy (hereafter referred to as SFAA) is a small, district-run public charter school in a mid-sized city situated in the western United States. The school serves students in Grades 6–12 and offers a rigorous science-focused curriculum. All students spend extra time in science classes and have a greater number of science credits required upon graduation than the minimum set by the state. In the 2014–2015 school year, the school reported a student population that identified as 47% White, 37% Hispanic, 6% Pacific Islander, 5% African American, 3% Multiracial, and 1% Asian. In addition, the school reported that 8% of students were classified as ELs.

The ninth-grade classroom that served as the site for this research was led by a teacher who had 10 years of teaching experience and bachelor's and master's degrees in physics education, as well as state licensure in physics and an ESL endorsement. Mr. Henderson (a pseudonym) had also won numerous awards for physics teaching.

The three lab groups were made up of six students who participated with one another in different configurations across the three labs: (1) Sofia, an EL from the Dominican Republic; (2) Rose, a Spanish-English bilingual Latina student from a non-affluent family; (3) Henry, a White middle-class male with parents who are scientists; (4) Alexis, a Biracial student from a non-affluent family; (5) Andrea, a bilingual Latina student with exceptional grades but non-scientist parents; and (6) Candace, a White middle-class student with parents who are both scientists. Henry, Alexis, and Candace were all native English speakers.

The focal participant of the research was Sofia. At the time of data collection, she was in her first year at SFAA and was designated an EL by the school as a result of language testing. Her socialization pathway was intricately connected to a student called Rose, who was present in all of the labs. Sofia often relied on Rose and another bilingual student, Andrea (present in Lab 3 only), to translate both linguistic and cultural information for her.

Research Questions Addressed

Two research questions motivated the study.

1. What pathway of socialization does one EL undergo while participating in science inquiry labs?
2. What language and education policies directly and indirectly shape the EL's socialization pathway?

Research Methods

The research methodology for this study employed both ethnographic and discourse analytic methods. In this section, we discuss our data collection and analysis procedures.

Data Collection

Data were collected weekly with one to three visits per week for seven months. Data sources included field notes, audio and video recordings of whole class and small group discussions, interviews with the teacher and students, and artifacts (e.g., copies of student work and photos of lab set-ups.). From over 200 hours of audio and video recordings, a corpus of 19 hours of classroom interaction was created for detailed discourse analysis. The corpus data were spread across three different inquiry tasks that were undertaken by students in the labs. The results presented here focus on the data from the discourse corpus.

Data Analysis Procedures Used

Data were analyzed using an iterative process (Glesne, 2011), and discourse was analyzed following the methods outlined by Wortham and Reyes (2015) for conducting discourse analysis within and across speech events. This process allowed us to identify links or pathways in social and linguistic activity across the three labs.

In order to answer Research Question 1, the data in the discourse corpus that involved Sofia were identified, and the interactions in which she was present were tagged according to participants' orientations to the three identity models. The discourse was subjected to a detailed analysis to identify and trace Sofia's pathway of socialization both within each of the labs and across the lab tasks. To answer Research Question 2, Sofia's pathway was reexamined to determine how it was shaped, both directly and indirectly, by the teacher's pedagogical choices and by policy.

Findings and Discussion

Sofia predominately exhibited practices of the good assistant and good student and did not occupy the science expert role in any of these labs. The following sections describe her participation in the three labs, showing how these data were used to answer the research questions. These data also show how the teacher directly and indirectly influenced the opportunities Sofia had for language and content learning during inquiry tasks.

Lab 1—Modeling Newton's Law of Gravitation

In Lab 1, students modeled the inverse square relationship $(1/x^2)$ found in Newton's Law of Gravitation by varying the distance of a light source from a device designed to measure or approximate a reading of light intensity. In this model, students determined the relationship between the variables of distance and light intensity as a metaphor for thinking about the relationship between distance and the gravitational force of attraction between two objects.

Sofia consistently participated in the role of a good assistant in this lab by listening to her peers and retrieving materials for them when they expressed a need. She was often silent during discussions with all group members, but she did participate in one-to-one conversations with Rose. To understand some of the language socialization processes for Sofia, a dialogue with four of the participants is presented in Extract 1. The transcription conventions used for the extracts appear in Figure 11.1.

Symbol	*Meaning*
H	Henry
A	Alexis
S	Sofia
R	Rose
.	end of intonation unit; falling intonation
,	end of intonation unit; fall–rise intonation
?	end of intonation unit; rising intonation
=	latching; no pause between intonation units
–	self-interruption; break in the word, sound abruptly cut off
(p.p)	measured pause of greater than 0.5 seconds
@	laughter; each token marks one pulse
[]	overlapping speech
()	uncertain transcription
#	unintelligible; each token marks one syllable
< >	transcriber comment, nonvocal noise, gesture, or gaze

FIGURE 11.1 Transcription Conventions

The Absence of Language-focused Policy **135**

As the dialogue in Lab 1 begins, students are constructing the light box for the experiment.

Extract 1

9. H: Wenh wenh wenh wenh wenh wenh, I feel like maybe we should get another
10. piece cause this isn't very flat especially when it's up there. No so we could like get
11. a piece of this paper and get like make our own paper. Or we could even just write
12. it, put it on the paper that's a good idea.
13. A: What is @@? =
14. H: =Get=
15. A: =You keep changing your mind @@ [as you're talking to me. *<smiling>*
16. H: [@   sorry. I'm sorry.
17. A: It's like or maybe we should or maybe hunh? mm that's a good idea *<funny*
18. *voice>*
19. H: wow <talking quietly to self>
20. R: Lost. (1.0) Can I make the little box thing?
21. H: Wow w-well you could make a b-a square. You wanna make a square?
22. R: @@ yay making a square @@
23. H: Yay making squares ow.
24. A: Ow @@
25. H: Ow
26. A: Ow
27. H: O:w (4.5) could you just cut, see where this mark is?
28. R: No I don't.
29. H: Cut that like that and the[n:
30. R: [Where's the other mark. Isn't it that one?
31. H: Wait there yeah.
32. R: [Okay
33. H: [Just cut it, cut a square out.
34. R: ## scissors ##
35. S: Okay I will get
36. R: Hunh?
37. H: Say what?
38. S: I will get the scissors. ## okay?

A number of factors point to Sofia's positioning as a good assistant in this interaction. First, she does not speak until Line 35, allowing the other students to talk about the light box they are constructing. When Sofia does speak, it is clear that she had been listening to her peers because she offers to collect scissors for the group in Lines 35 and 38. Although this task represents some level of participation, there is no indication that Sofia is participating in the negotiation of science concepts, and she does not use any lab-related technical vocabulary. To understand what might have prevented Sofia from participating in other ways in this interaction, it is important to study the interaction among all four participants.

Henry occupies the position of science expert, as he thinks aloud about how to modify the light box (Lines 9–12). Alexis uses the pronoun "me" in Line 15, indicating that she and Henry are aligned in a conversation that excludes Rose and Sofia. When Rose indicates that she is "Lost" (in Line 20), neither Henry nor Alexis respond to her. She follows the statement about being lost with a request to be included by making "the little box thing" (Line 23). In this way, Rose is trying to take up a good assistant position in the group as a way of actively participating in the lab despite not having control over the task. Sofia observed these interactions and many similar ones over the course of Lab 1. To participate in a conversation about the science content of the lab, Sofia would have had to force herself into a conversation to which she was not being invited.

Lab 2—Measuring Electrostatic Force

In Lab 2, students measured the electrostatic force between a packet of salt and a balloon charged with static electricity. Sofia worked with Rose and Henry in this lab as well; however, rather than allowing her peers to characterize her only as a good assistant, there were moments in Sofia's interactions in which she attempted to be recognized as a good student by her peers. In Extract 2, Sofia participates as a good student by engaging with Rose as she lowers the balloon over a packet of salt and, later, by giving Rose instructions.

Extract 2

72. H: You zero it no yeah. Yup okay. No! [you don't touch it to the envelope ## things
73. R: [A::::::::h!
74. S: [A::::::::h!
75. H: M-maybe hold it like this
76. S and/or R: We tried that
    ---Deleted one line, non-group member comment---
78. R: How much salt did you put in there?
79. H: Ah I don't know, I don't think it matters. Like that much I mean you can't put a
80. ton in.
81. R: It is so hard.

The Absence of Language-focused Policy **137**

82. S: Do it fast.
83. R: The hardest
84. H: Do it like all around
85. S: Yeah
86. H: Not just like that.
87. R: I know I am but it's pretty hard.
88. H: Don't don't let it touch anything.

In Lines 72–74, Henry instructs Rose not to touch the charged balloon to the salt packet because this action would transfer the charge from the balloon to the packet. When Rose accidentally touches the balloon to the packet, Sofia's overlapping exclamation in Line 74 indicates that she follows the logic. In Line 76, the use of "we" aligns Rose and Sofia, indicating that they are working together. Sofia's participation in the lab by working with Rose initially and by giving instructions to Rose (Line 82) indicates that Sofia participated in Lab 2 differently when compared to Lab 1. Despite demonstrating that she had the ability to participate in collaborative behaviors and issue commands, practices which align more with the good student or science expert identities, she was not able to maintain this type of participation throughout her lab experiences. For example, after the command Sofia issues to Rose in Line 82, Henry quickly assumes the science expert role. Despite some moves that showed she was capable of good student and science expert participation, Sofia still did not participate as a science expert in this lab. Participating as a science expert would have required her to compete for this role with Henry, who identified himself as a science expert across the different lab tasks.

Lab 3—Measuring the Speed of a Wave

In Lab 3, students measured the speed of a wave traveling through a rope that was suspended between two table legs. Two accelerometers were attached to the rope and a hand-held lab computer with a fixed distance between them. In this lab, Sofia again participated as a good student and a good assistant while she worked with Rose. Andrea and Candace participated as science experts in this group. Early in the lab Sofia held the lab computer but was unsure about changing the settings. She asked Andrea, "Do we have to go to rate to change it?" Andrea responded, "You know how to change it, right Candace?" After this exchange, Candace took the computer from Sofia and did not return it. As a result, Candace was the only student who had access to collecting the data and evaluating their quality. This interaction was pivotal in placing Candace in the position of science expert because her peers made adjustments to the lab setup as a result of Candace's interpretations of the data. Candace's prior knowledge of how to manipulate the lab computer allowed her to accumulate additional science expertise that was denied to the other members of the group who did not view or manipulate the lab computer. Although Sofia demonstrated interest in learning how to use the lab computer by asking how to change a setting at the beginning of the lab, she was denied the opportunity to develop that expertise because of the way in which she was socialized by her peers.

An analysis of Sofia's participation in the three labs demonstrates that her disciplinary identity and related expertise were shaped by the interactions with her peers as she conformed to their expectations. The fact that Sofia was unable to articulate an identity as a science expert is important because students who occupy the role of science expert have an advantage over other students; they have opportunities to test out their scientific content knowledge, to instruct others, and to have firsthand access to data and lab equipment. Sofia did not voluntarily and regularly participate in classroom discourse; she only verbally participated in peer groups. This behavior is not unusual for ELs who often choose not to participate in whole class discussions. Consequently, the interaction among her peers in labs may be even more important for her content and language learning than is teacher-led instruction. The way in which Sofia was socialized by her peers to participate in peer groups as a non-expert had important implications for her in-the-moment learning and may also impact how she will see herself relative to STEM disciplines in making future career choices.

Although the interactions described in this chapter took place in peer groups in labs, it is important to remember that it was the teacher who played an important role in how his students were socialized in their lab groups because he created the lab assignments and also the classroom culture that supported the peer interactions that ultimately developed in the lab groups. The teacher indirectly facilitated the creation of the roles that students carried out in their lab groups by not providing an explicit structure for determining which students in the lab would take leadership roles and by not providing instruction on the specific language that students needed for collaborating and for conducting and carrying out the scientific investigations. As a result, students relied on their pre-existing expertise and on ways to collaborate with one another in their lab groups that together resulted in the reproduction of social hierarchies that already existed when the students entered the classroom.

Implications for Policy, Practice, and Future Research

STEM education is of utmost importance in the United States and in developing countries throughout the world because modern economies revolve around expertise in STEM fields. To meet societal demands, local educational agencies, such as schools, strive to build stronger STEM curricula, as well as a strong core of STEM teachers. In these endeavors, strong teacher education programs for STEM teachers are vital. However, teacher education in STEM fields has traditionally focused on the need for teachers to develop high levels of content area expertise and some general pedagogical knowledge (e.g., planning lessons and

The Absence of Language-focused Policy **139**

using multi-media). These values are reflected in disciplinary standards and in the ways that teachers and their students are held accountable for science learning on standardized tests.

The data from the three labs show that language socialization plays a role in how high school students develop identities as science students and how they affiliate with the discipline. As Sofia's pathway in developing expertise as a science student was tracked and analyzed, it became apparent that the choices she made were in large part influenced by how she was socialized by her peers and by the lab practices that were put into play by her peers and her teacher. The teacher played a role in influencing and directing the language socialization pathways of the learners in his class. Although he was a highly qualified and experienced STEM teacher, his instructional practices demonstrated lack of awareness of his own potential for influencing the socialization pathways of his students. By not recognizing the important role he could play in helping students develop disciplinary language, the teacher had, unknowingly and against his desired outcomes, created an environment that enabled a subset of students to accumulate expertise as a result of the lab experiences, as opposed to creating labs in which all students were given the chance to develop expertise as scientists.

If the educational gaps are to be narrowed and more students from language minority backgrounds are to choose STEM professions, STEM teachers must be aware of the importance of disciplinary language and language socialization in their classrooms. The highly qualified teacher in this study met the state's requirements, but it was not enough to shift his attention to the ways in which language operated in his classroom. The standards that the teacher used to guide his instruction and for which he was held accountable by the state were not focused on the role of language in this particular science discipline. In addition, the ESL endorsement curriculum in the state does not provide explicit guidelines related to language socialization research. We argue that science content standards, such as NGSS, that focus teachers' attention on science practices and science content knowledge, should also include attention to science language. In addition, ESL endorsement programs that serve mainstream content-area teachers should include language socialization research in their curricula. Making these two policy changes would encourage teachers to develop an awareness of the role that language plays in constructing science knowledge and in influencing students' science-related identities.

References

Braden, S. K. (2016). *Scientific inquiry as social and linguistic practice: Language socialization pathways in a ninth-grade physics class* (Unpublished doctoral dissertation). University of Utah, Salt Lake City.

Carlone, H. B., Haun-Frank, J., & Webb, A. (2011). Assessing equity beyond knowledge- and skills-based outcomes: A comparative ethnography of two fourth-grade reform-based science classrooms. *Journal of Research in Science Teaching, 48*(5), 459–485.

Cohn, D., & Caumont, A. (2016). *Ten demographic trends that are shaping the U.S. and the world*. Retrieved May 24, 2017 from www.pewresearch.org/fact-tank/2016/03/31/10-demographic-trends-that-are-shaping-the-u-s-and-the-world/

Glesne, C. (2011). *Becoming qualitative researchers* (4th ed.). Boston, MA: Pearson.

Goldberg, C. (2008). Teaching English language learners: What the research does—and does not—say. *American Educator, 8*(23), 42–44. Retrieved May 24, 2017 from www.aft.org/sites/default/files/periodicals/goldenberg.pdf.

Lee, O., Quinn, H., & Valdés, G. (2013). Science and language for English language learners in relation to Next generation science standards and with implications for common core state standards for English language arts and mathematics. *Educational Researcher, 42*(4), 223–233.

Longman, J. (2008). Language socialization. In J. M. Gonzalez (Ed.), *Encyclopedia of bilingual education* (pp. 490–493). Thousand Oaks, CA: Sage Publications.

National Research Council. (2011). *Successful K-12 STEM education: Identifying effective approaches in science, technology, engineering, and mathematics*. Committee on Highly Successful Science Programs for K-12 Science Education. Board on Science Education and Board on Testing and Assessment, Division of Behavioral and Social Sciences and Education. Washington, DC: The National Academies Press.

NGSS Lead States. (2013). *Next generation science standards: For states, by states*. Retrieved May 24, 2017 from www.nextgenscience.org/

U.S. Census Bureau. (2011). *American community survey*. Retrieved May 24, 2017 from www.census.gov/acs/www/

U.S. Department of Commerce. (2011). STEM: *Good jobs now and for the future*. Retrieved May 24, 2017 from www.esa.doc.gov/sites/default/files/reports/documents/stemfinalyjuly14_1.pdf

Wortham, S., & Reyes, A. (2015). *Discourse analysis beyond the speech event*. London, UK: Routledge.

12

BILINGUALISM FOR ALL?

Interrogating Language and Equity in Dual Language Immersion in Wisconsin

Laura Hamman

In recent decades, bilingual education has gained renewed popularity in the United States in the form of dual language programs. Unlike earlier transitional bilingual models, which provided home language support until minority-language students could be 'transitioned' to mainstream classrooms, two-way dual language immersion (DLI) serves both minority language and majority language students and teaches academic content through two languages with the goal of bilingualism for all. Research has shown these programs to be largely successful in reconceptualizing minority languages and cultures as resources (Fitts, 2006; Palmer, Martínez, Mateus, & Henderson, 2014) and in bolstering the academic success of English learners (Lindholm-Leary & Hernandez, 2011; Thomas & Collier, 2012). However, there is growing concern that DLI is unsuccessful in meeting broader goals of linguistic, social, and cultural equity (Pérez, 2004). Understanding local discourses and policies that shape implementation of dual language models is essential for designing more equitable programs.

In this chapter, I present findings from a case study of a social justice–oriented DLI school in a mid-sized city in Wisconsin called Lakeville (a pseudonym, as are all subsequent names of people and places). I explore local policy and ideological discourses around bilingualism that shaped program design and implementation, including the potential for DLI to foster more equitable educational contexts. Language policy and planning scholars have called for increased attention to the role of local agents in shaping policy implementation (Johnson, 2013; Wiley & García, 2016); in response, this study considers the role of teachers, board members, administrators, and community activists in sustaining a social justice focus in their efforts to implement the district's first dual language program. Findings reveal the co-existence of multiple, competing discourses around bilingualism and

142 Laura Hamman

demonstrate the power of local policy actors to foster more equitable educational models.

Issues That Motivated the Research

Despite national enthusiasm for DLI, some scholars caution that these programs may be perpetuating the same inequities they aim to combat (Valdés, 1997). Some argue that DLI is largely framed around the interests of White, English-speaking parents, who view Spanish acquisition as a means to increase their children's employment opportunities (Scanlan & Palmer, 2009). This focus on majority language speakers contributes to the commodification of Spanish and might cause programs to de-emphasize goals of bilingualism and biliteracy (Cervantes-Soon, 2014). At present, we lack an adequate understanding of the ideologies that shape DLI program design, which limits our ability to foster more equitable programs. Additionally, while the empirical base for dual language programs has grown, much of the extant literature does not reflect the breadth of sociolinguistic contexts in which DLI programs are realized. We need deeper, contextual understanding of the competing discourses that shape how dual language programs are implemented to inform policy making and program design.

Context of the Research

In the early 2000s, a group of equity-minded teachers, administrators, parents, and community members in Lakeville approached the school board with the aim of establishing a dual language immersion charter school. While initially resistant, the district eventually granted approval, and Escuela Bilingüe (K–5) was established. In the immediate years following, the success and popularity of Escuela Bilingüe led the Lakeville school board to adopt DLI district-wide. Now, just over a decade later, I consider the ideologies that shaped the initial program design and those that continue to impact the social justice mission of Escuela Bilingüe.

Research Questions Addressed

Acknowledging the dialogic relationship between language ideologies and program implementation, this chapter addresses two research questions:

1. What are the local ideologies and policies around bilingualism?
2. How did they shape the design and implementation of a DLI program in a mid-sized city in Wisconsin?

Ultimately, I hope this research will inform policy making and program design by documenting the competing ideologies that shape program implementation

Bilingualism for All? **143**

and providing evidence for how equity-driven local policy actors can foster transformative dual language schools.

Research Methods

This research aligns with an ecological approach to language planning and policy, engaging in the process of "unpeeling the onion" (Ricento & Hornberger, 1996, p. 401) to explore how a local DLI program is embedded in discourses, ideologies, and policies around language at multiple, interrelated levels. Varied perspectives were sought from administrators, consultants, board members, and teachers who had participated in the implementation and/or cultivation of the program in Lakeville. The inclusion of teachers was particularly important, as critical policy analysts have argued that so-called "nonauthorized policy actors" (Levinson, Sutton, & Winstead, 2009, p. 768) have a significant role to play in program efficacy. In addition to interview data, local policies and media related to bilingualism and DLI were analyzed. These sources helped paint a rich picture of the multiple ideologies around language and education in this community—and the potential for both to act as catalysts for equity.

Data Collection

In my data collection, I first reviewed state- and district-level policies to uncover the 'official' discourses around bilingualism and bilingual education in this community. I also examined relevant newspaper articles from 2015, the year the district proposed expanding the existing DLI program. Next, key program implementers were interviewed, including three administrators, two teachers, two board members, and one program consultant. Everyone was interviewed once, with questions about his or her involvement in the DLI program in Lakeville and perceptions of the affordances and constraints of dual language immersion.

Data Analysis Procedures Used

State and district policies and local media underwent content analysis to identify, organize, and index words that clustered around the conceptual idea of bilingualism. Interview data were transcribed and analyzed from a critical discourse analytic perspective (Gee, 2011; Rogers, 2011) to interrogate power-laden values and ideologies that framed local policy actors' interpretations of DLI. In keeping with the poststructuralist tradition (Bakhtin, 1981; Foucault, 1980), I explored tensions within these discourses and considered how they intersect with issues of equity. All data were analyzed with multiple rounds of open-ended and thematic coding (Saldaña, 2009). Throughout this process, I attended to recurring patterns and contradictions to identify and construct

144 Laura Hamman

emergent conceptual categories and themes (LeCompte & Schensul, 2010), which evolved into my central findings.

Findings and Discussion

In his seminal article, Ruiz (1984) posited three orientations to language planning: language-as-a-problem, language-as-a-right, and language-as-a-resource. Applying these constructs to perspectives of bilingualism, I argue that all three approaches simultaneously shape bilingual education in Wisconsin, broadly, and the district's DLI program, in particular. Furthermore, I contend that all three orientations require the interrogative lens, "for whom?" That is, *for whom* is bilingualism perceived as a problem, something to be eradicated? *For whom* is bilingualism a right that must be advocated for and preserved? *For whom* is bilingualism a resource that can be leveraged for future success?

Bilingualism-as-a-problem

The framing of bilingualism-as-a-problem is salient in Chapter 115, Subchapter VII of Wisconsin Statutes (2009–10), entitled "Bilingual-Bicultural Education," the policy that addresses state alignment with federal guidelines on educating English learners. The statute begins with a deficit framing of bilingualism: "There are pupils in this state who enter elementary and secondary school with limited or nonexistent English-speaking ability due to the use of another language in their family or in their daily, non-school environment" (Wis. Stats. § 115.95(1a)). This description not only ignores the richness of students' linguistic resources but, further, affixes blame for their "limited or nonexistent" English skills on their home language.

Indeed, despite its nomenclature, Subchapter VII does not endorse bilingualism; rather, it outlines a transitional bilingual model that permits students' home languages only as bridge toward English language acquisition:

> It is the policy of this state that fundamental courses may be taught in the pupil's non-English language to support the understanding of concepts, while the ultimate objective shall be to provide a proficiency in those courses in the English language in order that the pupil will be able to participate fully in a society whose language is English.
>
> *(Wis. Stats. § 115.95(5))*

This description reflects a subtractive view of bilingual education (Lambert, 1975), as the goal is to attain English proficiency, not to maintain both languages. The justification for home language erasure is even more troubling. Whereas English proficiency enables students to take full advantage of U.S. systems and institutions, claiming that the language of society "is English" ignores the social and historical reality that multilingualism has always characterized this nation and that other languages are beneficial—and often necessary—for full participation in local communities. In sum, Subchapter VII does not recognize bilingualism and biculturalism as assets in and of themselves and establishes (monolingual) English acquisition as its principal objective.

Bilingualism-as-a-resource

In contrast to the state's position, local media tend to frame bilingualism as a resource, with tangible economic benefits. Wisconsin Public Radio described the DLI program as "a new way to teach a foreign language," and a local newspaper cited the program's potential for "building a world class school system" that prepares students to engage in the 21st-century economy (note: specific citations are not provided where the anonymity of the school might be threatened). These descriptions frame DLI around its ability to promote global competitiveness, not cross-cultural awareness. They also focus on native English speakers learning an additional (foreign) language, ignoring goals of bilingualism and biliteracy for all students. Indeed, when Spanish-dominant students in DLI were referenced in local media, they were often termed "students who don't speak English" or "foreign language–speaking kids." This view ignores the linguistic resources these students do possess and frames their home language as "foreign," despite the long history of Spanish in the US, which, in fact, predates English.

In interviews with local policy actors, there was also an underlying discourse of bilingualism-as-a-resource. For example, Kim Johnson, the program consultant, described bilingualism as an "essential 21st-century skill." For that reason, she pushed back against recent critiques of the gentrification of bilingual education (e.g., Valdez, Freire, & Delavan, 2016) that aim to reframe bilingual education around language minority children. Instead, Kim argued that bilingual programs ought to be designed to serve *all* students. In her view, dual language immersion accomplished this goal because it is "fundamentally designed to promote . . . bilingualism and biliteracy for all." She elaborated:

> It [the present-day bilingual education movement] reminds me of Trump's message: "I'm going to bring manufacturing back." Really? You're going to bring back coal mining? Have you looked around the world to see that we've become an information-based society? Have you looked around the world to see what impact coal mining and fossil fuel energy has had and where we are today and what our needs are today? . . . [Similarly,] the conversation has changed from monolingualism for all, which was really the U.S. agenda with bilingual education, to bilingualism and biliteracy for all, not just for some.

This analogy, comparing language education to natural resources, relays the consultant's position that returning to bilingualism for some (i.e., language minority

146 Laura Hamman

students) is as misguided as the attempt to reinstate manufacturing and mining within the current technological and information-based demands of U.S. society. From this perspective, then, bilingualism is a 21st-century resource that should be accessible to all.

Most local policy actors shared some vision of bilingualism as a resource, but they tended to emphasize this perspective in connection to fostering stronger global and local relationships. Raquel Salvador, a DLI teacher at Escuela Bilingüe, explained that bilingualism laid the groundwork for a global perspective: "We are giving our students the ability to look outside of our little community here in the classroom or the city . . . our kids are more open to what's going on in the world, and how they can affect the world." Another teacher, Gabriela Thompson, described bilingualism as a way for students to serve their local communities. She shared:

> I've had parents say that they hope their kids can be bilingual so that they can help their community, so they can be a resource for other immigrants who are coming to Lakeville . . . that they can be a lawyer or a policeman or someone that is able to bridge that cultural and linguistic divide.

Here, bilingualism does not serve the individual, but the community. Becoming bilingual enables a student to become a cultural and linguistic bridge between the Latino community and U.S. institutions.

When asked how bilingualism benefitted native-English-speaking students, Raquel shared an example of one former student who recently purchased property in Costa Rica, thanks to his strong Spanish skills. Bilingualism, in this case, did not serve a communal goal; rather, it provided one student with the chance to advance economically. Thus, the ability to leverage the resource of bilingualism depends upon material and ideational factors that shape how bilingualism can and should be utilized for group or personal advancement.

Bilingualism-as-a-right: A Social Justice Approach

Whereas discourses of bilingualism-as-a-problem and bilingualism-as-a-resource certainly resonate in the Lakeville community, the prevailing understanding of bilingualism at Escuela Bilingüe is bilingualism-as-a-right. Every policy actor interviewed referenced social justice in connection to DLI, albeit with different interpretations of what it means and how to achieve it. For many board members, achieving social justice was the primary reason for founding the school, which was often interwoven with discourses about students' 'right' to bilingualism. This perspective was especially evident from Rebecca Gonzalez, a parent on the Escuela Bilingüe board. She shared that it wasn't "just the language" that made Escuela Bilingüe a unique model. Rather, "there's a whole social justice thread that makes Escuela Bilingüe different." Rebecca went on to elaborate:

Bilingualism for All? **147**

[W]e're trying to raise racial justice warriors. These kids are the ones that grow up in an environment where the brown kids are actually seen as smarter because they know more than the non-Spanish-speaking kids. I mean, that can actually shift biases at such a young age. What it can do for the next generation is phenomenal.

Through this lens, bilingual education serves as a platform for upending societal power dynamics, a space for fostering racial justice.

Rebecca cited "White privilege" as one of the school's biggest challenges, explaining, "I think White parents are excited about their kids learning Spanish, and . . . they know the school system so they create barriers for Spanish-speaking families to get involved and really lead in a meaningful way." One way the school addressed that challenge was by conducting parent meetings in Spanish and offering translating machines to English-speaking parents, which Rebecca argued had been an important move to change participation dynamics. She explained:

I think there's a divide between White parents and parents of color because White parents say, "Well this is how we do it. Let me teach you." And if we turn that upside down and let other people lead in ways that work for them, that's going to make it more successful.

In this perspective, the 'right' to bilingualism shifts power dynamics inside the classroom and out, flipping who is seen as knowledgeable and who is able to participate.

According to Raquel, one of the DLI teachers, bilingual education was about empowering Latino students by validating their language and culture. She explained, "Most of the teachers [at Escuela Bilingüe] are Latinos. We feel the need to give those tools to our kids." When asked about the strengths of Escuela Bilingüe, Raquel stated, "I think that . . . our Latino parents feel proud of our language because it's the first thing that we're learning in kindergarten." This sense of ownership of the school community, expressed through the possessive "*our* kids" and "*our* Latino parents," reveals the connection between the right to bilingualism and the establishment of a Latino community. The Spanish language becomes a tool of empowerment and a mark of pride. Raquel explained that this ideology extends to students:

I've kept contact with a lot of students and . . . when I ask them, "What do you think about Spanish?" they say, "You know, I'm really proud, I'm really happy that my parents put me through the program because . . . I can read and write [in Spanish], and I went to Mexico and I could communicate with my family." So I think that's the kind of empowerment that we're giving to our students.

148   Laura Hamman

According to this teacher, bilingual education is empowerment, providing Latino students the chance to see their home language as valuable and fostering inter-generational connections.

The framing of bilingualism-as-a-right was also embodied in Raquel's right to teach bilingually and to integrate her culture and her experiences into the curriculum. Prior to teaching at Escuela Bilingüe, she worked at a mainstream public school where she felt limited in her ability to integrate culture and pedagogy. Raquel provided the example of a lesson she designed about *Las Posadas*, a traditional Mexican nativity celebration. When she submitted the lesson to the principal, she was told it had to be sent to the school board to determine if it was appropriate. She shared, "I had to explain myself so much that I did not feel the liberty of using it." Now, at Escuela Bilingüe, she finds it much easier to integrate culture: "Here we have the freedom, you know, language comes from other countries and so I have more freedom to give examples of how it is used and when it is used." It is clear that with language comes culture, and the right to integrate that culture into her teaching.

Raquel also shared that she incorporates more of herself into her pedagogy at Escuela Bilingüe. A former migrant farm worker who was the first in her family to attend college, she often shares stories with students about her experiences growing up across different communities. Reflecting upon her storytelling practices, she explained:

> I think it has helped.... I was talking to a fifth grader and he said, "I remember when you told us about you working in the fields. [One time] I didn't want to help my parents and then I thought of you and I got up and I went with my dad to sell churros." ... If I make a difference with one student that's good enough.

The ability—and the right—to teach bilingually provides the platform for the teacher to integrate language and culture and her life experiences into the curriculum.

For the current principal, Mark Lewis, the connection between bilingualism and social justice at Escuela Bilingüe moves beyond the 'right' to language toward the establishment of a strong school community that transcends linguistic boundaries. Mark shared:

> I feel like we have come a long way in really developing what it truly means to have a school that serves the community, and I feel very proud when I look at how our school community has responded to the recent presidential election and all of the campaign promises, particularly around immigration and deportation.

He explained that Escuela Bilingüe recently held a passport fair for immigrant parents to apply for documentation for their children. The school community

Bilingualism for All? **149**

raised $1,000 in three days to help offset costs, and 36 children received passports. Mark shared, "That's just the community coming together to support each other, to protect each other."

As further evidence, the day after the 2016 U.S. presidential election, parents hung signs around the school reminding students that they are all safe and welcome at Escuela Bilingüe. This message has been echoed in the school's announcement board, which frequently displays statements of support. Immediately after the election, the board read, "*Ningun ser humano es ilegal*" (No human being is illegal), and, after the inauguration, it displayed, "*El respeto al derecho ajeno es la paz*" (Respecting the rights of others is peace) (See Figure 12.1).

According to Mark, social justice is both mission and action at Escuela Bilingüe. "You've got to have symbolic acts of support, but you've also got to have real acts of support. . . . I think we've achieved a safe haven, an emotional safe haven."

Whereas most local policy actors framed the 'right' to bilingualism around the Latino community, the educational consultant offered a different perspective, one that sees social justice as fostering bilingualism for all students. She described bilingualism as a 21st-century skill that all students were entitled to receive: "I genuinely believe . . . [that] bilingualism and biliteracy skills are, in today's global marketplace, skills that every child should have access to, every child, regardless of your first language." Whereas this understanding is still framed around the resource of bilingualism (for success in the 'global marketplace'), it expresses the fundamental belief that becoming bilingual is not the 'right' of any one group but, rather, is something that every child deserves. These two perspectives—bilingualism for empowerment of linguistic minority children and bilingualism for all children—reflect the ongoing tension in national conversations about who should benefit from dual language programs. If bilingualism is indeed a 'right,' should it be extended to all children? Which fosters more equity: empowering language minority students or building a bilingual society? Can both goals be accomplished simultaneously or does one necessarily supplant the other?

Implications for Policy, Practice, and Future Research

Spanish-English dual language programs in the United States do not exist in a vacuum. These programs are interwoven with historical, ideological, and sociopolitical discourses that have shaped language-in-education policies across the nation. DLI carries the legacy of the civil rights movement of the 1960s, which provided the first legislation to address the educational rights of linguistic minority children. It exists in ongoing tension with the English-only movement, whose xenophobic cries resurfaced in the 1980s and live on today. Finally, DLI is embedded in broader shifts of globalization and neoliberalism, which have contributed to more asset-based views of multilingualism, but have also led to the commodification of minority languages and speakers (Cervantes-Soon, 2014; Flores, 2013).

FIGURE 12.1 Signs of Community Support at Escuela Bilingüe

In many ways, Escuela Bilingüe is a microcosm for the intersection of these broader discourses around bilingualism. The 'official' policy of the state still largely frames bilingualism-as-a-problem, undergirded by the nativist position that holds English as the language of society and non-English speakers as deficient. Reverberations of the economization of education have spurred the framing of DLI as a progressive model, preparing students to be more competitive in the global market. The school itself is grounded in discourses of equity—the right of (Latino) students to become bilingual, the right of teachers to teach culturally and bilingually, the right of (Latino) parents to become school leaders. These varying positions have implications for researchers and policy makers, who must interrogate the discourses around bilingualism within local communities to critically examine who or what is prioritized in DLI and find ways to build more equity-focused models.

This research also has implications for practice. Escuela Bilingüe demonstrates that, among the competing discourses, it is possible to maintain a social justice focus, but it requires an engagement with the "nonlinguistic dimensions of diversity" (Scanlan & Palmer, 2009, p. 4). To truly engage in transformative practice, schools must also acknowledge that students have differential access to resources outside of the classroom. Bilingualism allows some students to communicate with their grandparents and become leaders in their communities; it allows others to purchase property in Costa Rica. These realities must not be ignored when considering who and what to prioritize in DLI. It takes work to build cultural and linguistic bridges, to foster a school community where every member is valued. The creation of equitable DLI programs requires activism and the willingness to take a stand when some members of the community are threatened. Escuela Bilingüe presents one example of a school that is cognizant of the great opportunity—and great challenge—of becoming a transformative educational space.

References

Bakhtin, M. (1981). *The dialogic imagination*. Austin, TX: University of Texas Press.

Cervantes-Soon, C. G. (2014). A critical look at dual language immersion in the New Latin@ Diaspora. *Bilingual Research Journal, 37*(1), 64–82.

Fitts, S. (2006). Reconstructing the status quo: Linguistic interaction in a dual-language school. *Bilingual Research Journal, 30*(2), 337–365.

Flores, N. (2013). The unexamined relationship between neoliberalism and plurilingualism: A cautionary tale. *TESOL Quarterly, 47*(3), 500–520.

Foucault, M. (1980). *Power/knowledge: Selected interviews and other writings*. New York, NY: Pantheon.

Gee, J. P. (2011). *An introduction to discourse analysis: Theory and method* (3rd ed.). New York, NY: Routledge.

Johnson, D. (2013). Positioning the language policy arbiter: Govermentality and footing in the school district of Philadelphia. In J. Tollefson (Ed.), *Language policies in education: Critical issues* (2nd ed.) (pp. 116–135). New York, NY: Routledge.

Lambert, W. E. (1975). Culture and language as factors in learning and education. In A. Wolfgang (Ed.), *Education of immigrant students: Issues and answers* (pp. 55–83). Toronto, Canada: Ontario Institute for Studies in Education.

LeCompte, M. D., & Schensul, J. J. (2010). *Designing and conducting ethnographic research* (Vol. 1). Lanham, MD: Altamira Press.

Levinson, B. A. U., Sutton, M., & Winstead, T. (2009). Education policy as a practice of power theoretical tools, ethnographic methods, democratic options. *Educational Policy*, *23*(6), 767–795.

Lindholm-Leary, K. J., & Hernandez. A. (2011). Achievement and language proficiency of Latino students in dual language programmes: Native English speakers, fluent English/ previous ELLs, and current ELLs. *Journal of Multilingual and Multicultural Development*, *32*(6), 531–545.

Palmer, D. K., Martínez, R. A., Mateus, S. G., & Henderson, K. (2014). Reframing the debate on language separation: Toward a vision for translanguaging pedagogies in the dual language classroom. *The Modern Language Journal*, *98*(3), 757–772.

Pérez, B. (2004). *Becoming biliterate: A study of two-way bilingual immersion education*. Mahwah, NJ: Erlbaum.

Ricento, T. K., & Hornberger, N. H. (1996). Unpeeling the onion: Language planning and policy and the ELT professional. *TESOL Quarterly*, *30*(3), 401–427.

Rogers, R. (Ed.). (2011). *An introduction to critical discourse analysis in education*. New York, NY: Routledge.

Ruiz, R. (1984). Orientations in language planning. *NABE Journal*, *8*(2), 15–34.

Saldaña, J. (2009). *The coding manual for qualitative researchers*. Los Angeles, CA: Sage.

Scanlan, M., & Palmer, D. (2009). Race, power, and (in)equity within two-way immersion settings. *The Urban Review*, *41*(5), 391–415.

Thomas, W. P., & Collier, V. P. (2012). *Dual language education for a transformed world*. Albuquerque, NM: Dual Language Education of New Mexico Fuente Press.

Valdés, G. (1997). Dual language immersion programs: A cautionary note concerning the education of language-minority students. *Harvard Educational Review*, *67*, 391–429.

Valdez, V. E., Freire, J. A., & Delavan, M. G. (2016). The gentrification of dual language education. *The Urban Review*, *48*(4), 601–627.

Wiley, T. G., & García, O. (2016). Language policy and planning in language education: Legacies, consequences, and possibilities. *The Modern Language Journal*, *100*, 48–63.

Wisconsin Statutes. (2009–2010). *Chapter 115, Subchapter VII, Bilingual-Bicultural Education, 115.95–115.996*. Retrieved July 6, 2017 from https://docs.legis.wisconsin.gov/statutes/statutes/115/VII/

13

MEDIA DISCOURSES OF LANGUAGE POLICY AND THE "NEW" LATINO DIASPORA IN IOWA

Crissa Stephens

Issues That Motivated the Research

In response to changing student populations, school districts across the United States must implement equitable language policies that uphold bilingual students' civil rights. (For the sake of simplicity, the term *bilingual* is used throughout this chapter to include students who use more than one language.) Currently, 1 out of 10 U.S. students is labeled an English learner (EL) and is participating in a language education program. These students have the right to equal and meaningful education (Lau v. Nichols, 1974), and educational research has documented the effectiveness of multilingual approaches toward achieving this goal (Freeman, 1998; Rolstad, Mahoney, & Glass, 2005). However, national language policy affords states the power to choose the role non-English languages will play in education.

Historically, U.S. language policy has been determined by a blend of policy discourses, political perspectives, and ideologies, and it has been heavily influenced by social and economic factors apart from language itself (Gutierrez, Asato, Santos, & Gotanda, 2002; Ovando, 2003). Language policy is "always about more than language" (Ricento, 2006, p. 6). As schools with growing numbers of ELs develop policies, they draw on ideologies, beliefs, attitudes, and discourses (Hult & Pietikäinen, 2014; D. Johnson, 2015) that impact policy choices and shape the social environment in which language education takes place. Language policy processes in local contexts cannot be understood without an understanding of the ideologies, discourses, and beliefs at work in a particular context.

News media are potential sources of insight into the relevant beliefs, ideologies, and discourses in local contexts. To the extent that news media discuss and debate educational language policies, they provide a window into opinions and arguments circulating about those policies (Wodak, 2006). Like all language, the

154 Crissa Stephens

language of the media has the power to reflect and refract ideologies (Voloshinov, 1973). Because policies are couched in the contexts of language ideologies and societal attitudes (de Jong, 2011; Flores & Schissel, 2014; McCarty, 2011) and because the media play a role in mediating society back to itself (Matheson, 2005), the motivation for the present study is to explore media representations of the dual language education program in the small town of West Liberty, Iowa. This research used a multi-layered, intertextual analysis that considers connections between policy discourses and the language of local newspapers and a news radio program at the state, regional, and local levels as they relate to dual language education in Iowa.

Critical analyses of media language are timely. National focus has been drawn to the media's role in the 2016 presidential election through *fake news*—a term originally used to refer to websites falsely posing on social media as news sources covering the election. Shortly after the election, the term *fake news* was employed regularly by the Trump administration to criticize mainstream news organizations. As society grapples with media language on a national level, research that systematically analyzes such language offers a valuable empirical perspective on the truth claims, arguments, and production of media texts. In such an analysis, a critical perspective on the production of media texts is useful because power relations structure their construction (Fairclough, 2015). News media typically position themselves as objective observers of current events, projecting validity to make their claims more powerful for those who rely on them for information about current social issues (Matheson, 2005). In actuality, media texts are created by producers with an ideal audience in mind; those producers determine what is included and excluded and how events are represented while projecting an air of common sense. Therefore, there is always a hidden ideological power in media discourse (Fairclough, 1992, 2015) which must be considered.

Context of the Research

Some U.S. states have received ample attention from language policy researchers, whereas others have seen relatively little. Research has typically focused on states with markedly restrictive language policies or on urban centers with established concentrations of EL students (e.g., Fitzsimmons-Doolan, 2009; E. Johnson, 2005; Tarasawa, 2009). This research has found that bilingual education is often portrayed unfavorably in media coverage. In a 10-year analysis of major national newspapers, McQuillan and Tse (1996) found that articles, editorials, and opinion pieces were decidedly against bilingual education and that more space was devoted to pieces against it than in favor of it. Sutton-Jones (2013) found that news media often misinterpret educational research or ignore it altogether, and there are issues with the type of coverage provided—namely that the news industry often highlights controversy and manufactures educational crises (Rickford, 1999; Sutton-Jones, 2013; Waller, 2012). The existing research illuminates media representations of bilingual education found in national newspapers, in contexts where language policy debates are contentious, and in places where the public has voted in favor of monolingual education.

These studies lend valuable insight into media discourses of language policy, but less is known about suburban and rural school districts with changing student demographics and newly developing policies. A growing number of districts without previous policy structures for ELs are seeing exponential EL population growth and must develop and implement language policies accordingly. Iowa is one such context, experiencing 400% growth in the numbers of EL students over the last 20 years. Many of its small towns have more linguistic diversity per capita than some of the country's largest cities. Some research identifies Iowa as a site of the New Latino Diaspora (Johnson, Lynch, & Stephens, 2015; Wortham, Murillo, & Hamann, 2002). The concept of New Latino Diaspora may be used to situate the context of this study with a caveat: Language policy research itself is susceptible to the semiotic process of erasure identified by Irvine and Gal (2000), wherein counterpoints to a theory are bypassed. Although many nearby Iowa towns have experienced exponential growth in the numbers of Latino students, it is important to recognize that West Liberty's Latino population is not 'new.' The town is home to six generations of Latino residents, and West Liberty was the first school district in the state to implement *dual language education*—a form of bilingual education where both English- and Spanish-speaking students learn language and content through bilingual instruction.

Preliminary policy analysis revealed that Iowa's official language policies bear more intertextual and interdiscursive connections (explained in the following) to monoglossic language ideologies (where English monolingualism is seen as the norm) than to heteroglossic ideologies (where bilingualism is seen as the norm) (Flores & Schissel, 2014), but educators may choose a variety of programs to serve ELs. Iowa's Official English law (SF 165) draws on the monoglossic discourse of academic and social success through English and identifies social and economic achievement as reasons for upholding English proficiency in Iowa. Both SF 165 and Iowa's educational language policy (Iowa legislative code 280.4) suggest the use of and a transition to English inside and outside of education. Iowa's educational language policy guidance for educators, *Educating Iowa's ELLs* (Fairbarn & Jones-Vo, 2010), is based on Iowa Code 280.4. This guidance document identifies English mastery as the main goal of language programs, but bilingualism and biliteracy are listed under bilingual education subheadings. The policy simply lists bilingualism and biliteracy as goals of bilingual education program options; it does not specify whether or how they relate to the state's overarching monoglossic English policies. The appearance of these goals in the document implies that bilingualism and biliteracy are permissible, and the language leaves space for educators to interpret how these goals of bilingual education relate to the overarching goal of English mastery and to other state policies that privilege English. West Liberty's program includes these goals, listing them alongside the additional goals

156 Crissa Stephens

of increasing academic achievement, developing cross-cultural relationships, and forming home-school partnerships (West Liberty Community School District, 2016). Because other Iowa districts have the freedom to implement a variety of language policies in response to their changing populations, studying media representations in local, regional, and state newspapers may provide a useful glimpse into how discourse about West Liberty's language policy interacts with and influences other nearby contexts.

Research Questions Addressed

The following questions are addressed in this chapter:

1. What texts and discourses are drawn upon in the construction of media reports of West Liberty's dual language program?
2. What intertextual and interdiscursive connections exist between the larger social context, the language of news, the language of state policy, and the language of the program's communications?

A *text* can be thought of as any utterance or unit of linguistic production (Bauman & Briggs, 1990), and a *discourse* is a habitual way of representing knowledge about something (Foucault in Hall, 2001).

Research Methods

Data Collection

Data were gathered from three main sources: Iowa state policy documents, 39 newspaper articles and the transcript of a radio show about the bilingual program in West Liberty (primarily found in the Iowa City *Press-Citizen*, the *Des Moines Register*, and Iowa Public Radio), and communications published on the district's website. Within a multi-layered conception of language policy, these sources represent different levels or layers of policy (Ricento & Hornberger, 1996). The Iowa City *Press-Citizen* was chosen for its local and regional reach, and the *Des Moines Register* for its statewide reach. One piece from NPR was used as the only nationally syndicated article available at the time of the study. In addition to newspaper articles, the analysis included the transcript of an episode on Iowa Public Radio (Nebbe, 2013) about language learning in the state.

Data Analysis Procedures Used

This study relied on intertextual analysis (Fairclough, 1992; D. Johnson, 2015) to address the research questions. Intertextual analysis is a means of discourse analysis based on the work of Bakhtin (1981) and Kristeva (1986). It traces how and where particular texts appear inside of other texts with the assumption that all texts have social histories and are influenced by other texts. Whether incorporating state policy, quotes, research, political perspectives, or public opinion, news articles draw upon many different texts and discourses (and omit others) to produce their representations of social issues and language policy. Tracing which discourses local articles draw on (or the interdiscursive connections; Fairclough, 1992), as well as the texts they incorporate directly (or the intertextual connections; Fairclough, 1992), in reporting on language policy can help uncover the meaning of a language policy in that social context as it emerges across time (D. Johnson, 2015). *Intertextual connections* occur when one text is directly incorporated into another, e.g., a language policy (like Iowa's educator handbook) quotes other language policies (like the *Lau v. Nichols* decision). *Interdiscursive connections* occur when a discourse (or a habitual way of representing knowledge about something; Foucault in Hall, 2001) appears in a new context. An example would be when the discourse of the link between English proficiency and national identity—or the idea that, to be an American, you must speak English—appears in the speech of a community member giving an opinion about bilingual education. Using critical intertextual analysis to trace these connections disentangles the ways media representations of language policy are constructed to uncover more about the social context in which they produce and are produced.

Findings and Discussion

Positive Coverage, Exceptions, and Connections to Policy Language

The analysis revealed that news reporting aligned more closely with the program's stated goals than with the monoglossic facets of state legislation. In contrast to previous studies, coverage of West Liberty's program presented an overwhelmingly positive view of bilingual education as constituted by intertextual connections to research showing the benefits of bilingual education, the highlighting of awards and academic achievements in bilingual programs, the views of local residents and educators who expressed satisfaction, and the showcasing of academic gains by students in the programs. Altogether, 32 of the 39 articles and the radio episode displayed these connections, whereas the language of five articles displayed neither positive nor negative intertextual connections. Only one of the articles exhibited an overt connection to a monoglossic language ideology.

The positive impact on the community and state was an overarching theme, of which the following data excerpt is representative:

> "And in the end, all the students then become bilingual, biliterate and bicultural," Gardner says. . . . The program is so successful, several Anglo families have moved to West Liberty from nearby Iowa City, Muscatine and

158 Crissa Stephens

other towns specifically to enroll their kids. The program, which now has a waiting list, is being duplicated in a handful of other Iowa school districts with growing Hispanic populations.

(Inskeep & Montagne, 2011, paras. 22 & 24)

This excerpt uses a direct quote from an administrator, a reference to the success of the program, and references to the program's positive social impact for English-speaking families to construct its representation of the bilingual program. Notably, this article ran in NPR's *Morning Edition* as the only nationally syndicated article in the data set. Therefore, Gardner's direct quote, an intertextual connection to West Liberty's stated program goals, constitutes a positive media representation of bilingual education at the national level.

Another interesting sub-theme was community building through the program. Media touted the program's success in promoting tolerance, combatting racism, meeting social needs, and strengthening community relationships. Representative of this theme are the following excerpts:

Residents say improved relations between different cultures have reinvigorated the town of 6,050. The greater cooperation has led to building and renovation projects, supporters say.

(Boone, 2001, p. A1; note: the actual population of West Liberty is roughly 3,700.)

In many ways, West Liberty is unique with its cohesiveness within the community. The addition of the state's first Dual-Language Program to the school district will only help bring the English and Spanish speakers closer together.

(Hamilton, 2000, p. C14)

This language portrays an image of dual language programming that extends beyond the classroom and into the community. In the news, bilingual education is associated with community cohesiveness, social success, and revitalization of the town. Interestingly, the discourse of increased productivity and social success reported by the media as an effect of dual language education in West Liberty connects interdiscursively to SF 165, which utilizes the same discourse of increased productivity and social success to support its argument for making English the only official state language. Although the language of SF 165 implies that social success comes through English, the message in the media suggests that success is happening through bilingualism and biculturalism. As seen in the language of the prior data samples, the argument for the program's success is based in part on the benefit that is provided to English-speaking children who are given access to Spanish learning in the dual language program.

The only intertextual connection to an overtly monoglossic language ideology displayed in local newspapers was a quote from an out-of-state presidential candidate campaigning for a national election. Mitt Romney is quoted as saying, "To be successful in America, you have to speak the language of America" (Gallegos, 2007, p. A3). This language constitutes an interdiscursive connection to the discourse of social success through English in Iowa policy, but Romney's argument for English monolingual education grossly misaligns with the arguments for social success through bilingualism seen in media reporting and in West Liberty's program communications.

Educational Research and Reporting Style

Further analysis of the language that constituted positive reporting showed that a large percentage of media coverage was made up of direct quotes (i.e., intertextual connections to the speech of educators) and that, in contrast to previous findings, it included multiple intertextual and interdiscursive connections to educational research. Typically, these connections were embedded within the direct speech of educators quoted in the news, but in one instance (shown in the following) the reporter referenced educational research. An article by Boone (2001) contained multiple examples of these types of intertextual connections and interdiscursive connections. Several excerpts from Boone's (2001, p. A1) article are displayed here as a representative example of this facet of newspaper coverage of West Liberty's program:

> Sharon Halcomb, dual-language and ESL director, said quick oral fluency does not help students excel. She said students who are learning English don't usually earn high marks on standardized tests. She predicts dual-language students will eventually outperform all students, because the program helps students' cognitive abilities and enhances their knowledge of their native language. "Language is the barrier to higher performance," Halcomb said. "These students are going to outperform because the barrier has been broken down."
>
> Research by Wayne Thomas and Virginia Collier of George Mason University in Fairfax, [Virginia], shows that immigrant students excel academically when they continue to learn their native language, are taught both languages through the school's academic curriculum, and the community supports bilingual education.
>
> "This is a long-term process to help all children become academically bilingual," Galicia said. "A lot of places want children to learn English as fast as possible, but we are into learning quality English."
>
> Both populations benefit from becoming bilingual," Sosa said. "Research tells us that children who are bilingual have an advantage over children who are not."

160 Crissa Stephens

The first two quotes directly and indirectly reference the findings of Thomas and Collier (2002) and Collier and Thomas (2004) that, over time, language minority children in bilingual programs catch up to their language majority (English-speaking) peers. Halcomb's description of "quick oral fluency" and Galicia's conception of "quality English" connect interdiscursively to Cummins' (1979, 1981) theory of a rapid development of social language as compared with the long-term development of academic language. Their comments also connect to the findings of Thomas and Collier (2002) and Hakuta, Butler, and Witt (2000) that it takes several years of language instruction before language minority students catch up to their peers academically. Finally, Sosa's idea of a bilingual advantage is reflected in research summarized in Adesope, Lavin, Thompson, and Ungerleider (2010) pointing to the cognitive and linguistic advantages of bilingualism.

News articles were replete with direct educator quotes like these where information about bilingual education from educational research was disseminated. Fairclough (1992) notes that in reporting, indirect speech (such as "she said that . . .") denotes a space where the following words potentially represent the person reporting rather than the one who is being reported. When information is communicated through indirect speech, authors can combine the speaker's words with their own to represent discourse, but in the case of reporting about language policy in West Liberty, direct speech by educators is used more extensively than reported speech. These direct quotes contribute to a local understanding of bilingual education that is not usually represented in national media.

Opinion Pieces and Arguments for Change From the Ground Up

Opinion pieces featured in the newspapers made interdiscursive connections to the dual language program, suggesting that it has been influential in the region. Although these pieces are a different genre than general news articles, they are included here because they form part of the media's overall coverage of bilingual education. All four opinion articles argued for bilingual programs in other parts of the state using West Liberty's program as an example of effective language education. The following is an excerpt from an opinion piece from the editorial page of the *Press-Citizen* (Anonymous, 2010, p. A11):

> For example, West Liberty has offered a successful dual-language immersion program for more than a decade. It's not a bilingual program geared at teaching non-native English speakers in their own language; it's a dual-language program in which children are taught in both English and Spanish with the goal of making every student bilingual and bi-literate. If the Iowa City School District were to take the next two years and transform Twain or Wood into a magnet school focusing on elementary-age language

immersion, parents from all over the district would start viewing the south-east Iowa City schools in a new light.

Here, West Liberty's program model is portrayed as capable of causing "parents from all over the district" to see their schools in "a new light." Similar arguments were made for bilingual programming statewide based on West Liberty's program.

Implications for Policy, Practice, and Future Research

Media representations of West Liberty's program were not principally reflective of heavy emphasis on monoglossic ideologies found in the language of official state policies. Instead, they were replete with recontextualizations (Bauman & Briggs, 1990) of findings from educational research and interdiscursive connections to the community context of the bilingual program. Freeman (1998) and others have long highlighted the context-specific nature of bilingual programming—that is, the strong, often transformative relationships that these programs can have with the communities in which they exist. In the case of West Liberty's program, educator quotes and community members' positive responses to the impact of the program comprised the majority of the media coverage. Based on the intertextual analysis, there were micro-level forces at play in the shaping of communication about language policy in the news. The news coverage of the dual language program reflected local concerns and goals, suggesting that even though top-down policies can play a role in the life a policy takes on in education, movement at the community, school, district, and classroom levels can be powerful forces in shaping policies.

In contrast to previous findings in the broader U.S. context, media coverage of West Liberty's program was largely positive. In this case, media discourses of a small town bilingual program in a rural state run counter to those found in research on national news (e.g., McQuillan & Tse, 1996) and in media coverage of locations across the country (e.g., E. Johnson, 2005; Tarasawa, 2009; Sutton-Jones, 2013). If theory postulates that the media mediate society back to itself (Matheson, 2005), it may logically follow that in contexts where bilingual education for the benefit of language minoritized children is contentious, like California (Sutton-Jones, 2013) and Arizona (E. Johnson, 2005), media representations would be negative. However, media coverage in this specific community reflects positive attitudes toward bilingual/dual language education, suggesting that media representations of language policy are closely tied to the context in which they are found. In the context of West Liberty, English-speaking students learn together with English-learning students, providing a benefit to the English-speaking, socially dominant population. When past research is considered in light of present findings, media coverage of bilingual education for the benefit of Spanish speakers is characterized as negative in some media, whereas bilingual education benefitting English speakers is characterized more positively. This difference in media coverage depending on who benefits from bilingual education may corroborate Ovando's (2003) argument that language policy decisions in the US are often more influenced by economic and social factors than by language itself.

The local media discourses about minoritized language use and the access of that minoritized (although major world) language to English-speaking students may or may not supersede macro-level societal discourses of cultural and linguistic hegemony, but they may precipitate new local spaces for dual language education (Hornberger, 2005; D. Johnson, 2013). In support of this point, opinion pieces used West Liberty's program to argue for the development of similar programs in the region. Research suggests that bilingual education can have a transformative impact on communities, and studies have also illuminated cases of community-wide policy change generated by bilingual language programming (Hornberger, 2005; Paciotto & Delany-Barman, 2011). Although the number of opinion articles was small (four), all but one argued for more programs like that of West Liberty to meet the needs of Iowa's EL students and provide access to bilingualism to English-speaking students. This opinion coverage could be seen as early rumblings of advocacy for change from the ground up in Iowa's educational programming. Indeed, since this study was initiated (in 2014), the number of dual language programs in the state is in the process of rising from five to eight.

This study raises several implications for future research. Although media representations of bilingual education are useful for examining ideologies and discourses employed in a local context, they offer a limited perspective without explanatory power for understanding what is happening "on the ground." Ethnographic research is needed to understand how local actors make sense of overarching state policies and experience the claims made in news articles. For the theme of community building and success through bilingual education, one article argued that the program is successful because Anglos are moving to West Liberty; other articles included direct quotes from Latino residents to that effect. Valdés (1997) and others (e.g., Wright, 2015) have pointed out that bilingual education programs can still be undertaken from the standpoint of monoglossic ideologies and may hold disproportionate benefits for English-speaking students. Although communications from and about the program connect to heteroglossic ideologies, more research is needed to understand the ideological assumptions of the program and how non-English-using students in particular experience the benefits of bilingual education expressed in news media.

To conclude, media language about dual language education in West Liberty diverges from the state's official English policy stance, but it draws from the same discourses of achievement and economic and social prosperity as the monoglossic Official English policy and educational policy (Iowa Code 280.4; SF 165). In media reports, these outcomes are linked to dual language education rather than monolingual English education, and ethnographic research is needed to understand how participants experience these claims. Finally, media coverage of West Liberty's program is peppered with references to the local—the revitalizing and culturally validating impacts that bilingual education has on its own community and the impacts it has had on arguments for similar programs in surrounding communities.

References

Adesope, O., Lavin, T., Thompson, T., & Ungerleider, C. (2010). A systematic review and meta-analysis of the cognitive correlates of bilingualism. *Review of Educational Research*, *80*(2), 207–245.

Anonymous. (2010, February 13). Beyond keeping 'Magnet Schools' on the Table [Opinion]. *Press-Citizen*, p. A11.

Bakhtin, M. M. (1981). *The dialogic imagination: Four essays*. Austin, TX: University of Texas Press.

Bauman, R., & Briggs, C. (1990). Poetics and performance as critical perspectives on language and social life. *Annual Review of Anthropology*, *19*, 59–86.

Boone, D. (2001, February 6). Two languages; one purpose: Innovative instruction clicks for West Liberty. *Des Moines Register*, p. A1.

Collier, V. P., & Thomas, W. (2004). The astounding effectiveness of dual language education for all. *NABE Journal of Research and Practice*, *2*(1), 1–20.

Cummins, J. (1979). Cognitive/academic language proficiency, linguistic interdependence, the optimum age question and some other matters. *Working Papers on Bilingualism*, *19*, 121–129.

Cummins, J. (1981). The role of primary language development in promoting educational success for language minority students. In California State Department of Education (Ed.), *Schooling and language minority students: A theoretical framework*. Los Angeles, CA: Evaluation, Dissemination and Assessment Center, California State University.

de Jong, E. (2011). *Foundations for multilingualism in education: From principles to practice*. Philadelphia, PA: Caslon.

Fairbarn, S., & Jones-Vo, S. (2010). *Educating Iowa's English language learners (ELLs): A handbook for administrators and teachers*. Grimes, IA: Iowa Department of Education, State Office Building.

Fairclough, N. (1992). Intertextuality in critical discourse analysis. *Linguistics and Education*, *4*(3), 269–293.

Fairclough, N. (2015). *Language and power*. London, UK: Routledge.

Fitzsimmons-Doolan, S. (2009). Is public discourse about language policy really public discourse about immigration? A corpus-based study. *Language Policy*, *8*(4), 377–402.

Flores, N., & Schissel, J. L. (2014). Dynamic bilingualism as the norm: Envisioning a heteroglossic approach to standards-based reform. *TESOL Quarterly*, *48*(3), 454–479.

Freeman, R. (1998). *Bilingual education and social change*. Clevedon, UK: Multilingual Matters.

Gallegos, R. (2007, August 9). Romney stumps in Coralville. *Press-Citizen*, p. A3.

Gutierrez, K. D., Asato, J., Santos, M., & Gotanda, N. (2002). 'Backlash pedagogy': Language and culture and the politics of reform. *Review of Education, Pedagogy & Cultural Studies*, *24*(4), 335–351.

Hakuta, K., Butler, Y. G., & Witt, D. (2000). *How long does it take English language learners to attain proficiency?* (The University of California Linguistic Minority Research Institute Policy Report 2000–1). Stanford, CA: Stanford University.

164 Crissa Stephens

Hall, S. (2001). Foucault: Power, knowledge and discourse. In M. Wetherell, S. Taylor, & S. J. Yates (Eds.), *Discourse theory and practice: A reader* (pp. 72–81). London, UK: Sage.

Hamilton, R. (2000, February 25). West Liberty Revels in Town's Ethnic Diversity. *Press-Citizen*, p. C14.

Hornberger, N. H. (2005). Opening up and filling implementational and ideological spaces in heritage language education. *Modern Language Journal, (89)*4, 605–609.

Hult, F. M., & Pietikäinen, S. (2014). Shaping discourses of multilingualism through a language ideological debate: The case of Swedish in Finland. *Journal of Language and Politics, 13*(1), 1–20.

Inskeep, S., & Montagne, R. (Hosts). (2011). A look at Iowa's first majority Hispanic town [Radio Broadcast]. In S. Gilbert (Producer), *Morning Edition*. Washington, DC: National Public Radio. Retrieved from www.npr.org/2011/10/10/141150607/west-liberty-is-iowas-first-majority-hispanic-town.

Iowa Code 280.4.

Irvine, J. T., & Gal, S. (2000). Language ideology and linguistic differentiation. In P. V. Kroskrity (Ed.), *Regimes of language: Ideologies, polities and identities* (pp. 35–83). Santa Fe, NM: School of American Research Press.

Johnson, D. C. (2013). *Language policy*. London, UK: Palgrave McMillan.

Johnson, D. C. (2015). Intertextuality and language policy. In F. M. Hult & D. C. Johnson (Eds.), *Research methods in language policy and planning* (pp. 166–180). Hoboken, NJ: Wiley Blackwell.

Johnson, D. C., Lynch, S., & Stephens, C. (2016). Proceedings of the14th Annual Conference, 2015: Educational language policy and the new Latino diaspora in Iowa. In S. Jeanetta, C. Rector, L. Saunders & C. Valdivia (Eds.), *Cambio de colores: Latinos in the heartland: Shaping the future: Leadership for inclusive communities* (pp. 55–59). Kansas City, MO: Cambio Center at the University of Missouri.

Johnson, E. (2005). WAR in the media: Metaphors, ideology and the formation of language policy. *Bilingual Research Journal, 29*(3), 621–640.

Kristeva, J. (1986). *Revolution in poetic language* (M. Waller, Trans.). New York, NY: Columbia University Press.

Lau v. Nichols, 414 U.S. 563 (1974).

Matheson, D. (2005). *Media discourses: Analyzing media texts*. Maidenhead, UK: Open University Press.

McCarty, T. (2011). *Ethnography and language policy*. London, UK: Routledge.

McQuillan, J., & Tse, L. (1996). Does research matter? An analysis of media opinion on bilingual education, 1984–1994. *Bilingual Research Journal, 20*(1), 1–27.

Nebbe, C. (Host). (2013). Foreign language learning in elementary school [Radio Broadcast]. In B. Stanton (Producer)(Ed.), *Talk of Iowa*. Iowa City, IA: Iowa Public Radio.

Ovando, C. (2003). Bilingual education in the United States: Historical development and current issues. *Bilingual Research Journal, 27*(1), 1–24.

Paciotto, C., & Delany-Barmann, G. (2011). Planning micro-level language education reform in new diaspora sites: Two-way immersion education in the rural Midwest. *Language Policy, 10*(3), 221–243.

Ricento, T. K. (2006). Theoretical perspectives in language policy: An overview. In T. K. Ricento (Ed.), *An introduction to language policy* (pp. 3–9). Hoboken, NJ: Blackwell.

Ricento, T. K., & Hornberger, N. H. (1996). Unpeeling the onion: Language planning and policy and the ELT professional. *TESOL Quarterly, 30*(3), 401–427.

Rickford, J. (1999). The Ebonics controversy in my backyard: A sociolinguist's experiences and reflections. *Journal of Sociolinguistics, 3*(2), 267–275.

Rolstad, K., Mahoney, K., & Glass, G. V. (2005). The big picture: A meta-analysis of program effectiveness research on English language learners. *Educational Policy, 19*(4), 572–594.

SF 165, Iowa English Reaffirmation Act.

Sutton-Jones, K. (2013). Bilingual education in the Southern California press and proposition 227: A case study. Presentation given at *NABE*, 2013. Orlando, FL.

Tarasawa, B. (2009). Mixed messages in media coverage of bilingual education: The case of Atlanta, Georgia. *Bilingual Research Journal, 31*(1–2), 23–46.

Thomas, W. P., & Collier, V. P. (2002). *A national study of school effectiveness for language minority students' long-term academic achievement.* Berkeley, CA: UC Berkeley Center for Research on Education, Diversity and Excellence.

Valdés, G. (1997). Dual-language immersion programs: A cautionary note concerning the education of language-minority students. *Harvard Educational Review, 67*(3), 391–429.

Voloshinov, V. (1973). *Marxism and the philosophy of language.* Cambridge, MA: Harvard University Press.

Waller, L. J. (2012). Bilingual education and the language of news. *Australian Journal of Linguistics, 32*(4), 459–472.

West Liberty Community School District. (2016). *Bilingual program, program goals.* Retrieved from www.wl.k12.ia.us/Page/44

Wodak, R. (2006). Linguistic analyses in language policies. In T. K. Ricento (Ed.), *An introduction to language policy* (pp. 170–193). Hoboken, NJ: Blackwell.

Wortham, S. E. F., Murillo, E. G., & Hamann, E. T. (2002). *Education in the New Latino diaspora: Policy and the politics of identity* (Vol. 2). Westport, CT: Greenwood.

Wright, W. E. (2015). *Foundations for teaching English language learners: Research, theory, policy, and practice.* Philadelphia, PA: Caslon.

PART 4

Identity and Individual and "Invisible" Language Policy and Planning

14

RETHINKING CULTURALLY AND LINGUISTICALLY DIVERSE STUDENTS' PERCEPTIONS OF FAMILY LANGUAGE POLICIES AND IDENTITIES IN AN AMERICAN AFTERSCHOOL PROGRAM

Yu-Chi Wang

ANITA: *I don't talk about my parents a lot at school because I don't want other people to judge me. I think when people think about Spanish, they only think about that it's from Mexico. Spanish is the only language from Mexico, not from different countries. But I don't think they learned their geography well enough.*

ME: *So do you think that if you tell them about your parents, your friends or other people will feel something weird?*

ANITA: *Not my friends, because they trust me and I trust them about everything. But people who don't know me or they are dumb, they don't understand me that well, (I) probably won't tell them because they would get the wrong thing.*

This vignette comes from an informal interview with Anita, a sixth-grade elementary school girl who participates in an afterschool book club. Anita's discomfort and struggle are to balance her Honduran identity and the Hispanic American identity. As a researcher, an educator, and an international doctoral student, I had mixed feelings after listening to her story. I sympathized with Anita's discomfort at being seen as different because of how she looks and speaks. Anita's perspective was not the product of a single incident; it was the product of discursive practices formed over time (Weedon, 1987). I wondered how many students with culturally and linguistically diverse (CLD) backgrounds, like Anita, are still forced to choose one social identity and perhaps hide the others in order to avoid people's misconceptions of multilingualism, and how these choices and her perceptions of herself are influenced by language policies inside and outside of her home.

The chapter locates language policy as a field of inquiry within the study of CLD students' perceptions of their multilingual literacy practices and identities in an afterschool book club. In this chapter, the term *CLD students* refers to students who learn English as another language or grow up in bilingual or multilingual environments and have diverse cultural and linguistic backgrounds. This study emphasizes how participants' discourses influence and are influenced by their family language policies.

The inspiration for this study came from my three-year participation in an afterschool book club and research project called Strong Girls Read Strong Books. I paid attention to students' discourses of *invisible language planning*—language planning that is spontaneous and not directly linked to governmental language policy and planning (Curdt-Christiansen, 2009). In this chapter, I focus on three CLD students' invisible language policies inside and outside of school settings and the relationships between their multilingual identities and these language policies.

Issues That Motivated the Research

In 2013, I participated in the afterschool book club and research project. I participated in the group as a discussion leader, reading and discussing books with an ethnically diverse group of elementary school girls. We talked about various issues regarding gender roles and topics that emerged from our discussions. Throughout my participation, I noticed that the CLD elementary school girls showed strong interest in topics about our multicultural and multilingual backgrounds. I was fascinated by how they positioned and negotiated their bilingual identities inside and outside of school settings. The book club members brought diverse perspectives to uncovering the discourses of privilege, ambiguity, confusion, and resistance that they had acquired inside and outside of their homes. Discourse plays a significant role, not only in reflecting and reproducing society, but also in enabling individuals to exercise their agency to disrupt social norms (Fairclough, 2015; Gee, 2011). Thus, the purpose of this study is to investigate CLD students' perceptions of their multilingualism in their everyday discursive practices.

Many scholars have highlighted the important role of family in the domain of language policy and planning. It was not until recently, however, that scholars began considering family language policy individually (King, Fogle, & Logan-Terry, 2008; Spolsky, 2012). Curdt-Christiansen (2009) defines *family language policy* as "a deliberate attempt at practicing a particular language use pattern and particular literacy practices within home domains and among family members" (p. 352). The formation of family language policy is not fixed; it is shaped and reshaped by individuals' beliefs about languages and other cultural "baggage" that individuals from diverse cultures bring with them (Schiffman, 2006, p. 112). This cultural baggage helps shape discourses about national and local language planning and creates different power relationships in a society. Moreover, the power relationships can be transformed to active language practices and further impact language identities.

Language Practices and Identity

Drawing on a poststructuralist perspective, in this study, identities are considered multiple, dynamic across time and space, and a site of struggle (Norton, 2000). Individuals' identities are socially constructed, and we consciously and unconsciously construct our identities in relation to our understanding of the world and of ourselves (Weedon, 1987). That is, how CLD students employ their identities depends on how they position and are positioned by others in different social settings. Particular social identities are shaped and recognized through discursive practices where speakers and hearers actively participate in a shared community (Davies & Harré, 1990).

School and family are crucial social communities influencing school-age students' language practices and beliefs, especially students with diverse backgrounds (Conteh & Kawashima, 2008; Spolsky, 2012). However, little research has focused on elementary school students' perceptions of their multilingual identities. As Curdt-Christiansen (2009) points out, investigating pupils' views of their multilingualism can help contribute to researchers' and educators' understanding of the ideologies behind students' language, which reflect a broader view of multilingualism in a society and how language status affects students' multilingual development.

Language Practices at Home

Research suggests that immigrant parents' attitudes toward multilingualism strongly impact their children's heritage language maintenance and multilingual identities (King et al., 2008). For instance, mothers' consistent use of their native languages at home, traveling back to their heritage country, or contacting other speakers of their native language all influence their children's language identities (Takeuchi, 2006). In an ethnographic study of 10 Chinese immigrant families in Quebec, Curdt-Christiansen (2009) examined parents' perceptions of multiculturalism. The results indicated that parents' immigration experiences and connections between language proficiency and future job opportunities were key factors influencing Chinese immigrant parents' family language policies.

Additionally, parents' educational backgrounds, cultural backgrounds, and educational expectations contribute to their children's language identities. For instance, Chinese immigrant parents often carry high expectations for their children's successful multilingual development and educational results. These expectations are often shaped by their discursive practices from their sociocultural and Confucian values, which view education as the path to success (Curdt-Christiansen, 2009). Although studies show that families from different ethnic and cultural backgrounds make different language choices, taken together, the studies suggest strong connections between family language policy and children's language development and identities.

Language Practices at School

Schools are powerful institutions that directly and indirectly influence students' language practices and language beliefs. Research shows that CLD students often experience conflicts between school and home language policies (King et al., 2008). For instance, the promotion of monolingualism at school, given CLD students' diverse linguistic and cultural backgrounds, might privilege one language and minimize the value of others. As CLD students grow older, their multilingual identities and language development might be encouraged or hindered, depending on their relations to the world, especially their experiences with their peers.

The relationships between family language policy and children's language practices can be bidirectional. Research has shown that family language policies shape and are shaped by students' language and literacy practices outside their homes. Researchers have found that parents of multilingual children are influenced by their school-aged children when their children begin to identify with their peer groups and the mainstream culture outside of their homes (Tuominen, 1999). That is, when a language is more acceptable and can grant access to social power, then CLD parents might promote or discourage children's use of a certain language in order to support children's language development in a dominant social setting.

Context of the Research

The data come from the weekly book club meetings I attended that took place from 2013–2016 at a public elementary school in the Midwestern US. The research team consisted of two professors, six undergraduate students, and two graduate students. My role was both participant and researcher. I led book discussion groups and also observed the Strong Girls' interactions and participations.

The book club aimed to provide a comfortable reading environment for fourth- to sixth-grade girls to improve their reading comprehension and gender role awareness. We read and responded to children's and young adult literature by adopting various written and multimodal activities. The book club often began with a whole-group discussion in which we read and talked about a text together. We then split into intimate discussion groups where we talked about a book the girls had chosen to read together. In this process, my researcher lens became increasingly tuned to the stories they told about their multilingual and multicultural experiences.

Participants

In this chapter, I focus on three participants in my discussion group: Jamie, Kathy, and Anita (pseudonyms). The members in my group included three Caucasian Americans, one Asian American, two Hispanic Americans, and me. The data

I discuss in this chapter come from our small group discussions. I was particularly interested in the girls' talk about family language policy and their multilingual identities.

Like myself, the three CLD girls all come from households where English is not the dominant language or where more than one language is used at home. Moreover, they had all attended English language learning programs and passed the English language proficiency standard in the same elementary school.

Research Questions Addressed

This ethnographic study of the Strong Girls book club culture seeks to gain a better understanding of a bigger picture of processes of language policy as well as to provide a balanced picture between policy power and interpretative agency (Johnson, 2013). Although I was not an insider of the CLD girls' heritage cultures, the two-year relationships that members constructed and reconstructed and their active participation in the book club all contributed to the credibility of the data analysis.

In this chapter, I address the following research questions:

1. What does the students' language reveal about their perceptions of their multilingual identities?
2. What social factors affect their family language policy and use of their heritage languages?

Research Methods

Data Collection

Data collection took place from January 2013 to May 2016. Data resources included audio and video recordings from book club discussions, field notes from observations, semi-structured interviews, and the girls' oral and written responses that reflect their personal stories and participation in the book club.

Data Analysis Procedures Used

In my analysis of students' discourses regarding their perceptions of their family language policies and their multilingualism, I focused on how the students used language to create practices, identities, and politics (Gee, 2011). The term *practices*, according to Gee (2011), means "a socially recognized and institutionally or culturally supported endeavor that usually involves sequencing or combining actions in certain specific ways" (p. 17). The term *identities* means that individuals use language to get recognized as taking on a role. In this context, *politics* means that individuals use language to convey and construct a perspective of "social goods,"

174 Yu-Chi Wang

a term which refers to something or someone considered by individuals as being acceptable, normal, or good in a mainstream social group (Gee, 2011, p. 17).

My data analysis was not linear; it was retrospective, which enabled me to identify and confirm emerging themes. I categorized the data through open coding and analytical coding from various data resources in order to triangulate the findings. Specifically, the various types of data collection allowed me to carry out *methods triangulation*, which involved the use of multiple methods to investigate a given issue (Denzin, 1978).

Findings and Discussion

CLD Students' Family Language Practices

Findings across data resources show that family language practices and CLD parents' beliefs impact the girls' identity positions. The CLD students all demonstrated strong affiliations with their heritage backgrounds. Recognition of their multicultural backgrounds in various social contexts was crucial to these students' multilingual identities, including their languages, actions, interactions, values, beliefs, symbols, objects, and so on (Gee, 2011). These factors were present in Jamie's journal entries and served as evidence of her Vietnamese identities. Once I asked the girls to describe a neighborhood that represents who they are, and she chose to share about her neighborhood in Vietnam, as indicated in Figure 15.1.

Jamie was often the quietest girl in our group, but she became more vocal when our discussion topics were about Vietnamese culture, as her journal entry in Figure 14.1 illustrates. She also drew a map and a flag of Vietnam, revealing her knowledge of her heritage country.

CLD girls were not only aware of their multiple identities, but also constantly contesting and negotiating those multiple identities. An example of CLD girls' identification of the differences between various ethnic identities took place when I had an extended conversation with Kathy and Anita about their ethnicity. (The ellipses in this and subsequent transcripts are used to indicate deletion of the texts unrelated to or redundant of the findings.)

ME: So when you are at home, what did your mom and dad tell you about staying in the US?
ANITA: They always tell me that. If I was there (*pause*), if I have choice, where will I stay? I would always say that in USA because you will have way better life here.
ME: Will your parents go back to Honduras?
ANITA: No, it's only for vacation.
. . .
ANITA: Honduras is like poor, dirty, dangerous, only some parts are dangerous. And it is sad over there because there are lots of . . .

Rethinking Diverse Students' Perceptions **175**

FIGURE 14.1 Jamie's Response to Her Neighborhood

I am from Vietnam, I see street lights, cats, dogs, ducks, dry grass. . . . It's very very fun there. I like to go to the zoo. I see very "[sic] hard to find animals.

KATHY: Pollution
ANITA: Yeah, pollution.
. . .
KATHY: Home (*smiles awkwardly and pauses*) I would say Central America, all my families are in Colombia, so I would say Colombia.
ANITA: But it's more comfortable *here*. I like *here* because it's comfortable.

This vignette shows two different perspectives from Anita's and Kathy's definitions of home. When I asked them where they considered home to be, Anita replied "I would always say that in USA because you will have way better life here." Honduras, according to her understanding, is a place "only for vacation." When the discourse was related to her American citizen identity, she emphasized the comfort and the social, cultural, and economic capital that her family could not access in Honduras. She refers to Honduras as "poor," "dangerous" (in "some parts"), "dirty," or having "no opportunities for a good job." The language she used showed a conscious inclination toward her American identity. Kathy, however, portrayed a more positive image of living in Colombia, where she had a strong affiliation with her family outside of her American home. I found that Kathy's discourse about her Colombian identity was more prominent than that of the other CLD girls in the book club. Although those girls were born in the US, their positions and their definitions of home were complicated and influenced by the discourses they learned about their family home practices, as well as sociocultural and economic factors.

Although all three CLD girls identified the importance of their heritage languages, when I asked about their experiences of learning their heritage language, only Jamie mentioned language learning at home. She sometimes wrote her own stories in both English and Vietnamese in her journal. In an informal talk, she told me that she felt tired on the weekends because her mother insisted that she practice reading and writing Vietnamese at home. She explained that her mother thought that learning Vietnamese was important to communicate with her Vietnamese family and maintain her Vietnamese culture.

The data show that all the CLD parents valued their children's spoken skills in their heritage languages more than their written skills. The three CLD students shared different stories of their parents' beliefs toward their children's multilingual practices inside and outside school settings, but only Jamie clearly indicated her mother's insistence on practicing Vietnamese at home. Jamie's case corresponds to Curdt-Christiansen's (2009) study of Chinese immigrant families' belief that maintaining heritage languages and culturally significant knowledge contributes to CLD students' sense of belonging and identity.

However, Kathy's and Anita's mothers held a different belief about their children's multilingual practices at home. In a large group discussion with the fifth-grade girls about their standardized reading test scores, Kathy revealed her mother's worry that speaking Spanish might delay her English-learning development.

KATHY: Sometimes my mom thinks I should speak less Spanish and more English at home. She said I speak too many Spanish.
ME: Why?
KATHY: Because she thinks I speak too much Spanish and that is not good for my reading scores. She thinks I need to speak more English.

In this vignette, Kathy's mother's discourse treats spoken English as a social good that creates unequal power relationships between Spanish and English. Her mother's discourse of invisible language planning implies that speaking Spanish might hinder her reading in English, which is often the only language recognized as legitimate and used in mainstream academic communities. Kathy's mother's language belief echoes Spolsky's (2012) claim that if parents' family language policy is driven by myths, such as the idea that bilingualism is problematic, then one specific language might predominate over the others.

The findings show that participants viewed English not only as a social good that played a significant role in their reading development, but also as playing a crucial role in helping their parents assimilate into mainstream American culture. All three CLD students shared their parents' and family members' efforts to improve their English skills. For instance, Anita told the group that she and her sisters sometimes took turns teaching their mother English at home. This finding is consistent with Tuominen's (1999) description of the bidirectional relationships between parents' language choices and the language practices of school-age children from CLD families. These relationships have influenced CLD parents' language polices and planning by socializing their families to assimilate to American culture instead of maintaining their heritage culture. For the CLD parents, maintaining their children's heritage culture and language becomes more challenging when speaking English means gaining more social status than does speaking their heritage languages.

CLD Students' Positions of Their Multiple Identities

Discussions of the CLD girls' multiple identities revealed that they had high levels of awareness of their multilingual identities. These identities empowered the CLD students when their multilingual abilities were recognized and valued. All three CLD students had positive experiences with their multilingual abilities inside and outside of school settings. Kathy gave an example of being recognized as an expert multilingual speaker during an informal talk. She told me that she was like a teacher because her teacher sometimes asked her to assist a new Latino student with adapting to the new environment and learning more about Hispanic culture. The teacher's recognition of Kathy's bilingualism and the opportunities to be an insider of both cultures offered her social status in formal social institutions. In this case, Kathy's bilingual ability was a resource that empowered her bilingual identity. However, Kathy's bilingual ability was not always welcome at school. One time Kathy's Spanish language knowledge was teased by the other girls in the book club because they thought she sounded funny when speaking Spanish. She told me that was not the first time, and she was used to handling the embarrassing situation. Kathy's stories show that CLD students might encounter more complicated challenges when their bilingual identities are questioned and restricted by implicit and explicit school language policies.

Not only did Kathy recognize her bilingual ability, but other girls also perceived her as the Spanish expert in the group. When I asked them to provide a short description of each girl, one of the non-CLD students, Jennifer, described Kathy as a "Spanish dictionary." At the end of the 2015 spring semester, I asked the girls to write words and thoughts to each other. A Caucasian American,

Jennifer, wrote a note to Kathy to show her interest in her Colombian identities, as indicated in Figure 14.2.

Another example of Kathy's bilingual ability was highlighted when I asked the CLD girls if their identities were questioned by people of their heritage countries. Kathy described her interaction with people in Colombia:

KATHY: Yeah, they don't ask you if you are Mexican. They just "Oh, that girl, she is not American, she is Colombian" all that. Also because they can hear my Spanish and my Colombian accent, so they might say "Oh, she is obvious Colombian."

BELLA: Yeah, but people here know nothing about that stuff unless they really know you. Because I know you (*facing toward Anita*), I know you are Honduran. When I was little, I thought many Hispanics were from Mexico.

Both Kathy and Anita mentioned that speaking Spanish without accents in their heritage communities helped them blend into the community. As she indicated earlier, for Kathy, one advantage of having a Colombian accent is being recognized as a valid member in her Colombian community. However, as the preceding extract shows, when Bella, a non-CLD student, shared her understanding of the public's perception of Hispanic Americans in a larger social community, identity became a site of struggle.

Another example supporting identity as a site of struggle occurred when Anita shared how people perceived her Hispanic identity:

ANITA: I think when people think about Spanish, they only think about that it's from Mexico. Spanish is the only language from Mexico, not from different countries. But I don't think they learned their geography well enough. . . .

FIGURE 14.2 Jennifer's Note to Kathy

Your really talented with your Spanish and your like a Spanish dictionary. I wish I new Spanish.

You have a colorful personality. I like hearing your stories about Colombia. I read some where that Colombia mines a lot of emeralds. Like the emeralds, shine on!

I don't know why they would say that because I think they were dumb because they don't know the geography well.

ME: Did you get the chance to let other people know that not all people who speak Spanish are Mexican?

ANITA: Yeah, exactly. Like there are a ton of people (*who speak Spanish*). Most of them are in South America, like mostly Spanish, their language is Spanish and a little bit in Europe. Mostly the bottom of Central America. . . . a lot of people suspect, because a lot of people think that because this country is more popular, then they must speak this language.

Here, Anita discussed the assumption that Latino Americans are often categorized as a homogenous group from Mexico. This extract suggests the need to incorporate CLD students' diverse cultural backgrounds into elementary school curricula in order to benefit all students' awareness of people's diverse backgrounds.

Although this study focuses on only three CLD students' perceptions of their multilingual identities and discourses of their family's language beliefs, the findings show that the construction of students' multicultural identities is complicated and interwoven with factors from different visible and invisible social and power relationships. Thus, it is imperative to examine how these relationships directly and indirectly affect students' beliefs and their multilingual identities, especially because many CLD students and their immigrant families have been surrounded and threatened by the misleading racial information and portraits of diverse ethnic groups in America (Murphy, 2017). If the racial discourses and misinformation are not examined critically, then CLD students might be impeded from participating in schools, and social barriers among students might be created (Catalano, 2017).

Implications for Policy, Practice, and Future Research

In this chapter, I have presented three CLD students' perceptions of their multilingual identities and their relationships with their family and school language policies in an afterschool book club. The findings illustrate that CLD students' subtle strategies of negotiation, resistance, and reconfiguration of their multilingual identities suggest the need to provide spaces for CLD students' multilingual identities to be recognized and affirmed, both inside and outside of school settings (Cummins et al., 2005). For instance, providing safe and comfortable environments outside formal school settings for students to discuss questions about multilingual and multicultural practices can help create space for students to exercise their agency to resist unfavorable language policies that are shaped by inside and outside school settings, such as implementing English only language policy. Furthermore, teachers can use multicultural texts as windows and mirrors into their classroom practices to open opportunities for critical pedagogy (Glazier & Seo, 2005). For example, the CLD girls in the afterschool book club were offered more opportunities to share their backgrounds when reading multicultural texts.

Future research should focus on providing more ethnographic perspectives to explore factors affecting family language policies in relation to children's identities and language development. For instance, researchers can collaborate with teachers to examine pedagogies and opportunities for embracing CLD students' multilingual backgrounds. Additionally, researchers should work with stakeholders who have influence on local and national language policies to critically investigate the impact of language policies on different social communities in order to reduce the gap between language policies and day-to-day language practices.

References

Catalano, T. (2017). When children are water: Representation of Central American migrant children in public discourse and implications for educators. *Journal of Latinos and Education, 16*(2), 124–142.

Conteh, J., & Kawashima, Y. (2008). Diversity in family involvement in children's learning in English primary schools: Culture, language, and identity. *English teaching: Practice and critique, 7*(2), 113–125.

Cummins, J., Bismilla, V., Chow, P., Cohen, S., Giampapa, F., Leoni, L., Sandhu, P., & Sastri, P. (2005). Affirming identity in multicultural classrooms. *Educational Leadership, 63*(1), 38–43.

Curdt-Christiansen, X. L. (2009). Invisible and visible language planning: Ideological factors in the family language policy of Chinese immigrant families in Quebec. *Language Policy, 8*(4), 351–375.

Davies, B., & Harré, R. (1990). Positioning: The discursive production of selves. *Journal for the Theory of Social Behavior, 20*(1), 43–63.

Denzin, N. K. (1978). *The research act: A theoretical introduction to sociological methods* (2nd ed.). New York, NY: McGraw Hill.

Fairclough, N. (2015). *Language and power*. London, UK: Longman.

Gee, J. P. (2011). *An introduction to discourse analysis* (3rd ed.). New York, NY: Routledge.

Glazier, J., & Seo, J. A. (2005). Multicultural literature and discussion as mirror and window? *Journal of Adolescent & Adult Literacy, 48*(8), 686–700.

Johnson, D. C. (2013). *Language policy*. London, UK: Palgrave Macmillan UK.

King, K. A., Fogle, L., & Logan-Terry, A. (2008). Family language policy. *Language and Linguistics Compass, 2*(5), 907–922.

Murphy, J. P. (2017). Defending "all this Diversity Garbage": Multidimensional coalition-building in the age of Trump. *Mid-Atlantic Education Review, 5*(1), 12–18.

Norton, B. (2000). *Identity and language learning: Gender, ethnicity and educational change*. Harlow, UK: Longman.

Schiffman, H. (2006). Language policy and linguistic culture. In T. Ricento (Ed.), *An introduction to language policy: Theory and method* (pp. 111–125). Malden, MA: Blackwell.

Spolsky, B. (2012). Family language policy—the critical domain. *Journal of Multilingual and Multicultural Development, 33*(1), 3–11.

Takeuchi, M. (2006). *Raising children bilingually through the 'one parent-one language' approach: A case study of Japanese mothers in the Australian context*. Bern, Switzerland: Peter Lang.

Tuominen, A. K. (1999). Who decides the home language? A look at multilingual families. *International Journal of the Sociology of Language, 140*, 59–76.

Weedon, C. (1987). *Feminist practice and poststructuralist theory*. London, UK: Blackwell.

15

DIGITAL LITERACY, LANGUAGE LEARNING, AND EDUCATIONAL POLICY IN BRITISH COLUMBIA

Ron Darvin

In the Canadian province of British Columbia (BC), the Ministry of Education defines *digital literacy* as "the interest, attitude and ability of individuals to appropriately use digital technology and communication tools to access, manage, integrate, analyze and evaluate information, construct new knowledge, create and communicate with others" (Province of British Columbia, 2017, para. 2). In contrast to the definition provided by the Office for Information Technology Policy of the American Library Association (ALA, 2013), which refers to digital literacy as a singular ability, the BC definition highlights how digital literacy is not just a technical skill but one that involves "interest" and "attitude": that is, a certain disposition toward technology use. This distinction underlines how becoming truly digitally literate begins with and is sustained by adopting a mindset that recognizes the power of digital technologies.

Based on the National Educations Technology Standards for Students (NETS•S) developed by the International Society for Technology in Education (ISTE), the BC Digital Literacy Framework (Province of British Columbia, 2017) identifies six characteristics of digital literacy: research and information literacy; critical thinking, problem solving, and decision making; creativity and innovation; digital citizenship; communication and collaboration; and technology operations and concepts. By creating digital literacy profiles of four grade ranges (K-2, 3–5, 6–9, and 10–12), the framework outlines experiences with technology and digital resources expected at these different stages. Developing these characteristics of digital literacy is particularly crucial as BC implements a new curriculum that focuses on personalized, concept-based, and competency-driven learning. Based on a "Know-Do-Understand" model where the areas of learning have been structured according to Content, Curricular Competencies, and Big Ideas, this curriculum enables students to explore their own interests through technology-enabled

182 Ron Darvin

learning environments and inquiry and question-based approaches (Province of British Columbia, 2017). As technology becomes an increasingly important component of curricula and pedagogy in K–12 contexts, new opportunities and issues in language education and educational policy emerge. Drawing on data from a case study of two high school students in Vancouver, this chapter discusses how language education can contribute to the learning of digital literacies critical in the 21st century and how educational policies can shape digital pedagogy that is both agentive and equitable.

Issues That Motivated the Research

Technology has not only accelerated the flow of people, capital, and ideas (Appadurai, 1990; Basch, Schiller, & Blanc, 1994); it has also precipitated new forms of social participation, enabling new allegiances and social formations while expanding our conceptions of citizenship and community. It has also reshaped both the meaning and practice of literacy (Cope & Kalantzis, 2010, 2012; de Costa, 2010). By providing new modes of representation and socialization, digital media have instigated the growth of diverse semiotic modes and cross-language interaction (C. Luke, 2003; Warschauer, 2009). Social media platforms, online communities, and forums have become a significant arena in which identities and networks are negotiated. Through texting and instant messaging, speech and writing frequently converge, transforming literacy practices in unprecedented ways. With the popularity of textspeak and emoticons and the abundance of multimodal affordances made available through digital media, learners need to develop continually evolving literacies (Lankshear & Knobel, 2011).

In this new social landscape, digital literacy has become critical to assert one's place, to engage with others, and to claim the right to speak (Norton, 2013). Through continuously evolving digital tools, learners are able to identify, use, adapt, and create affordances to achieve diverse purposes such as the representation of identities, artistic expression, the facilitation of social relations, the consumption and production of knowledge, the exchange of goods and services, and entertainment. Technology has also transformed industries and workplaces, constructing new modes of production, and facilitating the shift to "knowledge work" (Jones & Hafner, 2012). Preparing students for this "technology-rich world" (Province of British Columbia, 2017), where knowledge is growing exponentially in various domains, has served as the primary impetus for redesigning the BC curriculum. Through digital affordances, learners are able to cross boundaries, enter multiple spaces, and perform diverse functions; critical to unlocking these possibilities is language. How teachers, researchers, and policy makers are able to design new curricula and reimagine pedagogy that addresses the specific needs of a digital age is perhaps the greatest challenge of language education in the 21st century (Darvin & Norton, 2015).

Context of the Research

Recognizing the increasing significance of digital literacies in the social and academic trajectories of learners, this research examines the digital practices of youth of contrasting class backgrounds. As teachers in British Columbia continue to experiment with different ways of integrating technology into their classrooms, the question of which digital literacies learners already come to school equipped with is critical in addressing issues of equity. In Canada, where 85% of students have their own mobile phones by Grade 11, and where 99% are able to access the internet outside school (Steeves, 2014), issues of digital access and connectivity may not appear to be a significant concern. This research, however, focuses on how learners perceive and use technology in different ways that may be valued unequally in school. It seeks to understand to what extent home settings and social networks shape learners' dispositions toward technology and their digital practices. As policy makers continue to build digital infrastructure in schools and design new learning standards, an understanding of the differences of these "digital natives" (Prensky, 2001, p. 1) needs to be taken into consideration to ensure these innovations do not exclude segments of the student population.

Research Questions Addressed

To demonstrate how today's learners are developing diverse digital literacies, we turn to Ayrton and John, two high school students in Vancouver, Canada, who participated in a two-month case study I conducted in 2013. (The names of the participants that appear here are pseudonyms that they chose for themselves.) The purpose of the study was to compare the language and literacy practices of immigrant learners of contrasting socioeconomic backgrounds. A more detailed discussion of the data that appears here can be found in Darvin (forthcoming) and Darvin and Norton (2014, 2015). The research questions were:

1. To what extent are there differences in the technology access and home contexts of these learners?
2. In what ways do these differences shape divergent digital practices?
3. How do these digital practices develop literacies that may or may not be valued in school?

Research Methods

Data Collection

Data were generated from observations of digital events in home settings, interviews of the learners and their parents, and literacy artifacts. Notes were written

Data Analysis Procedures Used

Transcripts of the interviews were represented for general readability and do not include silences, false starts, intonational contours, or similar interactional features, nor do they indicate subtle distinctions between sounds. Coding using Atlas.ti was done to determine salient themes, which are discussed in this chapter. Multimodal analysis of the literacy artifacts and the screen captures was also conducted.

Participants

Ayrton is a 16-year-old tenth-grade student at a private high school in Vancouver. His family immigrated from the Philippines three years before the study, through the Investor Class, which was designed to attract experienced business people who have a net worth of at least C$1.6M and requires them to invest C$800,000 in the country (Citizenship and Immigration Canada, 2012). The family lives in a three-bedroom apartment that they own in a wealthy part of Vancouver. Ayrton's father continues to own multiple businesses in the Philippines and uses technology to manage them remotely. An older sister is a university graduate who edits films and videos on her computer, while an older brother studies mechanical engineering at a prominent university. The language they speak at home is primarily English, which was also the case when they were living in a wealthy area of Manila. Everyone in the family has his or her own laptop, with the exception of the mother, who uses a desktop in a study room, which everyone shares. Ayrton owns a laptop, an iPad, and a Samsung phone. The computers are networked to a printer and a scanner, and all family members have their own computer-dedicated spaces. Because of his interest in currency trading, Ayrton, with the support of his parents, also registered for an e-learning course, Infinite Prosperity, which provides him with the information and analytical tools necessary to become a trader in the future.

Like Ayrton, John is also 16 but is an eleventh-grade student in a public school in an area of Vancouver largely populated by immigrant families. He moved to Canada when he was 10 years old, after six years of being separated from his mother, who started living in the country as a caregiver under temporary migrant worker arrangements. When she was eventually able to claim permanent residence, she arranged for John, his older sister, and his younger brother to immigrate through the Family Class, which enables residents to sponsor relatives to come to Canada (Citizenship and Immigration Canada, 2012). John's father, who is legally separated from John's mother, continues to live in the Philippines. The family of four live in a one-bedroom apartment, and they speak primarily Filipino at home. John's sister is studying to be a licensed practical nurse in a community college and supports her education by working at the same time. John's mother continues to work as a caregiver in a senior care facility, and she usually gets home from work later than 11 in the evening. The entire household shares one desktop. They have two iPads, one of which is used solely by John, who also has his own mobile phone. When the sister needs to use the desktop, John has to go to the public library and use the computer there.

Findings and Discussion

Both John and Ayrton are visibly very adept with technology and multitask with great ease. They can jump from one application to another as they talk about their interests and digital practices. Ayrton clicks swiftly on hyperlinks to get to a desired page and lists URLs from memory. John types swiftly without even looking once at the keyboard, which is completely hidden under the computer table. Both say there have been occasions where their teachers would ask them for help with operating digital projectors or navigating through PowerPoint. When asked about what he feels about his teachers asking for his assistance, John says "it's just usual" because "our generation is more into technology" (Darvin, forthcoming). Both demonstrate confidence in being able to use technology and view this ability as natural. From the observations and interviews, what emerges, though, are striking differences when it comes to the boys' views of what technology is for and how they use it at home.

For Ayrton, whose university-schooled family members are sophisticated technology users, technology is clearly an educational tool that promises social mobility: "With how the world is just connected and how information is at your fingertips, you can be anyone or anything you want to be and it's just right there" (Darvin & Norton, 2014, p. 115). Social futures and identities ("you can be anyone or anything you want to be") are imagined and realized through the access to and use of information. Ayrton recognizes the significance of information technology ("the world of computers today") and connectivity ("the world is just connected") and views the computer as the gateway to global flows of information. He also recognizes how this access is important in both school and non-school contexts. He said,

> Because of how school and everything is just structured nowadays, it's as if you need to spend that much time in front of the screen or else or you're gonna be left behind or you're gonna miss out on something important.
>
> *(Darvin, forthcoming)*

On a school night, Ayrton spends around four to five hours at the computer, and more than half of that time is spent on schoolwork. He registered for an online currency trading course, and he spends the rest of the evening monitoring currency trends, filling out his currency trading journal, reading about cars, and scrolling through his Facebook newsfeed. Through the online forum of the currency trading course, he is able to interact with finance professionals and exchange knowledge with them. Because Ayrton gets busy with schoolwork, he rarely gets a chance to play games, sometimes going without games for several weeks. He has dinner with his family, which provides a break from being in front of the computer the whole time. Apart from using his mobile phone to text and check email, Ayrton uses it to read the news in between classes. It contains a BBC app which he has installed "to have a general idea of what's going on." He also downloaded a CNN app "to see different perspectives of how the news is being reported," an indication of how he has adopted critical media literacy (Darvin, forthcoming). Ayrton has also been active in writing fan fiction and has posted online a 150,000-word story comprised of 18 chapters. He gets feedback from other writers about how to improve his craft.

In contrast, for John, the computer seems to be a tool primarily for games and data encoding, which reflects the early digital practices he was accustomed to when he was a young boy studying in the Philippines. In his old school, computer class only involved learning how to use the keyboard. Because his family did not own a computer then, he would go to internet cafes to play games. As a busy caregiver, John's mother hardly has any time to use the computer, and if she does, she uses it to check Facebook and watch soap operas. John's own views of technology appear to be shaped by his life experiences and social background. When asked what he uses technology for, he responds immediately with "League of Legends," a multiplayer online game.

RON: How about stuff for school? What do you use the computer for?
JOHN: Basically for printing.
RON: Do you think working with the computer helps you with English?
JOHN: No, not at all.

(Darvin, forthcoming)

On weekdays, John gets home at 3:30 in the afternoon to a usually empty house and goes straight to the computer, while his younger brother tinkers with the iPad. Because their mother is at work, John only has to microwave dinner for his brother and himself, and he usually has it in front of the computer. Most of John's evening is spent playing League of Legends and Minecraft, and he is not particularly active in producing digital texts. His hobby is sketching anime images, which he either copies from comic books or draws from his imagination. He uploads pictures of these creations on Facebook, but he receives only one or two likes at a time. He has attempted using Paint to draw manga images, but finds it difficult to control the mouse. Paid animation applications, he says, "have more colors, more different kinds of tools where you can change the animation" (Darvin, forthcoming), but he is only able to download free versions, which have limited functionality.

Implications for Practice, Policy, and Future Research

As demonstrated by Ayrton and John, learners of this generation may have access to technology, but because of a variety of factors, they will invest in diverse digital literacies. Whether it's because of differences in home environments, parental involvement, or the affordances and limitations of devices available to them, learners can develop different views of what technology is for, and these in turn shape their digital practices. Motivated by different interests and desires, they may invest in specific literacies to achieve a variety of benefits (Darvin & Norton, 2015) that can range from the economic (e.g., finding a job) to the social (e.g., connecting with friends). To realize these possibilities, learners need to be able to identify the affordances of different digital tools, adapt them for their specific needs, and create affordances of their own. They may use these affordances for different purposes:

1. Identity representation: e.g., taking selfies, constructing a Facebook profile
2. Artistic expression: e.g., posting pictures on Instagram, publishing fan fiction stories online
3. Facilitation of social relations: e.g., chatting with friends on Snapchat
4. Consumption and production of knowledge: e.g., reading news online, preparing a PowerPoint for science class
5. Exchange of goods and services: e.g., ordering books on Amazon
6. Entertainment: e.g., playing Minecraft, watching a movie on Netflix

There are different platforms, programs, and apps designed for specific purposes, but how their affordances are used may vary across users. YouTube, for instance, may be used for artistic expression, entertainment, and/or research.

Learning Language to Navigate the Digital World

Referring to the generation of students who grew up with digital technology, Prensky (2001) coined the term *digital natives*, which he defined as "'native speakers' of the digital language of computers, video games and the Internet" (p. 1). By achieving currency in both academic and journalistic discourse, this designation has helped construct the notion that these young users are naturally adept in using digital devices for different purposes. As we have seen from the data, however, the ascription of digital savvy to a generation simply because they were born into technology is problematic for a number of reasons. Users engage with digital devices in very diverse ways, and with varying conceptions of what purpose

188 Ron Darvin

technology serves. At the same time, the existence of one "digital language" in which these digital natives are naturally fluent is a problematic premise. Code, for instance, while providing the logical architecture of software, is not the language that allows users to interact with others in these networked publics, nor is there just one definitive coding language. Whereas English appears to be the de facto language of the internet, it is in fact only one of an astounding number of languages used online.

When we speak of learning language to navigate the digital world, we are reminded that digital literacy is still about literacy in its most foundational sense, a proficiency in reading and writing. It involves being able to decode skillfully the words and images in digitally mediated texts, and to select and assemble appropriate words and images to communicate and perform various digital functions. Emphasizing this core is particularly crucial as language, genres of texts, and multimodal conventions in the digital realm continue to evolve. Multiple studies have analyzed how participants in different online spaces—such as blogs, online games, and social networking sites—use language in ways that are specific to these contexts, resulting in social variations of digitally mediated discourse (see, e.g., Barton & Lee, 2013; Thurlow & Mroczek, 2011). By enabling the use of written language in ways that are similar to face-to-face oral language, digital media allow the interpretation of the written in flexible, dialogic, and interactive ways (Lankshear & Knobel, 2011; C. Luke, 2003; Warschauer, 2009). Control is less top-down than it is in traditional modes of communication, and there is a notable increase in the use of images such as icons, emoticons, and animated GIFs to communicate meaning. Online participation also enables cross-language interaction, where users, for instance, can shift between English and Romanized Cantonese and assemble mixed idiomatic expressions (Warschauer 2009).

In short, learners need to develop more complex linguistic and semiotic repertoires that will allow them to negotiate the multiplicity and diversity of digital spaces. They need to gain a sense of the communicative 'game' that has been transformed by technology. Borrowing from Bourdieu's (1986) conception of *sens pratique*, learners need to develop a 'practical sense' of how to use language effectively within the digital realm. This sense is 'practical' in that it is developed through practice and serves very practical purposes. Applied to language learning, this practical sense (Darvin & Norton, 2015) enables learners to:

> (a) master the rules, norms, genres, and multimodal features specific to different communicative contexts; (b) seamlessly shift codes, practices, and strategies while moving across spaces; and (c) use linguistic and nonlinguistic resources to gain access to, challenge, and transform these spaces.
>
> *(p. 48)*

To address this pedagogical need, policy makers need to design curricula that reflect this broader conception of literacy, one where digital literacy is viewed not as separate or supplementary but interwoven with and as essential as print literacy. While they use different media, these literacies both involve the fundamental processes of encoding and decoding meaning. To scaffold the development of these competencies, teachers need to be able to draw parallels between print and digital genres and their shared use of linguistic and semiotic resources.

Designing Policies for 21st-century Learning

Indeed, the need to equip learners with this practical sense to negotiate an increasingly digital world has tremendous implications for language planning and policy. Because language is a critical component of digital literacy, the performance of even the simplest digitally mediated interactions requires reading and writing. On the other hand, designing digital solutions and creating algorithms to address specific needs that are built on advanced reasoning and problem-solving skills require mastery of symbolic and formal language (OECD, 2015). Language education, therefore, needs to provide the foundational skills required to navigate digital environments.

The teaching of reading strategies also needs to extend to the reading of digital texts, such as websites and social media, and learners have to recognize the different structures and conventions of these digital genres to navigate online environments. This navigation requires metacognitive regulation, the ability to organize hypertext structures into mental maps and to evaluate the relevance of webpages (OECD, 2015). Conducting an online search, assessing the credibility of sources, locating information on a webpage, and evaluating its usefulness—all these digital literacies complement inquiry-based or project-based approaches that encourage learners to be more autonomous as they discover solutions to real-world issues. To align with this flexible, learner-centered paradigm, language education policies need to articulate more explicitly the language skills that enable deep conceptual understanding and higher-order thinking in digital contexts. Leveraging the potential of technology in education requires school-wide planning to determine how to scaffold the learning of digital literacies across grade levels and subject areas. Teachers need to be trained on how to blend technology meaningfully into curricula so that lessons are able to strike a balance between digital literacy and foundational skills.

As the new BC curriculum promotes a more inquiry-based approach to learning, students need to learn how to sift through large volumes of data available online and extract legitimate knowledge. In a post-truth age, where what is regarded as true has become more malleable and disputable, learners need to develop a *critical literacy* that will enable them to separate hoaxes from fact and to examine how mechanisms of power shape knowledge and social relations in digital contexts (Darvin, 2017). A. Luke (2014) points out that mere digital engagement is not a critical literacy approach. Rather, this criticality involves an examination of the complex interplay of information processing, software dynamics, linguistic processes, and cultural practices that are at work within digital platforms. By applying a critical lens, learners are able to use media "to analyze, critique, and transform the norms, rule systems, and practices governing the social fields of institutions and everyday life" (A. Luke, 2014, p. 20). To achieve this goal, educational policies need to indicate how critical literacy in the digital age requires a more sophisticated understanding of algorithmic processes, search engine optimization, graphic design, and the norms and conventions of online genres.

As policy makers lay the foundations for digital infrastructure and technology-centered learning standards in schools, they also need to employ the same critical lens to recognize the situatedness of technology use. How technology is perceived and used varies not just within a particular classroom, school, or pedagogy, but also within the social and cultural conditions of out-of-school contexts (North, Snyder & Bulfin, 2008; Prinsloo & Rowsell, 2012). An autonomous notion of digital literacies assumes that they have a general applicability and operate in a general manner, regardless of local configurations. Assuming this generality and universality of function and practice, however, disregards the "differentiated, situated and enculturated ways in which digital practices happen" (Snyder & Prinsloo, 2007, p. 173). Policy makers need to be aware that technology choices have social and economic implications, privileging some and marginalizing others. Hence, the construction and implementation of policies such as bring your own device (BYOD) or flipped learning require an understanding of how learners access and use technology in unequal ways. Educational policies need to consider these inequities to ensure that technology integration in curricula and pedagogy does not exclude, but provides agentive possibilities for, learners of different social backgrounds.

References

American Library Association Office for Information Technology Policy. (2013). *Digital literacy, libraries, and public policy*. Retrieved May 23, 2017 from www.districtdispatch.org/wp-content/uploads/2013/01/2012_OITP_digilitreport_1_22_13.pdf

Appadurai, A. (1990). Disjuncture and difference in the global cultural economy. *Theory, Culture and Society*, 7(2–3), 295–310.

Barton, D., & Lee, C. (2013). *Language online: Investigating digital texts and practices*. London, UK: Routledge.

Basch, L., Schiller, N., & Blanc, C. (1994). *Nations unbound: Transnational projects, postcolonial predicaments and deterritorialized nation-states*. Amsterdam, Netherlands: Gordon and Breach.

Bourdieu, P. (1986). The forms of capital. In J. F. Richardson (Ed.), *Handbook of theory of research for sociology of education* (pp. 241–58). New York, NY: Greenwood Press.

Citizenship and Immigration Canada. (2012). *Investors*. Retrieved May 23, 2017 from www.cic.gc.ca/english/immigrate/business/investors/index.asp

Cope, B., & Kalantzis, M. (2010). New media, new learning. In D. Cole & D. Pullen (Eds.), *Multiliteracies in motion: Current theory and practice* (pp. 87–104). London, UK: Routledge.

Cope, B., & Kalantzis, M. (2012). *Literacies*. Cambridge, UK: Cambridge University Press.

Darvin, R. (2017). Language, power, and critical digital literacy. In S. Thorne & S. May (Eds.), *Language education and technology: Encyclopedia of language and education* (Vol. 9). New York, NY: Springer.

Darvin, R. (forthcoming). Language, social class, and the acquisition of unequal digital literacies. *Language and Literacy*.

Darvin, R., & Norton, B. (2014). Social class, identity, and migrant students. *Journal of Language, Identity & Education, 13*(2), 111–117.

Darvin, R., & Norton, B. (2015). Identity and a model of investment in applied linguistics. *Annual Review of Applied Linguistics, 35*, 36–56.

De Costa, P. I. (2010). Reconceptualizing language, language learning, and the adolescent immigrant language learner in the age of postmodern globalization. *Language and Linguistics Compass, 4*(9), 769–781.

Jones, R. H., & Hafner, C. A. (2012). *Understanding digital literacies: A practical introduction*. Oxon, UK: Routledge.

Lankshear, C., & Knobel, M. (2011). *New literacies: Everyday practices and social learning* (3rd ed.). Maidenhead, UK: Open University Press.

Luke, A. (2014). Defining critical literacy. In J. Avila & J. Z. Pandya (Eds.), *Moving critical literacies forward: A new look at praxis across contexts* (pp. 19–31). New York, NY: Routledge.

Luke, C. (2003). Pedagogy, connectivity, multimodality, and interdisciplinarity. *Reading Research Quarterly, 38*(3), 397–403.

North, S., Snyder, I., & Bulfin, S. (2008). Digital tastes: Social class and young people's technology use. *Information, Communication & Society, 11*(7), 895–911.

Norton, B. (2013). *Identity and language learning: Extending the conversation* (2nd ed.). Bristol, UK: Multilingual Matters.

OECD. (2015). *Students, computers and learning: Making the connection*. Paris, France: OECD Publishing.

Prensky, M. (2001). Digital natives, digital immigrants part 1. *On the Horizon, 9*(5), 1–6.

Prinsloo, M., & Rowsell, J. (2012). Digital literacies as placed resources in the globalised periphery. *Language and Education, 26*(4), 271–277.

Province of British Columbia. (2017). *Digital literacy*. Retrieved July 27, 2017 from www2.gov.bc.ca/gov/content/education-training/k-12/teach/teaching-tools/digital-literacy

Snyder, I., & Prinsloo, M. (2007). Young people's engagement with digital literacies in marginal contexts in a globalised world. *Language and Education, 21*(3), 171–179.

Steeves, V. (2014). *Young Canadians in a wired world, Phase III: Life online*. Ottawa, Canada: MediaSmarts.

Thurlow, C., & Mroczek, K. (Eds.). (2011). *Digital discourse: Language in the new media*. Oxford, UK: Oxford University Press.

Warschauer, M. (2009). Digital literacy studies: Progress and prospects. In M. Baynham & M. Prinsloo (Eds.), *The future of literacy studies* (pp. 123–140). London, UK: Palgrave Macmillan.

16

SMALL STORIES OF/IN CHANGING TIMES IN PARAGUAY

A Resource for Identity Work in Language Policy Appropriation

Katherine S. Mortimer

In Paraguay, a major language policy change in 1992 represented a substantial change in Paraguayan education. Before the policy, Guarani[1]—despite being a dominant language for a majority of Paraguayans—had been prohibited in education. After the change, all children were required to learn Guarani and to learn *in* Guarani while learning Spanish and learning *in* Spanish. At the time of this study, one whole generation of school children had just passed through the new system. Their parents and teachers, however, had all been educated in a different time. As adults talked about this policy change, they often told a small story—or a very brief narrative—about the changing meaning of being a Guarani speaker. Here is an example:

> People from before said, in Guarani, it makes our children sound igno-rant. . . . And our people before, well, they didn't love Guarani. I, for example, have the experience that my father would tell my mother not to speak to us in Guarani, that we must not speak in Guarani because we [would be seen as] *guarangos*. And [so], Mamá, all her life, spoke to us in Spanish.
>
> *(Profesora Carla, interview, 5/7/2008)*

Profesora Carla (all names are pseudonyms), a sixth-grade teacher who pas-sionately supported Guarani instruction in school, told me here what her par-ents and others used to say about speaking Guarani when she was young. She told me about their changing times in connection to this policy, about changes in how people saw Guarani, but also about changes in how people saw Guarani speakers. Over the course of 11 months of fieldwork, I heard many stories of this kind, and as these stories accumulated in my data, they demanded analysis. If people once—or now—chose not to speak Guarani for fear of being seen as a *"guarango"* kind of person, someone ignorant and rude, then people's experiences of this threat seemed important to understand if I was to understand the implementation of Guarani instruction in schools. I asked, what are people telling me about the policy and about themselves when they tell these particular stories?

In this chapter, I analyze these short narratives as small stories (Bamberg, 2006; Bamberg & Georgakopoulou, 2008; Georgakopoulou, 2006), or as moments of social identification in interaction. Taken from the field of narrative analysis, this approach offers a way to uncover some of the work that participants did to identify themselves in relation to the major educational language policy change and in relation to master narratives—or dominant discourses—about what it meant to be a Guarani speaker. I argue that understanding this identity work is important to understanding people's alignments and disalignments with policy and, ultimately, with their practices of policy.

Issues That Motivated the Research

The larger ethnography on which this analysis is based was motivated by my broad interest in understanding the Paraguayan language policy that mandated that all school children—non-Indigenous as well as Indigenous, majoritized as well as minoritized speakers—learn in both the national language of Indigenous origin, Guarani, and the colonial language, Spanish. Wondering how such a policy (seeming rather uniquely counter-hegemonic on paper) was practiced in schools and classrooms, I have drawn on two turns, or theoretical shifts, in language policy scholarship addressing the relations between macro- and micro-levels of policy activity. A policy-as-discourse approach analyzes policy as both (micro) talk and written text and as (macro) normative frames for sociocultural experience (Ball, 1993; Barakos & Unger, 2016; Johnson, 2009). The related policy-as-practice approach analyzes policy as constituted not only in (macro) policy texts but also in the everyday (micro) language practices of many actors at many levels, such that implementation is seen not as linear or directly following from policy text, but as appropriation by multiple actors into different contexts in different ways (Sutton & Levinson, 2001). Both approaches highlight that policy texts and activities cannot be understood except in relationship to their contexts and the sociocultural systems of meaning in which they occur.

Social identification is one of these systems of meaning. I draw on linguistic anthropological and sociocultural linguistic work conceptualizing social identification also in terms of practices and discourse: that is, as constituted in the relationship between the master (macro) narratives of social types of people and moment-to-moment (micro) discursive practice (Bucholtz & Hall, 2005;

Wortham, 2006). I have argued that processes of social identification are implicated in language policy appropriation: Policy influences how people socially identify each other, and social identification influences how people put policy into practice (Mortimer, 2016; Mortimer & Wortham, 2015; also see Pérez-Milans, 2017). This analysis looks closely at one discursive resource for social identification, alignment, and policy processes: small stories.

Alexandra Georgakopoulou and Michael Bamberg offer the concept of a *small story* (Bamberg & Georgakopoulou, 2008; Georgakopoulou, 2006) as a very brief narrative otherwise embedded in everyday conversations. They argue that these stories can be sites of important interactional and identity work. In line with other work on narrative in interaction (Wortham, 2006), an important part of the analysis of small stories is not just what the stories tell about—or the narrated event—but also what they do interactionally in the moment of the telling—the narrating event. Small stories analysis examines "how people actually use stories in everyday, mundane situations in order to create (and perpetuate) a sense of who they are" (Bamberg & Georgakopoulou, 2008, pp. 378–379). Like analysis of how policy is constructed in everyday sociocultural practice, small stories analysis examines the construction of identities in interaction.

Bamberg and Georgakopoulou (2008) outline a three-level procedure for analyzing small stories as sites of identity work. Each level focuses on some aspect of positioning—or relationships between the narrated and narrating events, how the referential world is constructed, and how the teller wants to be understood (Bamberg, 2006). In the first level, the analyst asks how characters within the story are positioned in relation to each other; in the second, how interlocutors in the interaction are positioned in relation to each other; and in the third, how the narrator positions her/himself in relation to master narratives or dominant discourses. Small stories analysis helps illuminate how participants navigate competing and contradictory positions—who they are in relation to multiple master narratives about language and speakers. Thus, small stories analysis is a useful tool for language policy research where we want to understand how policy positions speakers and how speakers position themselves in relation to policy.

Context of the Research

Paraguayan Guarani is a language of Indigenous origin, now spoken by a majority of Paraguayans, most of whom do not identify as Indigenous. Despite Guarani being a language of the majority, and despite it being exalted as an essential sign of national identity, it has been minoritized and, like many other non-colonial languages, stigmatized and prohibited in education (Gynan, 2001). More importantly, Guarani speakers themselves have been minoritized, as well.

A new national constitution in 1992 and a broad educational reform mandated Guarani/Spanish bilingual education for all students throughout the country. The two languages were to be used both as languages of and subjects of instruction (Paraguay MEC, 2000). At the time the data for this study were collected (2008), the policy for bilingual education had been in place for 14 years. Because Guarani usage is more heavily concentrated in rural areas, and bilingualism and Spanish monolingualism are more common in urban areas, the study included two focal schools: one urban and one rural. (For additional details, see also Mortimer, 2013.)

Research Question Addressed

The larger ethnographic study, of which this analysis is a part, examined the appropriation of the major national educational language policy with specific attention to how different social identities for Guarani speakers were evident in policy texts, in talk about policy, and in classroom practices. This specific analysis takes a closer look at one of the social identities that emerged repeatedly in the data—a Guarani speaker as someone who is uneducated, rural, and socially rude/crude—a social type of person referred to by the term *guarango*. In this analysis, I ask what participants were doing in terms of social identification when they told me these stories about their changing sociolinguistic and policy landscape.

Research Methods

The larger study was an ethnography of language policy (Hornberger & Johnson, 2007; Johnson, 2009). It took a specifically discursive approach (Mortimer, 2016; and, more generally, Barakos & Unger, 2016) to data collection and analysis, as well as to the conceptualization of language policy. That is, viewing language policy as discourse, I collected primarily discursive data and used discourse analysis (narrative analysis in this case) to understand them.

Data Collection

Data sources include nearly 500 hours of participant observation and field notes over 11 months of fieldwork; audio-recorded interviews in Spanish with 91 individuals, including teachers, administrators, parents, students, and language scholars; 28 hours of videotaped classroom interaction; policy and school documents; and student work. The bulk of my time was spent in two public schools, one rural and one urban. The present analysis is based primarily on data from interviews with adults (and one group of children) and field notes of conversations with adults in both communities.

Data Analysis Procedures Used

Broadly, the analysis was ethnographic (Hammersley & Atkinson, 2007) and discourse analytic (Wortham & Reyes, 2015), including open coding, memos, and focused coding, with patterns triangulated across multiple sources, time periods,

196 Katherine S. Mortimer

and types of data. Having identified the pattern that adult participants often told small stories about how things used to be, I extracted all such narratives from the field notes and interviews in the larger corpus of data. This process resulted in a reduced corpus of 30 narratives that explicitly employed the term *guarango*.

I examined Bamberg and Georgakopoulou's (2008) three levels of positioning in each of the small stories: character positioning, interlocutor positioning, and positioning of the narrator in relation to master narratives. I also analyzed each narrative for a number of other qualities, including the recipient/person being called *guarango* in the narrated event; the people saying "don't be *guarango*" (e.g., parents, teachers, or a generic *they*); the presence of reported speech, and others. I then examined patterns among these features. Those patterns are the findings discussed in the following.

Findings and Discussion

Character Positioning in the Narrated Event: A Prototypical Small Story

Early in the analysis, a picture emerged of what seemed to be a prototypical story. Many of the narrated events sounded alike, and on analysis, they included a set of common characters and elements (represented in bold in the following excerpt):[2]

Excerpt 1

1. **Antes**, en mi época, la época de tus padres [**before**, in my time, in the time of your
2. **parents**,] **parents** would **tell** their **children** not to speak Guarani,
3. que **no sean guarangos** [that they **should not be** *guarangos*,] he says they would
4. say. What does *guarango* mean, I ask. Someone who speaks Guarani, he says.
   (conversation with Sr. Ávalos, field notes, 2/27/2008)

First, the story began with or included a past temporal frame, as in line 1: "Before, in my time, in the time of your parents." Second, the story included a first character, most often positioned as dominant, such as a parent (as in line 2) or teacher. Third, that dominant character would call a second character *guarango* (as in line 3). And fourth, the recipient or second character was usually positioned in some way as subordinate to the first character; that is, often the adult teller was positioned as a child or children in general (as in line 2). Just over half of the small stories included all of these elements. Excerpt 2 is an additional example following this pattern:

Excerpt 2

1. There are people who before said that if one speaks Guarani he was seen
2. contemptuously as *guarango* . . . that he speaks a lot of Guarani. Why? Because it's

Small Stories of/in Changing Times   **197**

3. a status thing, like it's always the people from the countryside who used Guarani
4. and so people before saw it with contempt, right, but that has improved.

(urban school administrator Vice Directora Wilma,
interview, 6/17/2008)

There are two striking features of positioning in these narrated events. First, the person saying *guarango* was positioned as dominant to the person to whom it was said, and usually it was a dominance of age and role (parent/child, teacher/student). Also striking is that these stories—half of the sample—were set in the past. The characters and their actions were positioned as historical. The past-located stories told of a time before and implicitly or explicitly contrast it with a time now (e.g., Excerpt 2, line 4); that is, things had changed. Narrated events in the other half of the stories in the corpus were located in present times, and whereas these events still generally included two characters, one saying *guarango* to the other, the relationships or positioning between the characters in the present-located stories varied more and did not show the same pattern of dominance (as in Excerpts 4, 5, 6 discussed in the following). What participants were telling me about policy and about themselves is not yet clear, but it was emerging with analysis of the other two levels of positioning.

Interlocutor Positioning in the Narrating Event

In examination of interlocutor positioning, I looked at the relationships between the persons telling the story—my study participants—and their interlocutors during the actual telling. In addition to their common temporal framing of the narrated event, a striking feature of the past-located stories was that, with only one exception, all of them were told to me by urban residents who were Spanish-dominant. In contrast, the present-located stories were told by a variety of urban and rural residents who were more bilingual or Guarani-dominant. Two of the past-located stories that were told by urban teachers point to a function that the past-located stories may have had in general: as a way to resolve tension and contradiction. Profesora Lidia, a coordinator for fourth through sixth grades in the urban school, told me this story:

Excerpt 3

1. There came a time before when one would speak Guarani, people hear you
2. speak Guarani on the bus and they look at you like this, and the people
3. (seems like) they're embarrassed of speaking Guarani because it seems that Guarani
4. was so repressed at one time that, even I remember that if we said words in
5. Guarani when we were little and they'd say, *guaranga*, and *guaranga* was more or
6. less, it was something low [class].

(Profesora Lidia, interview, 5/21/2008)

To understand what this story is doing in the interaction, the narrating event, it is important to examine what led up to the telling. Profesora Lidia knew of my specific interest in the language policy for Guarani instruction, and she knew that I had come to the school in part through an introduction by the Ministry of Education. In this interview, I had asked her how Guarani was used at the school. She said that while the policy required a 50/50 language allocation, they did not teach enough Guarani. I had then asked what kind of role she, as a coordinator or supervising teacher, had in what languages the teachers used in class. Rather than answering my question directly, she asserted her support for Guarani and her opinion that it should be used more in schools. Then she told the story in Excerpt 3 about her experience: that it used to be embarrassing to be a Guarani speaker.

In their study of the interactional work that narratives do, De Fina and Georgakopoulou (2008) found that narratives can often function as a discursive device for managing disagreement between interlocutors and for backing up claims. The story Profesora Lidia told me did something similar. Knowing of my enthusiasm for Guarani instruction, she had told me that they did not use it enough in school. Although not my intention, my question about her role may have implied that she was responsible for this situation, and together we established a potential conflict and a potential threat to her identification as a good teacher and a good Paraguayan. The story she told me (recounted in Excerpt 3), however, located both of us in positions of powerlessness and shame for speaking Guarani. In lines 1–2, she invited me, through the generic second-person pronoun, to take the position of a Guarani speaker on the bus who feels looked down upon. In lines 4–6, she positioned herself as a child and a Guarani speaker, subject to accusations of being low class.

In establishing these sympathetic and unilateral positions for both of us, the story functioned to resolve the tension between the importance of Paraguayan students being Guarani speakers and the fact that many are not. It provided a rational explanation for why parents did not teach their children Guarani; why teachers (who were once those children) did not teach it enough; and possibly why Profesora Lidia, as a supervising teacher, may not have ensured it was used more in school. In an interview with a teacher friend of Profesora Lidia's, the friend cited Lidia as someone who lamented that her (Lidia's) own children did not speak enough Guarani now that they were nearly grown. Lidia's story even serves, interactionally, as a rational explanation for why Lidia's own children did not speak Guarani enough. Although the specificities of other people's lives and stories varied from those in Lidia's story, the predominance of urban, Spanish-dominant speakers telling past-located stories points to a common function: as a discursive device for these speakers to rationalize to me, to themselves, perhaps to the Ministry of Education, the tension between their support for Guarani in schools and their own insufficient use of it (by

Small Stories of/in Changing Times **199**

their judgment). The past-located stories helped these Spanish-dominant speakers navigate the complex and unstable sociolinguistic, pragmatic terrain of what it meant to speak—or not be able to speak—Guarani in current times.

Positioning of the Narrator in Relation to Master Narratives

The past-located small stories functioned interactionally as a means of managing interactional tension. More importantly, however, this function suggests that the stories helped the narrators to manage disagreement between contradictory master narratives about Guarani speakers—on the one hand, that Guarani speakers are ignorant, and on the other hand, that Guarani speakers are the essential Paraguayans—with the Paraguayanness of non-Guarani speakers called into question. Because these Spanish-dominant participants position themselves as children and the origin of their non-Guarani-speaking present as originating long in the past, they would not be held responsible for not knowing Guarani. The stories help them construct sensible, comprehensible, and empathetic selves in problematic and risky pragmatic terrain. The stories allow them to be both Paraguayan—valuing Guarani—and non-Guarani-speaking. For some, the stories may have helped explain a painful loss of language. I find that the selves that these urban, Spanish-dominant speakers constructed in these moments were different, however, from the selves constructed by the participants who told me present-located stories.

The present-located stories represented the other half of the corpus. With two exceptions, these stories were told by participants at the rural school where people were more Guarani-dominant. The following is one of these stories, told to me by Profesora Romilda, the pre-K–first-grade teacher at the rural school.

Excerpt 4

1. She says, la gente todavía piensa que hablar el guaraní es que seas ignorante. Dicen,
2. no hables el guaraní nde[3] guarango [people still think that speaking Guarani means
3. that you're ignorant. They say don't speak Guarani, you *guarango*.] I ask what
4. *guarango* means. She says, que sos[4] campesino, indio, inculto, indígena [that you're
5. a *campesino*, Indian, uncultured, Indigenous.] She qualifies that, what should it
6. matter if you are Indigenous? That doesn't mean you are uncultured. But she
7. affirms that what people mean when they say that is that people are uncultured.
8. She says the people who say things like this are people in the [rural] community
9. who have already learned Spanish and they say this to their children. They are
10. trying to correct them but they do it wrong. They should correct the children's
11. Guarani rather than telling them not to speak it. This happens with people who
12. speak Spanish to their children and so the children speak Spanish better and they

200 Katherine S. Mortimer

13. try to speak Guarani and they make mistakes and then the parents make fun of
14. them and call them *guarango*.

(field notes, 10/22/2008)

That the story was set in the present is evident in Profesora Romilda's use of "people still" (lines 1–2) and her use of the present tense throughout. Whereas in her telling, parents call their children *guarango* (lines 13–14), Romilda positioned herself (lines 5–6) in opposition to those people. In disagreeing with the idea that being Indigenous (often linked to Guarani-speaking) was being uncultured, she positioned herself in opposition to the master narrative about a *guarango* type of person. In her oppositional stance to those who say *guarango*, she constructed positions of resistance for both herself and for Guarani speakers more broadly, resistance to the master narrative of Guarani speakers being ignorant.

A similar resistance is also seen in a small story told by Profesora Sara, another teacher at the rural school:

Excerpt 5

1. Muchas veces nosotros aquí tenemos vergüenza de hablar el guaraní, sentimos
2. inferiores por hablar guaraní, la gente del centro dice, guarango [many times we
3. here are embarrassed of speaking Guarani, we feel inferior for speaking Guarani,
4. people from the [urban] center say, *guarango*.] I ask about the word. People still say
5. It, she says. Who, I ask. People from the [urban] center. For example, when they go
6. for a tournament to a school in the [urban] center children say things like that in
7. the hall about their students. . . . They say, *campesino. ¿*Por qué vamos a tener
8. vergüenza de por la sola razón de ser del campo, de una zona rural? [Why are we
9. going to be embarrassed for the sole reason of being from the countryside, from a
10. rural area?] So that [our students] don't feel that way, inferior, Guarani should be
11. used in more primary places.

(field notes, 6/11/2008)

Like Romilda, Sara positioned herself in opposition to those who say *guarango* and *campesino* (lines 7–10). She also constructed a position of identification for herself as being in resistance to the master narrative linking Guarani-speaking and ignorance/ruralness. Overall, the present-located stories by Guarani-dominant or bilingual speakers positioned their narrators in opposition to the master narrative of a Guarani speaker as ignorant.

Urban, Spanish-dominant participants constructed positions for themselves in which they could be good Paraguayans who value Guarani even though they did not speak it. Overt opposition to the Guarani-ignorance narrative was not necessary because they simply located it in the past: 'people don't say that anymore.'

In contrast, rural, mostly Guarani-dominant participants constructed selves in which they could resist the still-active master narrative about Guarani speakers being ignorant, or empathetic selves in which their experience of pain might be understandable.

However, two small stories among those located in the present were different in an important way: They were the only two stories in the corpus in which the term *guarango* was not linked to ignorance. In the first of these stories, the mother of a student (Francisca) at the rural school told me about her cousin:

Excerpt 6

1. I have one of my cousins who is *guaranga*. She knows everything right up to the
2. numbers, Guarani she knows, knows how to handle Guarani but so well.

(Francisca's mother, interview, 9/4/2008)

Francisca's mother identified her cousin with the term *guaranga*, but she also described the cousin's knowledge of Guarani—knowing the numbers—in a way that would be read in Paraguay as the product of education. Francisca's mother, who identified as Guarani-dominant, positioned herself as admiring her cousin's linguistic skill, and, while not acknowledging the master narrative linking Guarani and ignorance, she constructed a Guarani-speaking identity that was most definitely not ignorant. In the second of these stories, a sixth-grade student at the rural school, Ramón, told how his father, in the present tense, calls him *guarango*, which Ramón defined as someone who did not speak enough Guarani. Ramón constructed himself not as lacking education for speaking Guarani, but as deficient in his not speaking enough Guarani. Like Francisca's mother, Ramón positioned himself not in alignment with or resistance to the *guarango* narrative, but outside of it and perhaps in a reappropriation of it.

What were participants doing in terms of social identification when they told me these stories about their changing sociolinguistic and policy landscape? Urban adult participants who were largely Spanish-dominant used small stories to identify themselves as sensible, comprehensible people in an ideologically problematic terrain. If to be Paraguayan is to speak Guarani, then their identifications as people with logical, understandable reasons for not speaking Guarani afforded them a way to avoid being perceived as unParaguayan, and even to affirm the importance of Guarani without being able to speak it. They were able to align themselves with the master narrative that Guarani is the essence of Paraguayan identity while denying the contemporary existence of the narrative of Guarani-speaking as ignorant. In contrast, rural adult participants, who were more frequent Guarani users, employed small stories to identify themselves as people still subject to the painful identification as a *guarango* type of person, but people with the agency to resist that identification. In the two exceptional stories, rural residents constructed alternatives to the master narrative of ignorance and Guarani-speaking, aligning themselves with perhaps an emergent narrative that speaking Guarani displays education and skill.

Adult participants in this study lived in a context of major educational language policy change over the course of their lifetimes. Children in the study were growing up in substantially different sociolinguistic terrain. The small stories provided participants with a manageable way to describe this terrain—and sometimes changes to it—and to locate themselves in it. They used small stories to locate themselves in relation to master narratives about Guarani speakers and, indeed, in relation to the national educational language policy. Whatever their actual language use was in relation to the policy, small stories were a resource for getting identified as sensible, patriotic, and agentive people. That is, whether teachers used Guarani in school or not, they could still be identifiable as good Paraguayans in alignment with the policy. Whether or not the policy had actually made it possible for speaking Guarani to be associated with school, they could still be identifiable as proud and agentive Guarani speakers.

Implications for Policy, Practice, and Future Research

We see in this analysis that social identification is an active part of the context in which language policy is practiced and appropriated. With our growing understanding of the multiple macro and micro scales of language policy activity, we must attend to how people identify themselves and others and how that identification is connected to what policies get made and how policies get practiced. In previous work I have described how social identities can influence the decisions policy actors make when they appropriate policy into various contexts (Mortimer, 2013), as well as how language policy can change what identities are available (Mortimer, 2016; Mortimer & Wortham, 2015). This chapter closely examines one discursive resource for that work: small stories. Pérez-Milans (2017) argues for greater attention in ethnographic language policy scholarship to performative action in policy contexts—how people perform the identities of different kinds of speakers, not just how they talk about those kinds of speakers. Small stories analysis is a useful tool in taking such a step.

Finally, we can see in these small stories of a language policy context that, just as identities are being constructed and reconstructed in moments of interaction, the sociolinguistic context of policy, too, is being made and remade in these moments. We see that even a major policy change that on the surface would seem to increase the value and status of a minoritized language can visit distress on people by destabilizing the value of their linguistic resources (or lack thereof): teachers whose Guarani-speaking parents ensured their children spoke Spanish and who now feel deficient in their obligation to teach bilingually. If language policy is to work as a tool for more inclusive education, it will need to take into account speakers' possibilities for trajectories of identification.

Notes

1 Throughout this chapter, I use *Guarani* as a non-specific term to refer to the varieties of the language used by a majority of Paraguayans. Indigenous varieties of Guarani are spoken in Paraguay, and other varieties are spoken in Bolivia, Brazil, and Argentina, but they are not referred to in this paper. *Guarani* is pronounced with stress on the final syllable, written in Spanish as *Guaraní*. When writing in English, I follow Guarani orthography and do not use the diacritic. When writing in Spanish, as in excerpts, I follow the practices of my participants, who did use the diacritic.

2 Excerpts are taken from field notes and audio-recorded interviews, as indicated. Following ethnographic practice, participants' words are represented differently in these two different data sources. Where excerpts come from field notes, I include participants' original words in Spanish or Guarani if I recorded them verbatim in my notes, followed by my English translation in brackets. Otherwise my notes include my English gloss of what they said in an indirect quotation or paraphrase, as well as my questions to them. Where excerpts come from interviews, I provide direct quotations of participants' words, although, for reasons of space, I provide my English translation of what they originally said in Spanish or Guarani.

3 *Nde* is the second-person singular pronoun in Guarani.

4 *Sos* is a second-person singular form of the verb *ser*, pertaining to the second-person singular pronoun *vos* that is used instead of *tú* in Paraguay (and Argentina and a few other places) (i.e., *vos sos* instead of *tú eres*).

References

Ball, S. J. (1993). What is policy? Texts, trajectories and toolboxes. *Discourse: The Australian Journal of Educational Studies, 13*(2), 10–17.

Bamberg, M. (2006). Stories: Big or small: Why do we care? *Narrative Inquiry, 16*(1), 139–147.

Bamberg, M., & Georgakopoulou, A. (2008). Small stories as a new perspective in narrative and identity analysis. *Text & Talk, 28*(3), 377–396.

Barakos, E., & Unger, J. W. (Eds.). (2016). *Discursive approaches to language policy.* New York, NY: Palgrave Macmillan.

Bucholtz, M., & Hall, K. (2005). Identity and interaction: A sociocultural linguistic approach. *Discourse Studies, 7*(4–5), 585–614.

De Fina, A., & Georgakopoulou, A. (2008). Analysing narratives as practices. *Qualitative Research, 8*(3), 379–387.

Georgakopoulou, A. (2006). Thinking big with small stories in narrative and identity analysis. *Narrative Inquiry, 16*(1), 122–130.

Gynan, S. N. (2001). Language planning and policy in Paraguay. *Current Issues in Language Planning, 2*(1), 53–118.

Hammersley, M., & Atkinson, P. (2007). *Ethnography: Principles in practice* (3rd ed.). New York, NY: Routledge.

Hornberger, N. H., & Johnson, D. C. (2007). Slicing the onion ethnographically: Layers and spaces in multilingual language education policy and practice. *TESOL Quarterly, 41*(3), 509–532.

Johnson, D. C. (2009). Ethnography of language policy. *Language Policy, 8*, 139–159. doi:10.1007/s10993-009-9136-9.

Mortimer, K. S. (2013). Communicative event chains in an ethnography of Paraguayan language policy. *International Journal of the Sociology of Language, 219*, 67–99.

Mortimer, K. S. (2016). Language policy as metapragmatic discourse: A focus on the intersection of language policy and social identification. In E. Barakos & J. W. Unger (Eds.), *Discursive approaches to language policy* (pp. 71–96). New York, NY: Palgrave Macmillan.

Mortimer, K. S., & Wortham, S. (2015). Analyzing language policy and social identification across heterogeneous scales. *Annual Review of Applied Linguistics, 35*, 160–172.

Paraguay MEC. (2000). *La educación bilingüe en la reforma educativa paraguaya.* Asunción: Paraguay.

Pérez-Milans, M. (2017). Metapragmatics in the ethnography of language policy. *Working Papers in Urban Language and Literacies, 208*, 1–15.

Sutton, M., & Levinson, B. A. U. (Eds.). (2001). *Policy as practice: Toward a comparative sociocultural analysis of educational policy.* Westport, CT: Ablex.

Wortham, S. (2006). *Learning identity: The joint emergence of social identity and academic learning.* New York, NY: Cambridge University Press.

Wortham, S., & Reyes, A. (2015). *Discourse analysis beyond the speech event.* New York, NY: Routledge.

17

CHALLENGES OF LANGUAGE EDUCATION POLICY DEVELOPMENT AND IMPLEMENTATION IN CREOLE-SPEAKING CONTEXTS

The Case of Jamaica

Shondel Nero

Language education policy development and implementation in contexts where Creoles are spoken by the majority of the population and a European language is the official language has been fraught with challenges dating back to the colonial period. Specifically, policies in these contexts historically sought to educate the populace to "speak a language they don't write, and write a language they don't speak," as Jamaican performance poet Mutabaruka so eloquently put it (cited in Cooper, 2010). This situation has led to generations of Creole speakers' underperforming academically in school while often internalizing conflicting linguistic identities that don't match their language practices. One such Creole-speaking context is the Caribbean island nation of Jamaica, a former British colony, where English is the official language and language of education, but Jamaican Creole (JC) is the mass vernacular. In this chapter, I discuss Jamaica as an illustrative case of the challenges of language education policy development and implementation in a Creole-speaking environment in the postcolonial era. The discussion is based upon a critical ethnographic study[1] of the Jamaican language education policy developed by the Ministry of Education (MOE, 2001) and linguists from the University of the West Indies (UWI) in Jamaica. I draw on tenets of linguistic imperialism (Phillipson, 1992) and postcolonial theory (Bhabha, 1994; Hall, 1994) to contextualize the study and analyze the findings.

Issues That Motivated the Research

This study was motivated by the persistent academic underachievement of an increasing number of Creole dominant-speakers in New York City (NYC) public schools over the past three decades who hail from the Commonwealth Caribbean,[2]

206 Shondel Nero

mainly Jamaica. Educators have struggled to provide appropriate placement and literacy instruction for Creole-dominant speakers in NYC schools, who publicly self-identify as native speakers of English but whose productive abilities in standardized English are below grade level (New York City Department of Education, 2012). My own pilot study (Nero, 2010) of Creole-dominant students in two NYC schools with large Jamaican populations unearthed the need for a deeper understanding of the Jamaican education system and language education policy there, which led to the current study.

Context of the Research

Creole Contexts

Before examining their language education policy, it is important to understand Jamaica as a prototypical Creole-speaking environment, which shares a number of common characteristics with other Creole contexts around the world. Creole contexts emanated from transatlantic slavery and the European exploitive enterprise of colonization (Phillipson, 1992). Whereas *all* languages emerge from some form of human contact, Creoles emerged in uniquely exploitive contact situations where the language of the dominant European group (a numerical minority in the colony) was imposed on the dominated group (the numerical majority) through institutionalized structures and ideologies, creating a new language— Creole. The vocabulary of Creole was primarily drawn from the colonial language, whereas the syntax was mostly influenced by African languages brought by the formerly enslaved majority populations (DeCamp, 1971). Two key features of Creole contexts are (1) The European language is privileged in all formal domains, and the Creole is generally stigmatized; and (2) sharp social stratification and a strong association between language and social class where proficiency in the European language is linked to high social class and academic achievement. Conversely, Creole-dominant speech is associated with low social status and academic underachievement.

Another critical aspect of colonization was to inculcate in the colonized population an ideology, identity, and set of dispositions around language based on a monolingual orientation. Canagarajah (2013) argues that the colonial language was used as a unifying force to create nation-states and construct linguistic identities among colonized peoples leading them to believe they were, for example, 'English-speaking' or 'French-speaking' only. In reality, the linguistic identities and dispositions in Creole contexts are much more complicated than originally intended.

Theorizing Language Education Policies in Creole Contexts

Language education policies in Creole contexts such as Jamaica can best be understood through theoretical frameworks that contextualize the institutionalized structures, language ideologies, dispositions, and practices in these contexts. These frameworks apply to the colonial and postcolonial eras, respectively.

Linguistic Imperialism

The first theory is what Phillipson (1992) calls *linguistic imperialism*. Specifically, he defines *English linguistic imperialism* as the "dominance of English ... asserted and maintained by the continuous reconstitution of structural and cultural inequalities between English and other languages" (p. 47). For example, the imposition and privileging of English in Creole contexts as the only language of instruction in school and the denigration of Creoles is an example of linguistic imperialism, and this was accomplished through language education policies. Linguistic imperialism also led to internalized dispositions, language attitudes, and practices that reinforced bias against Creole speakers in schools and beyond. However, language attitudes and practices in Creole contexts have evolved in the postcolonial era.

Postcolonial Theory

Scholars such as Bhabha (1994) and Hall (1994) have characterized the struggles of formerly colonized peoples to assert their own identities and counterdiscourses in the aftermath of colonization through postcolonial theory. One way that formerly colonized peoples have done so is through language by using the colonizer's language *against* them in independence movements (Canagarajah, 1999) *and* simultaneously reclaiming their own cultural identities by using their vernacular more widely. This dual linguistic identity (or what Bhabha [1994] terms *ambivalence*) is a hallmark of postcolonial Creole societies and a key factor in how language education policies are taken up.

Language Education Policy in Creole Contexts

Most language education policies in Creole contexts were originally developed during the colonial period with the purpose of promoting the colonial language and delegitimizing, if not eradicating, the mass vernacular (McCourtie, 1998). One major consequence of the policy of educating the population only through the colonial language has been academic underachievement of the Creole-speaking masses. Examples of this phenomenon can be found in Creole contexts such as the Republic of Seychelles, the Netherlands Antillean islands of Bonaire and Curaçao, and Haiti.

In the Commonwealth Caribbean, English as a mother tongue (Craig, 1999) was the dominant instructional approach for most of the colonial period and in the early post-independence years. The assumption was that students spoke English, albeit a nonstandard form with syntactic, phonological, and lexical

208 Shondel Nero

deviations that were perceived as a problem in need of correction. Devonish and Carpenter (2007) contend that language education policies in Creole contexts have been framed within this "problem" paradigm (p. 23), i.e., they are only introduced into the formal education system as a last resort, when it is perceived that existing policies have failed.

The Jamaican Context

The colonial history of plantation slavery in Jamaica left a rigidly stratified society in which the wealthy, minority upper class had access to better education and upward mobility, whereas the poor masses were deprived of access to education beyond the basic level (Sherlock & Bennett, 1998). Although this state of affairs has improved in the post-independence era, with more access to primary and secondary education for the masses (Márquez, 2010), Jamaica remains a sharply socially stratified society, and the education system is similarly stratified.

Language, Identity, and Education

In Jamaica, two dominant forms of language, Jamaican Creole (JC) and Standard Jamaican English (SJE), have co-existed, with the latter variety being the official language (Carrington, 2001). In everyday language use in Jamaica, "pure" forms of JC or SJE are rare. Rather, there is a seamless mixing of both forms, with a greater proportion of the population more JC-dominant. Despite wider use and acceptance of JC in the public sphere in the postcolonial era, most Jamaicans self-identify as native speakers of English.

There has been a long history of JC-dominant speakers being ostracized in schools. Their language, commonly referred to as "Patois," has been treated as deviant or "broken English" in need of repair or even eradication (Craig, 1999). For JC speakers, SJE is neither a mother tongue nor a foreign language, which means they are not likely to *perceive* English as a second or foreign language because their oral language is dominated by a largely English lexicon. The question then becomes how best to develop language education policy in a Creole-dominant environment where (1) language practices don't match linguistic self-identification; and (2) there is a significant disparity in academic performance among different types of Jamaican schools (MOE, 2011).

Language Education Policies in Jamaica in the Postcolonial Era[3]

In the postcolonial era, several language education policy initiatives have been proposed, including monoliterate transitional bilingualism (Craig, 1999) and full bilingual education, piloted with a four-year-long Bilingual Education Project (BEP) in two primary schools (Devonish & Carpenter, 2007).

In 2001, the Jamaican MOE, in collaboration with linguists at UWI, drafted the policy under investigation in this study. Responding to the persistently poor performance in language and literacy among many Jamaican children, the goal of the draft policy was to "provide direction for the treatment of language issues in the Jamaican educational context, in order to improve language and literacy competencies" (MOE, 2001, p. 6). It proposed an approach of transitional bilingualism and took as its premise that Jamaica is a bilingual country with JC and SJE as the two languages in operation. The policy includes four key objectives:

1. to acknowledge that Jamaica is a bilingual country and to maintain SJE as the official language;
2. to promote oral use of the home language in the early primary and secondary years, using bilingual teaching strategies, while facilitating the development of literacy in SJE;
3. to employ strategies of immersion in SJE through wide use of literature, content-based language teaching, and modeling the target language in the classroom; and
4. to ensure that children are competent in the use of SJE and reading at grade level by the end of grade four (MOE, 2001, pp. 23–25).

These four objectives are important because they show that despite acknowledgment of the population's bilingual practices, literacy in SJE *only* dominates the policy.

On arrival in Jamaica, I learned that this draft policy was never formally ratified by the Jamaican Parliament, owing to a refusal to accept its central premise that Jamaica is a bilingual country. To do so would have been politically contentious and sparked public outrage, as it would have given JC the status of a language. Thus, the policy was never officially disseminated to schools, but remains a draft on the MOE's website with little or no knowledge of its existence among most classroom teachers. However, in this study it was used as a tool to uncover teachers' ideologies with regard to language teaching and learning in a Creole-speaking environment by my asking them to read it prior to my interviewing them about it.

Research Questions Addressed

This was a nine-month-long critical ethnographic study in three Jamaican schools guided by three research questions:

1. What are teachers' understandings of the draft language education policy once they are made aware of it?
2. What are teachers' attitudes toward Jamaican Creole?
3. What are the differences among teachers' language practices and instructional approaches to language and literacy development in different types of schools?

Research Methods

A critical ethnographic approach was chosen for this study because it allowed me to capture the explicit and implicit controls on language practices via institutionalized structures and policies as they are played out in Jamaican schools. This approach also allowed me to critically examine the dispositions, underlying assumptions, and attitudes of stakeholders with regard to language and literacy in a Creole context and how these are enacted in practice.

Data Collection

The study was conducted at three Jamaican public schools representing the different types of schools that Jamaican students attend, e.g., in terms of their socioeconomic status (SES). The names of the schools and teachers have been changed to protect their identities. (See Table 17.1.)

There were 30 participants, including 3 educators who participated in drafting the policy, 3 principals, and 6 English language arts (ELA) teachers—Grades 5–9 (two at each school). There were also 18 students—6 students from each school, 3 per class. My focus here is on the teachers.

Data included weekly classroom observations and field notes on the teachers; questionnaires seeking demographic data on each teacher; and two audiotaped interviews with each teacher. In addition, I examined ELA textbooks for Grades 5–9, curricular documents for those grades, and samples of local standardized tests.

TABLE 17.1 Profile of Three Jamaican Schools and Teachers

School[a]	Kingston Primary (KP)	St. Andrew Primary and Junior High (SAPJH)	Kingston Traditional High (KTH)
Location	Kingston (capital city)	Suburb of Kingston	Kingston
Students' SES	Low	Low	Middle-upper middle
Academic standing[b]	Low achievement	Low achievement	High achievement
School hours	Shift system (two five-hour shifts with different students)	Shift system	Regular full school day
Teachers	Ms. L.—Grade 5 (top stream)	Ms. V.—Grade 8 (middle stream)	Ms. C.—Grade 7 (no streaming)
	Ms. R.—Grade 6 (middle stream)	Ms. D.—Grade 9 (top stream)	Mr. J.—Grade 9 (no streaming)

Sources

a School data provided by principals.

b Ministry of Education Student Assessment Unit (2011).

Data Analysis Procedures Used

I conducted a qualitative data analysis (Miles & Huberman, 1994), first separating the data related to each research question, then coding for emerging themes using Nvivo 9 software. Each teacher was treated as a case. I analyzed and compared interview data related to research questions 1 and 2 across the cases within and among the schools. Observation data for research question 3 focusing on teachers' language and instructional practices were compared with their views on the policy followed by analyses across the cases.

Findings and Discussion

Teachers' Understanding of the Language Education Policy

The teachers expressed a range of understandings of the policy. For example, Ms. L. from KP said, "While we do speak Creole and English, they are more pushing for Standard English per se." Ms. V. of SAPJH understood the policy as "trying to sensitize teachers as to what are the expectations of getting students to use standard English." Mr. J. of KTH noted that he liked the idea of students being competent in SJE by Grade 4 but "worried that if we start to dabble with Creole in the classroom, it means we have failed in teaching standard English." Although the range of responses showed consensus among the teachers that the acquisition of SJE was the ultimate goal of the policy, we see clear differences among their dispositions. Ms. L. *explicitly* acknowledged Jamaicans speak Creole and English (a more postcolonial disposition), whereas Ms. V. *implicitly* acknowledged that students speak JC. Mr. J., too, implicitly acknowledged the existence of JC in the policy, but framed it in the "problem" paradigm alluded to earlier, i.e., a policy that "dabbles with" JC has failed at teaching SJE (a decidedly anti-postcolonial disposition). The differences in the teachers' understandings of the policy reflected their various language attitudes.

Teachers' Language Attitudes

Given the contentious nature of the debate on the role of JC in schools, any question that seeks to elicit a teacher's attitude toward JC is, by definition, political and highly sensitive. When I asked the teachers how they felt about Creole, Mr. J. responded emphatically, "I *hate* [his emphasis] Creole; I don't like it, I don't use it, I don't like it in school, I don't like it in church, I don't want my daughter speaking it at home . . . you get my point." Ms. L.'s attitude, by contrast, was more ambivalent. She replied, "I don't have a problem with it [Creole], because Creole comes naturally *even* [her emphasis] to me, yes it does!" I followed up by asking her whether she defined herself as a Creole speaker, an English speaker, or a bilingual, to which she laughed and then replied:

> I would say "yes," because as I was explaining to you earlier, I *will* teach in the Standard English but if I'm teaching a concept and realize they not *getting* it, I will go *down to the Creole*, and explain it as best and then say, "Okay, do you understand it now?"

We see here Ms. L.'s grappling with her own acceptance of Creole, offering a kind of grudging confession that it comes naturally even to *her*, as if to suggest it would not be normal for someone of her class or stature (a teacher perhaps) to be a Creole speaker. Ms. L. displays a conflicted attitude toward JC, typical in Creole contexts—a removed acceptance of the mass vernacular while simultaneously seeming surprised that, in fact, she is not removed from it. Furthermore, her emphatic statement that she *will* teach in SJE but go *down* to Creole to explain difficult concepts to students shows (1) the lower status accorded to JC implied in her use of the word *down*; and (2) the 'generally understood' policy of teaching in SJE *only* is not taken up so absolutely in practice.

Overall, the teachers' attitudes toward JC ranged from embracing it (Ms. R., KP), to acceptance (Ms. L., KP and Ms. C., KTH), to tolerance (Ms. V. and Ms. D., SAPJH), to rejection (Mr. J., KTH). The teachers' range of language attitudes has implications for their instructional practices and the uptake of a language education policy if and when one is formally ratified.

Teachers' Language and Instructional Practices

The variation among the teachers' instructional practices can be attributed to a host of interrelated factors including the type of school and population of students; how the 'understood' policy was taken up by teachers; the curriculum and national exams; individual teacher's training (or not) in linguistics; and teachers' language attitudes.

At KP, a school operating on two five-hour shifts due to overcrowding, known as a *shift school*, the students were from mostly low socioeconomic backgrounds and were predominantly JC speakers; they could be heard speaking JC routinely inside and outside the classroom. In Ms. L.'s top stream fifth-grade class (*streams* are groupings of students by ability level), her ELA lessons were mostly taught in SJE, except when she selectively used JC to scold, mock, be affectionate with, or, as noted earlier, explain difficult concepts to students. Given that Ms. L.'s class was the top stream, she routinely reminded students that they had to comport themselves as top stream students and produce "5P work," implying work written in SJE befitting of students in the top stream. Evans (2001) correctly notes that in Jamaican schools, streams mark students' identities, which are subtly reinforced by teachers and internalized by students themselves, often through classroom-sanctioned language practices.

Both Ms. L. and Ms. R. at KP, and Ms. D. and Ms. V at SAPJH, routinely 'corrected' students when they spoke JC in class. For example, when students pronounced *three* as *tree*,[4] this 'correction' was not effective, as students' speech reflected Creole pronunciations rather than lack of understanding of the content. The attempted correction by teachers is part of the tendency to frame Creoles as badly pronounced or poorly spelled versions of the colonial language rather than languages in their own right. To be fair to teachers, given that (1) MOE (1999) curriculum guides state that students' mastery of SJE is an important goal in ELA; (2) few teachers are offered linguistic training in JC as part of their teacher preparation; and (3) a codified writing system of JC is not permitted in schools,[5] they are left with no choice but to approach JC from a corrective stance. Moreover, what counts as mastery of SJE was heavily focused on short written grammatical exercises or reading comprehension questions that mirrored the format of the high-stakes Grade Six Achievement Test (GSAT) (MOE, 2006). Thus, as Menken (2008) notes in her study of English language learners (ELLs) in New York City, standardized tests become *de facto* language policy, leaving many ELLs behind, as they drive teachers' instructional practices and constrain students' written language practices in class. For JC-speaking students at KP and SAPJH who had little opportunity to use SJE outside of school, the policy of SJE only in class left them, too, further behind, given that they attended shift schools with fewer hours of instruction, had less time to prepare for the GSAT, and had no option to use their vernacular in writing.

At KTH, a different situation emerged. Students at this high-performing secondary school were mostly middle to upper class and were already fluent in both spoken and written SJE. It was a full-day school, so students had many more hours of instruction in SJE. In fact, ELA teachers at KTH wrote their own English curriculum, which superseded the MOE's curriculum guides, creating affordances for higher levels of literacy in SJE among the students. The policy focus on acquisition of SJE, then, could easily be realized at KTH or a similar type of school.

Mr. J.'s ninth-grade class was typical of KTH, a neatly arranged room with students speaking mostly in SJE. He spoke to students exclusively in SJE, reminding them that this was an "English" class, so he expected them to speak and write English. Given his stated dislike for JC, he did not allow students to use it in class, except when writing dialogues in a narrative. (I call this his personal language policy.) When one student who took him up on the option to write a few sentences of dialogue in JC asked him how to spell a word in JC, he quipped, "Spell it however you like; there's no rule," thus potentially reinforcing the notion that JC has no structure.

Ideological Tensions in the Postcolonial Era

The foregoing examination of language education policy in Jamaica illustrates the challenges of policy development and implementation in Creole contexts. First, the development of the policy itself was framed within the "problem" paradigm

214 Shondel Nero

(a response to a literacy crisis among the masses of JC-speaking children), but the policy could only have a chance to pass muster if acquisition of SJE was the ultimate goal, evidence of the deeply embedded legacy of linguistic imperialism in Jamaica, even more than 50 years after independence. The policy's approach of transitional bilingualism was a compromise between educators at the MOE, whose focus was promoting literacy in SJE (their take on solving the problem), and linguists at UWI whose focus was recognition of JC as a language. The linguists were attempting to shift the ideology from language-as-problem to language-as-right and language-as-resource (Ruiz, 1988), within a larger frame of educational equity in the post-colonial era (Devonish & Carpenter, 2007). The attempted ideological shift didn't work; i.e., even the compromise policy was not ratified by the parliament. Its central premise of Jamaica being a bilingual country was too much of a radical disruption to the monolingual (English) orientation cultivated during the colonial era. It's one thing to 'know' that JC exists; it's quite another to give it institutionalized recognition. This issue was the biggest obstacle to the policy's ratification.

Testing Language Attitudes, Practices, and Agency in Policy Implementation

The teachers' consensus reading of the policy as primarily focused on the acquisition of literacy in SJE was correct; however, we see among them different levels of recognition of JC as a language spoken by most Jamaicans—from explicit (Ms. L.) to implicit (Ms. V.) to acknowledgment of its existence but dismissal of its validity in school (Mr. J.). We can surmise that these different levels of recognition of JC would have had implications for how the policy might have been differentially taken up by each of these teachers, had it been ratified.

Policy ratification aside, the teachers' attitudes toward JC and their instructional practices, as well as students' language practices, present challenges for language education policy implementation in a postcolonial context. For example, Ms. L's conflicted attitude toward JC is a very common postcolonial one, as it illustrates Bhabha's (1994) notion of "ambivalence." Furthermore, the postcolonial era brought with it greater access to primary and secondary education for many JC speakers, who are disproportionately tracked into schools like KTH or SAPJH. Teachers at such schools are thus confronted daily with large numbers of students speaking JC in the classroom and elsewhere on the school premises, which makes it difficult for them to deny its existence. Thus, despite a policy that insists on their instruction being only in SJE, teachers exercise their own agency, as Ms. L. did, by selectively using JC in order to connect with the students affectively and academically.

British Colonial Education Structure Versus Postcolonial Language Attitudes and Practices

Had the language education policy been ratified, its implementation would still have been challenged by the tensions between the enduring British colonial education system in Jamaica and the changing language attitudes and practices in the postcolonial era. Not only did the system enforce English as the only language of instruction in schools and of high-stakes national exams, but a particular standardized variety of English, thereby institutionalizing what Lippi-Green (1997) calls *standard language ideology* (SLI). She defines SLI as "the pervasive belief in the superiority of an abstracted and idealized form of language, based on the spoken language of the upper middle classes—the 'standard language'" (p. 64). This ideology privileges those who already speak SJE or are fortunate enough to be tracked into the 'right' schools like KTH where their language is accorded respect and symbolic power. At the same time, postcolonial attitudes have shifted toward acceptance, and even celebration, of JC in the wider society, owing to its use in popular culture, reggae music, and reclaiming of Jamaican identity, especially among the younger generation (JLU, 2005). As a result, JC is increasingly spoken in more domains heretofore considered formal, e.g., on university campuses or even at academically high-ranked schools like KTH. Thus, a policy that seeks to 'transition' youth from JC to SJE is constantly tested by the use of JC everywhere. Furthermore, the fact that JC speakers do not have the option to read and write in their language in school makes the acquisition of SJE that much harder, as the only access to school-based literacy is via a language that they do not speak. I would argue that the phenomenon of the *majority* being forcibly schooled in the language of the *minority* is unique to Creole and postcolonial contexts. Language education policies that are based on this phenomenon end up, unfortunately, reproducing social inequities.

Despite this inequitable linguistic situation, and the loosening up of language attitudes in the postcolonial era, the fiercest resistance to policies that recognize Creoles in schools often comes from JC speakers themselves. The contradictory attitude of simultaneously celebrating and resisting the vernacular is exacerbated by the fact that most Jamaicans are deeply invested in an 'English-speaking' identity, despite their actual language practices (the ultimate legacy of linguistic imperialism). Thus, the intentional focus on English as a language to be learned is more challenging, if perceived and actual language practices are, in reality, far apart.

Implications for Policy, Practice, and Future Research

The language-as-problem orientation in Creole contexts has been the driving force in language education policy development, as exemplified in Jamaica. This orientation has failed to serve a large segment of the population by framing *them* (via their language) as a problem. Any chance for real policy change must start with a different orientation, one that moves beyond the problem paradigm. In the postcolonial era in Jamaica, that change has been mostly driven by linguists at UWI (with some support from the MOE) who have advocated for language education policies based on *equity*. Devonish and Carpenter's (2007) BEP is one example of an equity-driven study based on language-as-resource for *all* rather than a problem for many. Even as a pilot study, though, the BEP's approval and implementation was highly contentious, as it sought to disrupt the 'problem frame,' which begs the question, who should develop language education policy? Linguists or educators or both? I would say all stakeholders who have expertise and a vested interest in language and educational outcomes should be involved in policy development.

In Jamaica and other Creole contexts, language education policies are not only approved by the MOE, but also ratified by Parliament or a similar governmental body, which make them likely to be highly politicized and contentious. The non-ratification of the Jamaican policy is a case in point. But this level of contention should not be avoided. Language education policy development is, by definition, political work. In Creole contexts, the task of developing policies attuned to the postcolonial era is one of reckoning with the legacy of colonization. It is a task of creating a "counterdiscourse" (Hall, 1994) to ensure equity for linguistically marginalized groups. In order for policies to move from a problem frame to an equity frame, larger issues must be simultaneously addressed. They include truly recognizing Jamaicans as bilinguals; re-examining the broader goals of education; institutionalizing an orthographic system in JC so that literacy can be practiced in the language; dismantling structures that perpetuate linguistic hierarchies, such as shift schools and the practice of streaming; confronting ambivalent language attitudes; and building stronger alliances among linguists, educators, and Creole-speaking communities. Language education policy development and implementation in Jamaica will require commensurate teacher training in sociolinguistics, focusing on best practices for language teaching and learning in a Creole environment (Bryan, 2010). Siegel's (2007) language awareness approach has proven to be successful in raising metalinguistic awareness for Creole speakers to address the paradox of an 'English-speaking' identity coupled with complex JC-dominant discursive practices.

Finally, future policy research needs to investigate implementation and outcomes of language education policies in Creole contexts both quantitatively and qualitatively, especially around language assessment and instructional practices. In contexts like Haiti, where Creole already has official status, more research on the academic outcomes and societal effects of bilingual education there can help inform policy development and implementation elsewhere. Greater collaboration between language education policy researchers and practitioners in Creole contexts and those working with Creole speakers in the diaspora such as New York can strengthen the linguistic support provided to Creole speakers to ensure equity in academic outcomes.

Notes

1 This study was supported by a Fulbright Grant (#11–21111). Research support was provided by the Jamaican Ministry of Education and the University of the West Indies, Jamaica. Special thanks to the participating school principals, teachers, students, and policy developers without whom this study would not have been possible.

Challenges of Language Education Policy 217

2 The Commonwealth Caribbean consists of all the island nations in the Caribbean, as well as the mainland countries of Guyana in South America and Belize in Central America, that were former British colonies (now independent and part of the British Commonwealth) where English is the official language and medium of instruction in schools, but the mass vernacular is an English-lexified Creole.
3 The postcolonial era in Jamaica is understood as any time after 1962, when Jamaica gained independence from Britain.
4 The "th" sound does not exist in Creole.
5 Linguists at UWI developed a revised version of the Cassidy orthographic system for JC, which was used in Devonish and Carpenter's (2007) BEP.

References

Bhabha, H. (1994). *The location of culture*. New York, NY: Routledge.

Bryan, B. (2010). *Between two grammars: Research and practice for language learning and teaching in a Creole-speaking environment*. Miami, FL and Kingston, Jamaica: Ian Randle Publishers.

Canagarajah, A. S. (1999). *Resisting linguistic imperialism in English teaching*. Oxford, UK: Oxford University Press.

Canagarajah, A. S. (2013). *Translingual practice: Global Englishes and cosmopolitan relations*. New York, NY: Routledge.

Carrington, L. (2001). The status of Creole in the Caribbean. In P. Christie (Ed.), *Due respect: Papers on English and English-related creoles in the Caribbean in honour of Professor Robert Le Page* (pp. 24–36). Kingston, Jamaica: UWI Press.

Cooper, C. (2010, August 8). Reading and writing. *The Jamaica Gleaner*. Retrieved July 5, 2017 from www.jamaica-gleaner.com

Craig, D. (1999). *Teaching language and literacy: Policies and practices for vernacular situations*. Georgetown, Guyana: Education and Development Services.

DeCamp, D. (1971). Introduction: The study of pidgin and creole languages. In D. Hymes (Ed.), *Pidginization and creolization of languages* (pp. 13–39). Cambridge, UK: Cambridge University Press.

Devonish, H., & Carpenter, K. (2007). Full bilingual education in a creole situation: The Jamaican bilingual primary education project. *Occasional Paper, No. 35*. Society for Caribbean Linguistics. Port of Spain, Trinidad & Tobago: UWI, St. Augustine.

Evans, H. (2001). *Inside Jamaican schools*. Kingston, Jamaica: UWI Press.

Hall, S. (1994). Cultural identity and diaspora. In P. Williams & L. Chrisman (Eds.), *Colonial discourse and postcolonial theory: A reader* (pp. 392–401). New York, NY: Columbia UP.

Jamaican Language Unit. (2005). *Language attitudes survey*. Kingston, Jamaica: UWI, Mona. Retrieved July 5 2017 from www.mona.uwi.edu/dllp/jlu/projects/Report%20for%20 Language%20Attitude%20Survey%20of%20Jamaica.pdf

Lippi-Green, R. (1997). *English with an accent*. New York, NY: Taylor and Francis.

Márquez, R. (2010). *A world among these islands: Essays on literature, race, and national identity in Antillean America*. Boston, MA: University of Massachusetts Press.

McCourtie, L. (1998). The politics of Creole language education in Jamaica: 1891–1921 and the 1990s. *Journal of Multilingual and Multicultural Development, 19*(2), 108–127.

Menken, K. (2008). *English learners left behind: Standardized testing as language policy*. Clevedon, UK: Multilingual Matters.

Miles, M., & Huberman, A. M. (1994). *Qualitative data analysis: An expanded sourcebook*. Thousand Oaks, CA: Sage.

Ministry of Education. (1999). *Curriculum Guide Grade 5*. Kingston, Jamaica. Retrieved July 5, 2017 from www.moe.gov.jm/curricula

Ministry of Education. (2001). *Language Education Policy*. Kingston, Jamaica. Retrieved July 5, 2017 from www.moec.gov.jm/policies/languagepolicy.pdf

Ministry of Education. (2006). *What is the Grade Six Achievement Test (GSAT)?* Kingston, Jamaica. Retrieved July 5, 2017 from www.moe.gov.jm/

Ministry of Education. (2011). *Student achievement data*. Kingston, Jamaica. Retrieved July 5, 2017 from www.moec.gov.jm/divisions/ed/assessment/index.html

Nero, S. (2010). Language, literacy, and pedagogy of Caribbean Creole English speakers. In M. Farr, L. Seloni, & J. Song (Eds.), *Ethnolinguistic diversity and education: Language, literacy, and culture* (pp. 212–240). New York, NY: Routledge.

New York City Department of Education (2012). Retrieved July 5, 2017 from schools.nyc.gov

Phillipson, R. (1992). *Linguistic imperialism*. Oxford, UK: Oxford University Press.

Ruiz, R. (1988). Orientations in language planning. In S. L. McKay & S. C. Wong (Eds.), *Language diversity: Problem or resource?* (pp. 3–26). Boston, MA: Heinle & Heinle.

Sherlock, P., & Bennett, H. (1998). *The story of the Jamaican people*. Kingston, Jamaica: Ian Randle Publishers.

Siegel, J. (2007). Creoles and minority dialects in education: An update. *Language and Education, 21*(1), 66–86.

18
SUMMARY AND CONCLUDING OBSERVATIONS

G. Richard Tucker

As the authors in this monograph note, we live in a time of enormous economic, political, and social change and development—a time in which the role of languages and the ability to communicate effectively and efficiently to diverse stakeholders have become increasingly important. This volume focuses on aspects of private and more public language planning and policy in national settings ranging across North and South America and parts of Asia and the Pacific. Authors in diverse settings note that a highly skilled workforce is a national priority and that language proficiency will be a critical asset, whether the language is Mandarin Chinese for students graduating from Nepali schools or English for students in Vietnam. The authors describe the diverse ways in which 'actors'—be they administrators, teachers, parents, students, or refugees—are attempting to gain access to languages that will facilitate their ability to thrive in the global knowledge economy of the 21st century.

Major Cross-cutting Themes

There are four major foci represented in the studies in this monograph: (1) a focus on the individual—the classroom teacher as the policy maker at levels ranging from primary education to university level; (2) a focus on policy making at the institutional level, such as the K–12 educational system or a university; (3) a focus on so-called diverse stakeholders; and (4) a focus on invisible language policy and planning—either at the individual or the family level.

Focus on Policy Making by the Classroom Teacher

Four of the contributors to this volume examine diverse aspects of the role of teachers in affecting or influencing policy implementation at the local level, whether this be in a primary classroom in northwestern Pakistan (Khan) or Vietnam (Le), a university classroom in Brazil (Galante), or a family literacy program in the southeastern United States (Pettitt).

The chapter by Khan illustrates quite clearly how difficult it is in reality to implement a policy from above (i.e., the teaching of Pashto) in primary schools in Northwestern Pakistan when the teachers have neither the skills that they need nor the academic proficiency to teach their students Pashto—all the more difficult in a setting in which English has positive instrumental value. This notion of the lack of support for the classroom teacher is reflected once again in the chapter by Le, when the classroom teachers—all of whom value the role of English in Vietnam in the 21st century—nevertheless have limited resources, inappropriate classroom settings for effective language teaching, and insufficient professional support. The teachers actively sought solutions to these challenges and exercised their agency, for example by purchasing additional supplies with their own funds, by deviating from the prescribed syllabi, etc. This example illustrates the important role that teachers play as stakeholders for the successful implementation of a top-down policy.

Galante examines the English language teaching situation at a federal university in Brasilia, in which at least six foreign languages are offered. The main research question examines the ways in which English teachers draw upon the linguistic and cultural diversity of their students in their teaching. The teachers reported that an awareness and critical analysis of linguistic and cultural diversity are major assets in preparing their students to participate in "a diverse national and global landscape" (Galante, this volume, p. 54).

In the final chapter in this part, Pettitt examines the ways in which the teacher in a program for refugee women acts as classroom-level policy planner and maker. She did so by creating materials for classroom use and structuring the class experience for the women, instead of using the funder-provided textbook.

Focus on Policy Making at the Institutional Level

Four of the contributors to this volume examine diverse aspects of the ways in which language policies are adopted or adapted for the teaching of oral or written languages at the institutional level. These studies were conducted in settings as diverse as Japan (Okuda and Yokoyama), Nepal (Sharma), and the United States (Subtirelu).

As Okuda observes, the past decade has seen an enormous spread in the number of writing centers at universities around the world. (Indeed, Carnegie Mellon University established a Global Communication Center in 2013 in Pittsburgh.) A major premise for establishing such centers is the belief that writing competence will be an increasingly important skill for workers participating in the world of work in the 21st century. In Japan, Okuda describes the emergence of English writing centers for Japanese students and similarly the spread of Japanese writing

Summary and Concluding Observations **221**

centers for international students. Okuda traces the ways in which the structure and goals of the emerging writing centers have been shaped by existing centers as well as by the work of the International Writing Center Association.

Yokoyama, on the other hand, investigates the ways in which differing priorities or policies of national ministries in Japan may affect the implementation of educational practice in the classroom. He examined the credentials of a number of Assistant Language Teachers who participated in the Japan Exchange and Teaching Program during 2014 and found that there was extremely wide variation in the extent to which the participants were sufficiently qualified to serve as assistant English teachers. Some of the participants were indeed well trained, whereas others were there primarily to learn more about the culture of Japan.

Sharma describes a very different situation in which a policy to promote multilingualism has been implemented in two elite schools in Nepal. In these schools, in which English is the medium of instruction from kindergarten on, Mandarin Chinese has recently been introduced beginning at the fourth grade. The school administrators see the value of Chinese proficiency for their graduates, who will increasingly do business in East Asia upon completing school. The students, as well as their parents, view Chinese as an economically powerful language that will be necessary if they wish to contribute to their families' and their country's growth and prosperity.

Subtirelu explores a very different theme in his chapter—namely the ways in which international teaching assistants (ITAs) are selected, trained, and utilized in five academic departments at a university in the United States. As he notes, there is extremely wide variation throughout tertiary institutions concerning the ways in which such ITAs are selected, the duties that they are assigned, the training that they receive, and the ways in which they are observed and evaluated. In my own hometown of Pittsburgh, we note distinct variations among the selection, training, mentoring, and evaluation of ITAs at Carnegie Mellon University, the University of Pittsburgh, and Duquesne University.

Focus on Diverse Stakeholders

Four of the chapters focus on the role of other stakeholders, such as university teachers, school principals, and participants in local news media, in shaping the implementation of language programs. For example, Newman notes that Timorese lecturers are faced with the problem of how best to train their students to participate in the "new global political economy" (Carneiro, 2014, p. 206). The situation is complicated because many of these lecturers have received their own training in Indonesian, rather than English. In other cases, they have been sent to Portugal for advanced study in Portuguese, but none of their students speak this language or wish to learn it. Newman notes a distinct separation of language instruction from disciplinary expertise: That is, the notion of language for specific purposes is not realized in the university classrooms, and so the instructors

222 G. Richard Tucker

are called upon to innovate, to try as best they can to meet the needs of their plurilingual students. A contrast can be made here between *plurilingualism* and *multilingualism*. The latter is "the characteristics of a place—city, society, nation state—where many languages are spoken" (King, 2017, p. 6). In contrast, *plurilingualism* is defined as "the repertoire of varieties of language which many individuals use . . . [including] 'first language' and any number of other languages and varieties" (King, 2017, p. 6, drawing on work by the Council of Europe).

The chapter by Braden and Christison examines an immensely important but under-examined topic—namely the need for teachers of science in today's schools to be adequately prepared to assist their (rapidly growing numbers of) English language learners gain mastery of content material in the STEM areas. As a nation, the United States, like many other countries, faces the distinct challenge of ensuring that students, including language minority individuals, are prepared to participate effectively in science, technology, engineering, and mathematical fields in the 21st century. And, today, educators are not adequately meeting this challenge.

In her chapter, Hamman contrasts the official position of the state of Wisconsin, which views bilingualism as a problem, with the role of local agents, such as school board members, teachers, and parents, who view bilingualism as a resource and indeed as a right (Ruiz, 1984). In fact, she notes that the Spanish-English dual language immersion program that she studied is viewed by social activists in the community as carrying on the legacy of the civil rights movement of the 1960s. Her analysis provides a clear example of stakeholders other than teachers helping shape an educational policy for students that infuses bilingualism and biculturalism into the various curricula.

Similarly, in her chapter, Stephens describes the ways in which the media in West Liberty, Iowa, portray a Spanish-English dual language immersion program in an extremely positive light. The media describe the program's positive impact on the community, which is leading to the transformation of this small town. Once again, the strong contribution that can be made by diverse local stakeholders is noted and reaffirmed.

Focus on Invisible Language Planning and Policy

Four of the chapters in this volume focus on the ways in which individual identities shape language policies and practices in a seemingly invisible manner. Wang, for example, examines the ways in which the personal experiences of heritage language–speaking parents influence and interact with the experiences that their children confront in an American afterschool program. Young girls participating in an afterschool book club struggle to balance their dual identities, and Wang discusses the ways in which these girls are constantly renegotiating their identities.

The chapter by Darvin investigates a topic that I predict will become increasingly salient in the decade ahead—namely the role of digital literacies in pedagogy and the ways in which people interact with diverse others over boundaries of time and space and ethnicity and language. Darvin interviews students from two very different social backgrounds. They both have access to the internet, but they use it for quite different purposes—one as a tool that facilitates social mobility and the other for fun and games. An emerging challenge for all educators will be to design curricula that support this broader—and increasingly broadening—concept of literacy.

Mortimer, on the other hand, describes the diverse ways in which beliefs about the roles and the status of Guarani and Spanish emerge in stories that are told among participants in two very different communities in Paraguay. Although both are official languages of the country, interviewees from a rural area view speakers of Guarani as uneducated, rude, and crude, whereas those in an urban area may claim to value Guarani although they themselves do not speak the language. So in a very real sense, policy—or at least practice—can be shaped by *people's* positioning of the roles and importance of languages rather than by federal policy shaping autocratically the views and practices that the government expects will be accepted and followed throughout the country.

As Nero describes in her chapter, the situation in Jamaica mirrors that in many of the postcolonial nations throughout the world in which diglossia is common. *Diglossia* occurs when "two or more varieties of the same language are used by some speakers under different conditions" (Ferguson, 1959, p. 325), often with a language such as English or French or Portuguese being privileged, while a local, widely spoken language is stigmatized. Nero refers to an attempt by individuals at the Jamaican Ministry of Education working with linguists from the University of the West Indies to develop a language education policy. In that policy, the view of language was to be systematically shifted from "problem" to "right" or "resource" (Ruiz, 1984) with the use of Jamaican Creole and Standard Jamaican English as dual media of bilingual instruction until Grade 4. Unfortunately, as Nero notes, Parliament never approved the policy, nor were teachers aware of it, despite the posting of the policy on the Ministry website. Therefore, the school administrators, teachers, and Creole-speaking students are left on their own to try to implement a consistent pedagogical practice.

Relatively Neglected Areas

A major unanswered question for everyone is posed in the chapter by Darvin, who wonders how policy makers, teachers, students, and researchers will reimagine pedagogy as digital literacy emerges as ubiquitous across the globe. In this day and age, when digital connectivity is so widespread in many parts of the world, language education is being offered in ways that would not have been imagined a decade ago. For example, in the *Plan Ceibal en Inglés in Uruguay* (British Council, 2017), remote teachers deliver English instruction to students in Grades 4 to 6. (See also Stanley, 2017, for a report on the use of technology in teaching English to primary school children in Uruguay.)

A second area that has been receiving a great deal of quiet attention has been the ongoing work to preserve Native American indigenous languages. See, for example, the website Native Languages of the Americas (2016), and also the work of Lewis and Simons (2016), who focus on indigenous languages in other parts of the world. Each of these areas will warrant our careful attention over the coming decade.

A third relatively neglected area is that described by Braden and Christison—namely ensuring that classroom teachers are adequately prepared to teach STEM subjects to the growing number of English language learners. There has been a concern among many American agencies (e.g., www.ed.gov/stem) about increasing the numbers of students specializing in the study of STEM subjects, but much remains to be done.

Concluding Observations

In reading this monograph, one is reminded of the recent report by the American Academy of Arts and Sciences (2017), which recommends a national strategy "to improve access to as many languages as possible for people of every age, ethnicity, and socioeconomic background" (para. 3). The goal here is valuing language education as a persistent national need, similar to education in math or English, and to ensure that reaching proficiency is within every student's reach. This same view was articulated by Saville (2017), who notes that "business, employment, and scholarship are increasingly global and multilingual, and citizens of the 21st century need a new range of skills and strategies . . . to supplement their core language learning skills" (p. 1). Clearly, in order to participate fully and meaningfully in the global knowledge economy of the 21st century, individuals around the world will require proficiency in multiple languages—a daunting challenge!

References

American Academy of Arts and Sciences. (2017). *America's languages: Investing in language education for the 21st century*. Retrieved July 18, 2017 from www.amacad.org/language

British Council. (2017). *Plan Ceibal en Inglés in Uruguay*. Retrieved July 18, 2017 from www.britishcouncil.uy/en/programmes/education/ceibal-en-ingles

Carneiro, A. S. R. (2014). Conflicts around the (de-)construction of legitimate language(s): The situation of Portuguese in the multilingual context of East Timor. In L. P. Moita-Lopes (Ed.), *Global Portuguese: Linguistic ideologies in late modernity* (pp. 204–221). New York, NY: Routledge.

Ferguson, C. A. (1959). Diglossia. *Word, 15*(2), 325–340.

King, L. (2017). *The impact of multilingualism on global education and language learning*. Cambridge, UK: Cambridge English Language Assessment.

Lewis, M. P., & Simons, G. F. (2016). *Sustaining language use: Perspectives on community-based language development*. Dallas, TX: SIL International.

Native Languages of the Americas. (2016). *Native languages of the Americas: Preserving and promoting American Indian languages*. Retrieved July 23, 2017 from www.native-lan guages.org/

Ruiz, R. (1984). Orientations in language planning. *NABE Journal, 8*(2), 15–34.
Saville, N. (2017). Foreword to L. King, *The impact of multilingualism on global education and language learning* (p. 1). Cambridge, UK: Cambridge English Language Assessment.
Stanley, G. (2017). Remote teaching: A case study in teaching English to primary school children in Uruguay via videoconferencing. In M. Carrier, R. Damerow, & K. M. Bailey (Eds.), *Digital language learning and teaching: Research, theory, and practice* (pp. 188–197). New York, NY: Routledge.

ABOUT THE CONTRIBUTORS

Kathleen M. Bailey is a Professor in the TESOL-TFL MA Program at the Middlebury Institute of International Studies at Monterey and a professor in the Anaheim University TESOL MA and EdD programs. She is a past president of both TESOL and AAAL, as well as the current president of TIRF.

Sarah Braden is an Assistant Professor of English Language Learner Education in The School of Teacher Education and Leadership at Utah State University. Her research centers on disciplinary language socialization in the sciences.

MaryAnn Christison is a Professor in the Department of Linguistics and the Urban Institute for Teacher Education at the University of Utah. She teaches graduate and undergraduate courses in applied linguistics and education. Christison is a member of the TIRF Board of Trustees and is a past president of TESOL.

JoAnn (Jodi) Crandall is a Professor Emerita of Education at the University of Maryland, Baltimore County, where she co-directed the MA TESOL Program and directed the PhD Program in Language, Literacy, and Culture. She is a former president of TESOL, WATESOL, and AAAL and a founding and current member of the TIRF Board.

Ron Darvin is a Vanier and Public Scholar at the University of British Columbia in Vancouver, Canada. He is the recipient of the 2017 Language and Social Processes SIG Emerging Scholar Award of the American Educational Research Association (AERA) and a co-recipient of the 2016 TESOL Award for Distinguished Research.

About the Contributors **227**

Angelica Galante is a PhD candidate in Language and Literacies Education at OISE, University of Toronto. She has extensive English language teaching experience in both Brazil and Canada and currently teaches at Brock University and York University. Her research interests include plurilingual education, innovative pedagogical applications, and classroom research.

Laura Hamman is a PhD candidate in Curriculum and Instruction at the University of Wisconsin-Madison, with a focus on ESL and bilingual education. Her current research explores the discourse practices, language ideologies, and identity enactments of young learners in two-way immersion programs, in order to better understand how students experience the process of be(com)-ing bilingual.

Aziz U. Khan holds a PhD degree in Applied Linguistics from the University of Auckland, New Zealand. He is currently working as an assistant professor at Abdul Wali Khan University, Mardan, Pakistan. His research interests include language-in-education policy, language teaching and identity, and social contexts of language learning and teaching.

Duc Manh Le is currently a PhD candidate of the School of Education, the University of New South Wales, Australia. He used to work as a language teacher trainer in Haiphong University, Vietnam. His current research interests include language policy enactment, teacher education, and teacher professional development.

Joseph Lo Bianco is a Professor of Language and Literacy Education at the University of Melbourne and chair of Language and Literacy Education and associate dean in the Melbourne Graduate School of Education there. He currently has an Australian Research Council three-year project underway investigating Intercultural Approaches to Teaching Chinese in English-speaking Settings.

Katherine S. Mortimer is Assistant Professor of Bilingual/Biliteracy Education at the University of Texas at El Paso, where she also co-directs the Ethnography of Languages, Literacies, and Learning Lab. Her research examines policies and practices for bilingual education in Paraguay and in the USA. She won the 2017 TIRF James E. Alatis Prize for her research on Paraguayan language education policy.

Shondel Nero is Associate Professor of Language Education at New York University. Her research examines linguistic and educational issues of Caribbean Creole English speakers, language and identity, language education policy, and intercultural competence. She was awarded the inaugural TIRF James E. Alatis Prize for her research on language education policy in Jamaica.

228 About the Contributors

Trent Newman is a PhD candidate in Language and Literacy Education at the University of Melbourne. He has a professional background in academic literacies, language teaching, and intercultural communication, as well as peace education, including human rights and anti-racism education. His current work focusses on the connections between language, education, and development.

Tomoyo Okuda is a PhD candidate in the Department of Language and Literacy Education at the University of British Columbia. Her research interests include writing center studies, higher education research, and language policy. She has co-authored a book chapter with Ryuko Kubota in *Why English?: Confronting the Hydra* (Multilingual Matters).

Nicole Pettitt is Assistant Professor of TESOL at Youngstown State University in Ohio. A former ESOL and Spanish teacher, her current research and teaching center on literacy and language learning in contexts of migration, focusing on the historical, political, and social contexts that shape learners' experiences, identities, and investments.

Bal Krishna Sharma is an Assistant Professor of English at the University of Idaho. He received his PhD from the University of Hawaii at Manoa in 2016. His research interests include discourse analysis, sociolinguistics, intercultural communication, and qualitative research methods.

Crissa Stephens is a doctoral candidate at the University of Iowa. She uses a critical sociocultural lens to examine how language policies impact social identity development and opportunity in education. Her recent publications utilize ethnography and discourse analysis to explore language policy and educational equity in local contexts.

Nicholas Close Subtirelu is Assistant Teaching Professor of Applied Linguistics at Georgetown University. His research looks at the circulation of ideologies pertaining to racial and linguistic diversity in educational discourse. Recent publications have appeared in *Applied Linguistics*, *Language in Society*, and *Multilingua*.

G. Richard Tucker, PhD, McGill University, is a Paul Mellon University Professor of Applied Linguistics Emeritus at Carnegie Mellon University. He is a former president of the Center for Applied Linguistics in Washington, DC, and professor of Psychology and Linguistics at McGill University. Dr. Tucker is a founding trustee of TIRF.

Yu-Chi Wang is an Assistant Professor in the Foreign Language Center at Feng Chia University in Taiwan. She received her doctoral degree in the Foreign

Language and ESL Education Program at the University of Iowa. She was a recipient of a TIRF Doctoral Dissertation Grant in 2015.

Takahiro Yokoyama is a Senior Lecturer in Japanese at the Ara Institute of Canterbury in New Zealand. He was a Lecturer in TESOL and Teaching Japanese as a Foreign Language in Australia and a recipient of a 2015 TIRF Doctoral Dissertation Grant.

INDEX

21st century xviii, 13, 15, 25, 129, 145–146, 149, 182, 189, 219–220, 222, 224

Abiria, D. M. 47–49
Abraham, R. 8
Adamson, B. 34
Adesope, O. 160
agency xiii, 2, 4–5, 7, 13, 17, 31–32, 34–35, 41–45, 85, 94
agriculture 10, 119, 122–123, 125–127
Alatis Prize xix, 1, 227
Alexander, N. 28
Aline, D. 108
American Academy of Arts and Sciences 224
American Library Association Office for Information Technology Policy 181
Anderson, A. 56
Anderson, J. 56
Andrade, A. I. 47–49
Anonymous 160
Appadurai, A. 182
Arthur, J. 23
Asato, J. 153
assessment xii, 9, 17, 47, 57, 100–103, 108, 131, 210, 216
Atkinson, P. 195
attitudes xiii–xix, xxi

Bailey, K. M. xii, xvii, xix, xx, xxii, 1, 8, 95, 100, 102, 226
Bakhtin, M. 121, 124, 143, 156

Baldauf, R. B. 1, 4, 34–35
Ball, S. J. 193
Bamberg, M. 193–194, 196
Baniabdelrahman, A. 106
Barakos, E. 193, 195
Barkhuizen, G. 25
Barratt, L. 106
Barton, D. 188
Basch, L. 182
Bauman, R. 161
Bennett, H. 208
Benson, C. 30
Bhabha, H. 205, 207, 214
Bianco, J. L. xv, xviii, xxii, 121, 227
Biesta, G. 35
bilingual education xvi, xix, 12, 14, 141, 143, 145, 147–148, 154–155, 157–163, 194, 208, 216, 227
bilingualism 7, 11, 23, 92–93, 141–151, 155, 158–160, 162, 177, 208–209, 214, 222
Bismilla, V. 179
Blackledge, A. 122–123
Blanc, C. 182
Bliss, B. 57
Blumenfeld, H. K. 109
Bohlke, D. 113
Bollinger, K. M. 74
Bonacina-Pugh, F. 120
book club 12–13, 15, 169–170, 172–173, 176–177, 179, 222
Boone, D. 158–159

Boquet, E. H. 73
Bourdieu, P. 188
Braden, S. K. xiii, xiv, xix–xx, 3, 10–11, 131, 222, 224, 226
Bräuer, G. 73
Brazilian foreign language policy 5, 46, 53
Briggs, C. 156, 161
Briggs, S. 8
British Council 46, 48–50, 223
Brock-Utne, B. 23
Broekhoff, M. 73, 74
Brown, K. 103
Bruffee, K. A. 73
Bryan, B. 216
Bucholtz, M. 193
Bui, T. T. N. 34
Bulfin, S. 190
Bunyi, G. W. 23
Burkhalter, A. J. 100
Butler, Y. G. 160
Byram, M. 73
Byrd, P. 8

Cabinet's Office 77
Cain, C. 43
Canagarajah, S. 31, 99, 121, 206–207
Carless, D. 106–107
Carlino, P. 73
Carlone, H. B. 131
Carneiro, A. S. R. 120–121, 221
Carpenter, K. 208, 214–215, 217
Carrington, L. 208
case study 95, 97, 141, 182–183
Catalano, T. 179
Caumont, A. 130
CEFR 46–54
Charmaz, K. 87
Chick, K. 23
Chinese 2, 8–9, 49, 63, 79, 84–93, 171, 176, 219, 221, 227
Christensen, E. 106–107
Christison, M. A. xiii–xiv, xix–xx, 3, 10–11, 130, 222, 224, 226
Christopher, V. 107
Citizenship and Immigration Canada 184–185
Clyne, M. 1
Codó, E. 123
Cohn, D. 130
Collier, V. P. 159–160
colonization 52, 54, 206, 207, 216
Commonwealth Caribbean 205, 207

communication skills 48, 74, 77–78, 114, 119, 122, 124–128
communicative: competence 3, 5, 34–35, 124, 126; language teaching 5, 34, 36
community development 10, 119
Constantinides, J. C. 8
Conteh, J. 171
Cook, V. 47, 51
Cooper, C. 205
Cooper, R. L. 1, 35
Cope, B. 182
Cornwell, S. 73
Corson, D. 35
Coste, D. 47–48
Coulmas, F. 1
Council of Europe 1, 6, 47–48, 52, 222
Council of Local Authorities for International Relations (CLAIR) 106–108, 110–114
Craig, D. 207–208
Crandall, J. A. xii, xxii, 1, 226
Creese, A. 16, 122
Creole xiv, 2, 14–15, 205–216, 223, 227
Creole contexts 14, 206–208, 210, 212–213, 215–216
Cuban, S. 56
culturally and linguistically diverse (CLD) 169–180
Cummins, J. 47, 160, 179
Curdt-Christiansen, X. L. 4, 170–171, 176
curriculum xvi, 2, 36, 39, 47, 53, 103, 106, 132, 139, 148, 159, 181–182, 189, 212–213, 227; development 108; and instruction 58, 64–65

Darvin, R. xiv, xix–xx, 4, 13, 15, 181, 183, 185–189, 222–223, 226
Davies, B. 87, 171
DeCamp, D. 206
De Costa, P. I. 182
Decree 1400 35–36
De Fina, A. 198
Delany-Barmann, G. 162
Delavan, M. G. 145
De Mejía, A. M. 92
Denzin, N. K. 174
Devonish, H. 208, 214–215
Dewaele, J. M. 49, 52
digital natives 4, 15, 187–188
diglossia 223
Dippold, D. 95
disciplinary discourse socialization 126, 128

232 Index

discourse 13, 15, 56, 65, 84–85, 87, 91–93, 99, 107, 119, 127, 145–146, 157–160, 170, 173, 175–176, 179, 187–188, 194; analysis 58, 124, 133, 143, 156; classroom 138; competing 141–142, 151; counter 207, 216; media 153–155, 161–162; planning 121; policy-as- 193, 195; political 149
diversity xiv, 8, 49, 51–52, 95, 114, 155, 188, 228; cultural 6, 46–47, 49–50, 53, 220
Doctoral Dissertation Grants i, xviii–xix, xxii, 229
dual language xiv, 141, 149, 154–156, 158–162; immersion xvi, 3, 10–12, 142–145, 222
Dudley-Marling, C. 57
Duff, P. A. ii, xvii, xx

Earls, C. 92–93
Early, M. 47
economic market xiii, 8, 84, 86–88, 92
Edwards, A. 43
Edwards, R. 43
EFL 35, 46, 50, 52, 53–54; classroom 6, 51–52; teacher xvi, 47, 49, 53–54; teaching 49, 51; university 5–6
Elder, G. H. 35
elementary school 60, 112, 144, 160, 170–173, 179
Ellis, E. 47, 49
ELT 51, 106, 108–114
Emirbayer, M. 35
English-speaking identity 215–216
equity 11, 100, 130, 139, 141–143, 149, 151, 183, 214–216, 228
Ertl, J. 74, 81
ESOL 6, 57, 63–65, 228
ethnography 25, 193, 227–228; of language policy 195
Evans, H. 212
expertise xvii, 107–108, 111, 113–114, 127, 130, 132, 137–139, 216, 221

Fairbarn, S. 155
Fairclough, N. 154, 156–157, 160, 170
Falout, J. 106, 114
Ferguson, C. A. 223
Fishman, P. 103
Fitch, F. 95
Fitts, S. 141
Fitzsimmons-Doolan, S. 154
Flores, N. 10, 122, 149, 154–155
focused group interview 87, 123

Fogle, L. W. 4, 12, 170
foreign language 7, 9, 23, 34, 36, 46–48, 53–54, 74, 85, 106, 145, 208, 220, 228–229; class/course 3, 8; classroom xvi, 107; education 47, 48; teaching 47, 48–49, 108, 112
Foucault, M. 143, 156
Freebody, P. xviii
Freeman, R. 42, 153, 161
Freire, J. A. 145
Freire, P. 6, 49
Friedrich, N. 56
Fujishima, H. 81

Gaffikin, F. 98
Gajo, L. 49, 120, 122, 123–124
Gal, S. 155
Galante, A. xiii–xix, 3, 5, 6, 46, 48, 51, 220, 227
Gallegos, R. 159
Ganobcsik-Williams, L. 74
García, O. 2, 3, 10, 24–25, 31–32, 35, 42, 48, 51, 85, 122, 141
García-Arroyo, M. 73–74
Gedye, S. 103
Gee, J. P. 143, 170, 173–174
Geluso, J. 106–107
Georgakopoulou, A. 193–194, 196
Ghazali, F. A. 87
Giri, R. A. 85
Glass, G. V. 153
Glazier, J. 179
Glesne, C. 133
global xiii, 15, 35, 42, 52, 73–74, 76–78, 80, 84, 90–93, 95, 124, 146, 185, 221, 224; citizen 6, 48, 51; community 52; competency 98–99; competitiveness 98, 145; English xviii; knowledge economy 219, 224; landscape 48–49, 54, 220; language 2, 9, 46, 84–85, 93–94; market 149, 151
globalization xiii, xviii, 3, 8, 9, 34, 49, 81, 84–85, 98, 121, 149
Göbel, K. 48
Goldberg, C. 130
Gotanda, N. 153
Government of Pakistan 24, 31
government school 5, 24–25, 31
Graddol, D. 93
Grant, V. 103
Griffith, A. 56
Grommes, P. 49
Guba, E. G. 25
Gustafsson, M. 74

Gutierrez, K. D. 153
Gynan, S. N. 194

Hafner, C. A. 182
Hakuta, K. 160
Hall, K. 193
Hall, S. 156–157, 216
Hamann, E. T. 155
Hamid, M. O. 4, 35, 42
Hamilton, R. 158
Hamman, L. xiii–xiv, 3, 11–12, 141, 222, 227
Hammersley, M. 195
Han, S. A. 106–107
Harré, R. 43, 87, 171
Hashimoto, K. 9, 110
Haun-Frank, J. 131
Hayes, E. 56
Heller, M. 93, 125
Henderson, K. 141
Hendrix, S. 57
Hernandez, A. 141
Herrmann, S. 57
higher education xii, 7, 10, 74, 78, 80, 89–90, 97, 101, 103, 119–123, 126–127, 228
Hinofotis, F. B. 8
Hitlin, S. 35
Hoekje, B. 100
Hofer, B. 8
Holland, D. 43
Holliday, A. 98, 107
Hope, J. 64
Horiguchi, S. 75
Hornberger, N. H. 2–3, 10, 15, 24–25, 35, 84, 107, 110, 122, 143, 156, 162, 195
Hosoda, Y. 108
Houghton, S. 107
Hu, A. 49
Huberman, A. M. 211
Hult, F. M. 153
human capital 74, 93
Hutchison, K. 57, 64

IBGE 46
identity xiv, 4, 12–15, 59, 86, 92, 133, 138, 169, 171, 175–178, 191–194, 202; Jamaican 206–208, 215–216; multilingual 174; national 157; representation 187
ideology xii–xiii, 85, 96, 124, 142–143, 147, 153, 171, 206, 214–215; heteroglossic 11, 155, 162; language 42, 121, 142, 154–155, 207, 227;

monoglossic language 12, 157; monolingual 50–51, 161; political-economic 88; teaching 34, 209
Igawa, K. 108
Imoto, Y. 75
implementation xvii–xiii, xx, 3, 9, 14, 42, 47, 54, 77, 106, 110; policy xix, 3, 16, 30–31, 34–36, 41, 107, 141, 190, 193, 205, 213–214, 216, 219–221; program 142–143
indigenous languages xviii, xx, 1, 14–15, 27, 46, 92–93, 224
inquiry tasks 131, 133–134
Inskeep, S. 158
insufficient support 5, 37
Internal Affairs and Communications Ministry 79
Internationalization 3, 73, 78–79, 81, 95, 97–99, 107, 110, 112
international students xvii, 3, 7, 76, 78–80, 221
international teaching assistants xvii, 3, 7–9, 95
International Writing Center Association 74–75, 221
Iowa Code 280.4 155, 162
Irvine, J. T. 155
Ishikawa, M. 81
Iwamoto, T. 77–78
Izumi, S. 113

Jamaican Creole 2, 9, 15, 205–216
Jamaican Language Unit 215
Japan Exchange and Teaching Program 106–114
Japan Student Services Organization 78
Jenkins, J. 79, 95–96
Jeon, M. 106–107
Johnson, D. C. 3–4, 15, 24–25, 34, 85, 97, 121, 124, 141, 153, 156–157, 162
Johnson, E. 154, 161
Johnson, E. J. 3–4, 15, 34, 85
Johnston, S. 73–74
Jones, N. 103
Jones, R. H. 182
Jones-Vo, S. 155
Jong, E. de 154

Kabel, A. 107
Kachru, B. B. 107
Kaewnuch, S. 35
Kalantzis, M. 182
Kamwangamalu, N. 34
Kang, O. 95, 99, 102

234 Index

Kano, A. 113
Kaplan, R. B. xi, 34–35, 97
Kaushanskaya, M. 109
Kawashima, Y. 171
Kendrick, M. 47
Kerfoot, C. 10, 122
Khan, A. xiii–xx, 3–5, 23, 27, 220, 227
Kim, J. E. 56
King, K. A. 4, 12, 103, 170–172
King, L. 6, 222
Kırkgöz, Y. 34
Kirkpatrick, A. 30
Kirkpatrick, R. 34
Kling, J. 3
Knobel, M. 182, 188
Kobayashi, Y. 85, 93, 112
Kontra, E. 106
Kristeva, J. 156
Krueger, R. 87
Kubota, R. 47, 93, 228

labs 132–134, 138–139
Lachicotte Jr., W. 43
Lambert, W. E. 11, 144
Landis, D. 6, 59
language: attitudes 207, 211–212,
    214–216; experience approach 2, 6,
    58–59; perceptions 25; planning xi, xiii,
    xvii–xx, 1, 15, 57, 80, 121, 143, 170,
    189, 219; practices 26, 30, 56, 177, 180,
    193, 205, 208–210, 212–215; target xvi,
    49, 52, 76, 209
language-as-problem 214–215
Lankshear, C. 182, 188
Lantolf, J. P. 43, 58
Lau v. Nichols 153, 157
Lavin, T. 160
Le, D. M. xiii, xix, 5, 34, 227
Le, V. C. 38
LeCompte, M. D. 144
Lee, C. 188
Lee, O. 131
Lee, Y. C. 35
Levinson, B. A. U. 11, 143, 193
Lewis, M. P. 148, 224
Li, M. 34
Lichtman, M. 98
Liddicoat, A. J. 35
Lin, A. 114
Lincoln, Y. S. 25
Lindemann, S. 96, 99, 102
Lindholm-Leary, K. J. 141
linguistic: diversity 8, 46–47, 49–50, 53, 95,
    155, 220, 228; imperialism 205, 207, 214

Lippi-Green, R. 215
literacies xii, xiv, 1–2, 14, 35, 74, 76, 81,
    169–170, 182–184, 186–187, 189–190,
    206, 213–216, 222–223, 226–228;
    bi- 12, 142, 145, 149, 155, 227; critical
    189–190; digital xvii, 13, 181–182,
    188–189; family 6–7, 56–57, 64–65,
    220; functional 126; Japanese 77–78;
    Language and xvi, 14, 58, 63, 90, 172,
    183, 209–210, 227, 228;
    participatory 59
Litosseliti, L. 87
Liu, L. 107
Llurda, E. 114
Lo Bianco, J. xv, xviii, xxii, 121, 227
Logan-Terry, A. 12, 170
Longman, J. 130
Luke, A. 189–190
Luke, C. 182, 188
Luttrell, W. 57
Lynch, S. 155
Lynham, S. A. 25

Mace, J. 59
Mahboob, A. 27, 114
Mahoney, K. 153
Mancha, S. 6, 59
Marian, V. 109
Márquez, R. 208
Marshall, S. 47
Martin, P. 23, 35, 122
Martínez, R. A. 141
Martin-Jones, M. 124
Martins Tilman, C. 127
Masamune, S. 29
Mateus, S. G. 141
Matheson, D. 154, 161
Matsuda, P. K. 103
Matsuta, Y. 79
McCarty, T. 4, 58, 15
McConnell, D. L. 109–110, 112–114
McCourtie, L. 207
McQuillan, J. 154, 161
mediated discourse analysis 58
medium of instruction 1–3, 5, 12, 126;
    English as the 31, 86, 91, 120, 221;
    Pastho as the 23–25, 28–30
Mein, E. 56
Menard-Warwick, J. 56
Menken, K. 2, 3, 24–25, 31, 35, 42, 85, 213
MEXT 76, 78–79, 107, 111–112
Meyers, C. M. 100
Miles, M. 211
Miller, K. 43

Ministério da Educação 47–48
Ministry of Education 205, 208–209, 213
Mische, A. 35
Molinsky, S. 57
monolingual orientation 53–54, 206, 214
Montagne, R. 158
Moore, D. 47, 49, 120, 122, 124
Morgan, S. E. 95
Mortimer, K. S. xiv, xix–xx, 4, 13–14, 192–193, 195, 203, 223, 227
Moussu, L. 114
Mroczek, K. 188
multilingualism 1, 13, 57, 65, 92–93, 122, 126, 144, 171, 222; elite 8, 92
Murillo, E. G. 155
Muro, A. 56
Murphy, J. P. 179

Nagoya University Writing Center 77
narrative 96, 192–196, 198–202, 213; analysis xx, 193, 195; counter 84; ethnographic research 23, 25; inquiry 25
Nash, P. 103
national development 123, 127–128
National Research Council 131
native-English-speaking teachers 106
Native Languages of the Americas 224
native speakers xvi–xvii, 102; of English 12, 50, 96, 113, 132, 145, 206, 208; of Japanese 7
Nebbe, C. 156
Nepal xii, 2, 8–9, 84–93
Nero, S. xiv, xix–xx, 2, 14, 205–206, 223, 227
New Latino diaspora 11, 155
Newman, T. P. xiii, xix–xx, 3, 10, 119, 221, 228
New York City Department of Education 206
NGSS Lead States 131, 139
Nguyen, H. T. M. 35, 42
Nishino, T. 34
nonnative speakers 12, 95–96, 100, 103, 160
North, S. 190
North, S. M. 73–74, 79
Norton, B. 13, 56, 90, 171, 182–183, 185, 187–188
Nunan, D. xix, xx, 31, 34
Nurul Islam, M. 106

Ochs, K. 7, 75
OECD 189
Ollerhead, S. 35

Osaka Jogakuin University 76–77
Otani, M. 108, 112
Oudenhoven, J. P. van 49, 52
Ovando, C. 153, 162

Paciotto, C. 162
Paiva, V. L. M. O. 47
Palmer, D. 151, 142
Palmer, D. K. 141
Paraguay xiv, 4, 12–15, 47, 192, 223, 227
Paraguay MEC 194
parents xiii, xvi–xvii, 2, 8–12, 14, 87–88, 92, 132, 142, 146–148, 151, 161, 169, 171–172, 174, 176–177, 183–184, 192, 195–196, 198, 200, 203, 219, 221–222
Park, J. 3
Park, J. S. Y. 92
Parmenter, L. 73
Pashto 3–5, 24–31, 220
Pauwels, A. 47–49, 54
Pavlenko, A. 123
Pawan, F. 3
Pearson, P. 5, 31, 69
Pérez, B. 141
Pérez-Milans, M. 193, 203
Perry, D. C. 98
petroleum 10, 119–122, 125–126
Pettitt, N. xiii, xix–xx, 2, 4, 6, 56, 220, 228
Phillips, D. 7, 75
Phillipson, R. 16, 205–207
Phyak, P. 85
Piccardo, E. 47–48, 51–52
Pietikäinen, S. 153
Pinho, A. S. 47–49
Plakans, B. S. 8, 95, 97
Plüddemann, P. 1, 107
plurilingualism 6, 10, 47–54, 122, 124, 127, 222
Pohl, K. 59, 66
policy: analysis xx; bilingual 14–15; borrowing 7, 73, 75; dumping 42; educational language 4, 6, 7, 9, 12, 16, 47, 53; English-only 51, 91, 179; family language 12, 170–173; global policy 10, 119, 127; hiring — of language teachers 9; invisible language 12, 14, 219; language-in-education 1, 9, 23, 25, 31, 86, 120; local 10–11, 141–143, 145–146, 149; medium-of-instruction 29–30; national xvi, 2, 107, 111, 153; nonauthorized — actors 11, 143; official language 12; state 10–11, 156–157; top-down 1, 31, 35, 42, 121, 161, 188, 220
political economy 8, 88, 121, 124, 221

postcolonial 23, 121, 128, 205, 207–208, 211, 213–216, 223
Preece, S. 122
Prensky, M. 13, 183, 187
Priestley, A. 43
Priestley, M. 43
primary teachers 4–5, 12, 25–26, 34, 36, 38
Prinsloo, M. 190
private schools 7–9, 13, 24, 84–86, 88, 91, 184
proficiency xvi–xvii, 14, 23, 48, 50, 100, 111, 131, 144, 171, 188, 206, 219–220, 224; Chinese 221; English 8, 11, 77, 97, 99, 112, 155, 157, 173; Japanese 9, 79, 109, 114; Pastho 30; test 100–101
Province of British Columbia 181–182

qualitative data xix, 36, 50, 86, 97–98, 123, 211
Quinn, H. 131
Quinn, M. 10, 119
Quintana, H. E. 73–74

Rahman, T. 23, 27
Rao, G. 23
Rappleye, J. 75
RDTL (República Democrática de Timor-Leste) 121–122, 128
refugee xii–xiii, xxi, 2, 6–7, 56–57, 64–65, 219–220
Reichelt, M. 73–74
repertoires 6, 10, 48, 51, 53, 57, 63–64, 84, 93, 120, 122, 124–125, 127–128, 222
Reyes, A. 133, 195
Ricento, T. K. 2, 3, 15, 24–25, 35, 84–85, 88, 107, 110, 124, 143, 153, 156
Richards, J. C. 30, 113
Rickford, J. 154
Ritsumeikan Asia Pacific University 79–80
Rivers, D. 107
Rogers, R. 143
Rolstad, K. 153
Ronesi, L. 73–74
Rowsell, J. 190
Rubin, D. 95, 99
Ruiz, R. 4, 11, 144, 214, 222, 223

Saldaña, J. 36, 143
Santos, M. 153
Saunders, R. A. 85
Saville, N. 224

Scanlan, M. 142, 151
Schensul, J. J. 144
Schiffman, H. 170
Schiller, N. 182
Schissel, J. L. 154–155
science 1, 3, 9–12, 15, 26, 29, 77, 97, 107, 125–126, 130–134, 136–139, 187, 222, 224, 226
Scollon, R. 58
Scott, P. 97
second language 23, 30, 88, 99, 108, 114, 130
Senaha, E. 79
Seo, J. A. 179
SF 165 155, 158, 162
Shackle, C. 27
Sherlock, P. 208
shift schools 212–213, 216
Shimizu, T. 113
Shohamy, E. 1, 3, 42
Shor, I. 6
Shuck, G. 96
Siegel, J. 216
Silva, T. 103
Silva Ribeiro, L. da 127
Simons, G. F. 224
Skinner, D. 43
Skutnabb-Kangas, T. 16, 92
Smith, D. 56
Smith, G. 63–64
Smith, J. A. 100
Snoddon, K. 47
Snyder, I. 190
Sobel, D. 63–64
social: identification 193–195, 202; media 154, 182, 189; mobility 92, 185
socialization xiv, 7, 10, 11, 78, 101–102, 126, 128, 130, 132–134, 139, 182
Sophia University 76
Spener, D. 6
Spolsky, B. 12, 35, 58, 170–171, 177
Standard Jamaican English 14, 208, 223
standards 47, 50, 57, 62, 131, 139, 181, 183, 190
Stanley, G. 223
Staples, S. 99, 102
Steeves, V. 183
Steiner-Khamsi, G. 7, 73, 75, 80
STEM 11, 15, 130–132, 138–139
Stephens, C. xiii–xiv, xx, 2, 11, 12, 153, 155, 222, 228

Stern, S. L. 8
streaming 210, 216
Stritikus, T. T. 42
Stroud, C. 10, 122
Subtirelu, N. C. xiii, xx, 3, 8, 95–99, 102–103, 220–221, 228
Sutton, M. 11, 143, 193
Sutton-Jones, K. 154, 161
Sylvan, C. 48, 51
symbolic capital 92

Takahashi, Y. 78
Takeuchi, M. 171
Tan, B. H. 73
Taniguchi, M. 79
Tarasawa, B. 154, 161
Taylor, D. 57
Taylor, S. K. 47
Taylor-Leech, K. 120
teacher: agency xiii, 2, 4–5, 7, 31, 34–35, 37, 42–43; education xiv, 109, 138; response 39–40
teaching assistants xvi, 3, 7, 9, 106
technology xii, xvii, 1, 4, 9, 11–13, 15, 107, 123, 130–131, 181–190, 222–223
Techopedia 13
Tedder, M. 35
TEFL 109, 114
TESOL xix–xx, 9, 47, 63, 107, 109–110, 113–114, 226, 228–229
tests xii, xvii, 8, 64, 84, 97, 99–101, 108–109, 130–132, 138–139, 159, 176, 210, 213–215
textbook xvi–xvii, xx, 2, 3, 5–6, 26, 28–31, 38–39, 50–54, 57, 100, 210, 220
Thomas, W. 159
Thomas, W. P. 141, 160
Thompson, T. 160
Thurlow, C. 188
Timor-Leste xiii, 3, 10, 12, 119, 122–123, 128
TIRF xiv–xv, xvii–xx, xxii, 1, 226–229
tourism xiii, 8, 10, 84, 89–90, 93, 119–122, 126
translanguaging 10, 121
Trend, D. 63
Tse, L. 154, 161
Tsuido, K. 112–114
Tsuruta, Y. 77
Tuominen, A. K. 172, 177
Turner, R. 103
tutoring 79, 101–102

Umolu, J. 6, 59
under-resourced and prescribed conditions 34, 41
UNESCO Institute for Statistic 108
Unger, J. W. 193, 195
Ungerleider, C. 160
United Nations High Commissioner on Refugees 56
university xvii, 4–8, 14, 36, 47, 49, 51–52, 74–80, 95–99, 102–103, 120, 123, 128, 159, 184–185, 205, 215, 219–221, 223; language planning 73; language program 53
the University of Tokyo 77
Uruguay 223
U.S. Census Bureau 63, 130
U.S. Department of Commerce 130

Valdés, G. 131, 142, 162
Valdez, V. E. 145
Valdiviezo, L. A. 24
Van Langenhove, L. 43
Varghese, M. M. 42
Vieluf, S. 48
Voloshinov, V. 154
Vygotsky, L. S. 58, 73

Waller, L. J. 154, 164
Walter, S. L. 30
Walters, J. 1
Waseda University 76, 79
Wasik, B. H. 57
Webb, A. 132
Wee, L. 92
Weedon, C. 169, 171
West Liberty Community School District 156
Wiley, T. G. xxii, 3, 141
Williams, J. 100
Williams-van Klinken, C. 127
Wingate, U. 79
Winstead, T. 11, 143
Winter, J. 103
Wisconsin Statutes 11, 144
Witt, D. 160
Wittner, E. 99
Wodak, R. 153
Wohlwend, K. 58–59
women xiii, 2, 6–7, 12, 56–57, 59, 62–64, 220
Woodin T. 59
workforce development 128
Wortham, S. 133, 193–195, 203

Wortham, S. E. F. 155
Wright, W. E. 162
writing: centers 7, 9, 73–81, 220–221; Japanese 7, 9, 73–81, 220; support 73, 7
Wurr, A. J. 59

Xi, X. 99

Yang, H. 35
Yoshida, H. 73
Yoshida, K. 113
Yoshikawa, M. 81

Zacharias, N. T. 4, 35
Zarate, G. 47
Zhu, L. 4, 35